PENGUIN BOOKS
ENLIGHTENED LEADERSHIP

Tshering Tobgay is a Bhutanese politician, environmentalist, and cultural advocate who has served as Bhutan's first leader of the opposition party from 2008 to 2013 and as its prime minister from 2013 to 2018. He has been recently re-elected for his second term as prime minister from 2024 to 2029.

PM Tshering was a civil servant before he joined active politics. He was the first official to resign from his work to take part in his country's transition to a parliamentary democracy. He was responsible for establishing the People's Democratic Party as the first registered political party in Bhutan and continues to serve as its president.

As an advocate of Gross National Happiness, he has spoken about conservation, climate change, poverty, democracy, and happiness at various international conferences.

Enlightened Leadership

Inside Bhutan's Inspiring Transition from Monarchy to Democracy

Tshering Tobgay

PENGUIN BOOKS

An imprint of Penguin Random House

PENGUIN BOOKS

Penguin Books is an imprint of the Penguin Random House group of
companies whose addresses can be found at global.penguinrandomhouse.com

Published by Penguin Random House SEA Pte Ltd
40 Penjuru Lane, #03-12, Block 2
Singapore 609216

First published in Penguin Books by Penguin Random House SEA 2025

ISBN 9789815162011

BICMA Registration Number 100001224

Typeset in Garamond by MAP Systems, Bengaluru, India
Printed at Repro India Limited

www.penguin.sg

For sale in the Indian Subcontinent only

To His Royal Highness Prince Jigme Namgyal Wangchuck,

In you, we see the future of Bhutan—a promise of hope, wisdom and unwavering dedication. Your generation carries the dreams of those who came before, and it is our sacred duty to nurture this land for you.

Just as our ancestors sacrificed for us, we shall protect Bhutan's heritage for you and your contemporaries. May the blessings of our guardian deities guide your path and may our nation's spirit fuel your endeavours.

In you, we envision a future where Bhutan's glory shines ever brighter.

Contents

Introduction

Promise and Paradox

The Kingdom of Bhutan made the commitment to remain carbon neutral in 2009 despite our status as a small, mountainous developing country with many other pressing social and economic development needs and priorities. This commitment was made with the view that there is no need greater, or more important, than keeping the planet safe for life to continue.

—Bhutan's climate action plan,
submitted in 2015, for the Paris Agreement

The Druk Air plane was just beginning its descent as I peered out of the window to my left. The clouds parted, unveiling boundless mountains that stretched for as far as my eyes could see. Somewhere in the distance, snow-capped peaks jutted up through thin wisps of clouds. For several minutes, we cruised at the same height, allowing me to take in the familiar snowy summits that greet all travellers who venture to Bhutan. Those who are unaccustomed to seeing mountain ranges outside their plane window while flying marvel in awe at the sight of these jagged peaks; it feels as if we are not flying down towards the mountains, but that they are rising up to meet us!

Reflecting a shade of gold from the rays of the sun, these snowy mountains look almost like celestial ice cities, with gods residing in white palaces unreachable by mere mortals. To us Bhutanese, this is exactly what our mountains are—abodes of the deities, summits that are not meant to be conquered. They are best left untouched for fear of offending supernatural forces that are beyond our comprehension.

Despite having taken dozens of flights in and out of Bhutan, I have never grown tired of the sights that welcome me home. There is always an air of excitement among passengers (including me) each time the plane enters Bhutanese airspace. Every single time, I instinctively grab my phone to snap a few pictures. After all, there are not many places in the world where your aircraft can be soaring above the clouds one moment, then suddenly be at the same height as the peaks of nearby mountains.

Indeed, passengers know that they have entered Bhutan's airspace when they suddenly see swathes of green forests with snow, trees, and buildings right outside their window. Flying into Bhutan is one of the most breathtaking and scenic experiences in the world—if there is another experience more like riding a real-life magic carpet, I am not aware of it!

I often speak of the climate change threats that are melting our glaciers in the Himalayas, a problem of importance to the critical area often known as the 'third pole'. The Himalayan region is the world's third largest repository of ice after the north and south poles, hence the nickname.

The headwaters of ten major rivers that flow into Asia originate from the Himalayan region. Along with snow and rain from the mountains, the ice that melts during spring and summer provides rivers much-needed meltwater for the food and energy needs of the 1.4 billion people (almost a fifth of humanity) who live downstream—mainly in India and China but also in comparatively smaller countries like Bangladesh, Pakistan, and Myanmar. It is not for nothing that the Himalayas are known as the water towers of Asia!

Just as we were preoccupied with getting a picture that we hoped would do justice to the view from above, the plane made a quick descent. We soon found ourselves flying lower than the mountain peaks around us, and also seemingly too close to them. From the window, the wings of the plane looked as though they were about to graze the trees and houses on the hills. We could spot a towering white structure in the distance below us. (This, I knew, was Paro Dzong, the fortified monastery where film director Bernardo Bertolucci shot scenes for his 1993 movie *Little Buddha*.)

We could also see rice terraces, traditional farmhouses, and temples on the surrounding slopes. As the plane made a sharp turn around a mountainside, I could spot a small structure sitting precariously on the side of a cliff. Although it was some distance away, I knew that this was the world famous Taktsang (or 'Tiger's Nest') Monastery, that every tourist who visits Bhutan inevitably makes a trip to.

Many people who have never been to Bhutan may think it is nothing but green trees and mountains. To some extent, this is true. Bhutan is one of the few spots in the world virtually untouched by modernization—there are no skyscrapers here, no flyovers, no traffic lights, no busy, jammed highways, and not a Starbucks, McDonald's, or KFC in sight. I could hear a lot of camera shutters going off and people chattering excitedly around me. I knew these were tourists who were flying to Bhutan for the first time.

The sights out the window are not the only unique thing about flying into Bhutan. Something about the shared experience loosens the tongue, and people often strike up conversations with total strangers. Whether they are from neighbouring countries like India, Nepal or Bangladesh, or distant lands like Japan or America, it is always a pleasure to be the first one to welcome them to my country. People might be curious on their flight in while those flying out may be eager to share their experiences from their stay.

In other places, travellers often plug themselves into the in-flight entertainment and retreat into isolation, and I wonder to this day how members of a species that needs social contact can somehow sit next to someone for hours on end, and not say hello. This is what's different about Druk Air. Since the journey into Bhutan is so special, people cannot help but open up to one another. This is even the case for celebrities. Someone once told me he had spoken to an unassuming Chinese tourist beside him on a flight . . . only realizing later that it had been tycoon Jack Ma!

A number of famous personalities have helped spotlight Bhutan, including Hong Kongese celebrity couple Tony Leung and Carina Lau, who hosted their star-studded wedding in Bhutan in 2008; Prince William and Kate Middleton in 2016; as well as Japan's Princess Mako in 2017; and Crown Prince Fumihito in 2019.

Another famed personality who is usually instantly recognizable to most tourists who have visited Bhutan is our King. His Majesty has never taken a chartered flight and always flies commercial according to his flight schedule. Unlike most dignitaries, he never changes it to suit his convenience. It is indeed a privilege to be able to travel with him on the same flight, but it is the foreigners who really get a kick out of it.

Once airborne, His Majesty always makes it a point to walk through the airplane greeting passengers, Bhutanese and foreigners alike. When His Majesty returns to Bhutan, there is also no red carpet or grand reception to welcome him home; indeed, there is no tradition of doing so, and His Majesty's travels are often low-profile. After all, he embodies humble service to his people, and nothing about that requires him to make an ostentatious displays of wealth and power.

The Paro Paradox

'Good morning. If you are travelling to Bhutan for the first time, do not be afraid if the mountains appear closer than usual,' the captain says over the PA system. 'We are not that close to them, so please do not worry.' Thankfully, the passengers around me usually take this announcement well. Any signs of fear are quickly overcome by excitement and adrenaline.

But when I fly to destinations around the world and speak to political, academic, and business leaders on the topics close to my heart—environmental conservation, democracy in Bhutan, and

Gross National Happiness (GNH)—and share in their amazement that Bhutan, a small country amid the vast Himalayas, is capable of big ideas and big promises, I confront a paradox over and over again that may shed some light on how we can tackle the greatest issues of our time.

In the 2022 film *Top Gun: Maverick*, to avoid detection and interception by a hostile aircraft, the protagonists must fly their F/A-18E and F Super Hornets at high speed down a narrow trench. Their target lies at the end of this trench. They must pop up to deliver their bombs, execute a treacherous climb, and then escape through a barrage of missile fire. Tom Cruise's character even points out the absurd danger and the pinpoint precision needed under fire, calling it 'two consecutive miracles'.

What if I told you sixteen such miracles happen every single day in Bhutan as of 2023? Bhutan's Paro International Airport is one of the world's most treacherous, unforgiving airports to land a commercial airliner. Surrounded by sharp peaks up to 5,000 metres high, its runway is concealed from sight and tucked away in a narrow valley 2,100 metres above sea level. The approach to Paro has the aircraft diving over rough terrain, dodging mountains while maintaining a suitably low altitude to commence landing. Captains only get visual on the runway after a perilous ingress, and they must prepare for an immediate landing where everything must go exactly right. It is so difficult that flights can only take off and land during daylight hours—that too under favourable weather conditions.

Due to the immense expertise and experience required, most captains require at least eight years before gaining the experience and special certification needed to land here. As I write this, only twenty-one airliner captains hold this status. This number may grow in the years to come, but it is by design not a quick process!

If a private flight arrives at Paro, the foreign pilot is required to have completed a simulator training programme on flying into and out of the airport. During the approach, the aircraft is required to have one of our certified pilots aboard, accompanying the crew and serving as a navigator when they make the dangerous ingress through our valleys.

Paradoxically, while Paro is justly known as the world's most challenging airport for landing, it also has one of the best safety records. In its three decades of serving commercial flights, with a service rate of sixteen flights per day, there has never been a major accident. This expertise ensures that flights operating in and out of Paro are managed by highly skilled professionals who can be trusted to deliver a safe experience, day in and out.

Once safely on the ground, travellers do not simply disembark into a bustling terminal. We do not use aerobridges, so passengers are greeted by Paro's fresh air as they descend the stairs. Paro sits in an open valley with lush, green forested mountains on both sides, and without fail, everyone stops to take photos before the leisurely walk into the terminal. As for me, I can't help but inhale deeply, gratefully filling my lungs with the fresh, crisp air of home.

Understanding the unique paradox of Paro Airport could help us unleash the human potential and talent needed to usher in sweeping social change—the kind that is necessary to keep civilisation running in a sustainable, environmentally friendly way. Because landing at the airport is so dangerous, it requires a combination of state-of-the-art navigation aids and communication systems to assist these skilled pilots during their approach and departure, and a culture that prioritizes safety above all else, even revenue.

Our aviation authorities continuously invest in infrastructure improvements, conduct regular safety audits and implement strict regulations to ensure that all stakeholders adhere to the highest safety standards. We have also established communication and collaboration as ways of life for everyone, be it air traffic controllers or even ground staff.

The danger and constant stress vastly increase the need to work together and achieve a common goal; the staff at Paro is incentivized to stay alert, learn from others' mistakes, and never be complacent. Paro (and the planet) can only function if its leaders are credible, forward-thinking, and dedicated to its success over their own enrichment. While we could theoretically open up bad-weather and low-light flights, this will not happen until we can be sure advancements in aeronautical technology and practice have made them as safe as possible—however long that takes.

Seen this way, our culture of expertise, emphasis on safety, and open communication enables one of the most dangerously-situated airports in the world to continuously and safely service flights day in and day out. Success and growth are possible even in the most challenging circumstances, and Paro shows why every day. As *Top Gun: Maverick* puts it, the possibility of completing the mission 'will come down to the pilot in the box'.

The Paro Paradox is a reminder that cooperation, safety consciousness, and careful development and integration of the best practices we know *can* indeed bring security out of danger, order out of chaos, and serenity out of fear. It is through unity and wisdom that we overcome the hazards of the natural world and create experiences of incredible beauty that bring everyone together. Here are the lessons that I seek to illustrate through my personal thoughts and experiences over the course of this book:

1. **Wisdom:** This is not just about having the smarts, knowledge, or even intelligence, as valuable as those things are. Wisdom is about how we use what we do, how we approach what we do not, and evaluating pros and cons for both the small and big pictures. It is also about listening to and learning from the experiences of others, and considering how today's decisions might shape our future. Here in Bhutan, we apply this wisdom by integrating the best practices from around the globe. We learn from others' experiences and successes, adapt those strategies to our unique context, and create solutions that are not only effective but also sustainable.

2. **Courage:** By this, the people of Bhutan mean having the willingness to ensure safe, controlled progress. Rather

than chasing silver bullets or immediate results, we also prioritize environmental sustainability and the well-being of everyone involved in our endeavours. This means doing things differently—not just for their own sake but also because they may be better alternatives to conventionally accepted options.

Our approach to development reflects this. I am not for one moment saying our problems do not need urgent attention but that we and our people are better served if we consider the potential impacts of our decisions on various stakeholders and the environment. We make sure we're moving forward in a way that minimizes negative consequences and ensures long-term viability. It takes courage to stand against the tide of rapid, unchecked progress, but we believe it is worth it.

3. **Compassion:** In a diverse society like ours, unity is key. We strive to foster unity among all groups and individuals, emphasizing shared goals and values to bridge divides and encourage collective action. It's not about everyone agreeing on everything, which just isn't possible! Instead, it's about coming together to build a stronger, more cohesive society and recognizing that what unites us must come first.

But compassion doesn't stop there. It's also about appreciating the beauty around us and cherishing our shared experiences. There's something about having a sense of wonder, about experiences that evoke awe or beauty that bring people together. These shared moments strengthen our bonds and foster a sense of belonging among us.

4. **Selfless service:** What makes all this possible is trust in one another through selfless service, which is the bedrock of cooperation. It is about service to others over yourself, benefiting others as opposed to being motivated by personal gain.

We believe in collaborative efforts among all stakeholders—governments, communities, organizations, you name it. By working together, we can harness diverse perspectives and resources to tackle complex challenges and develop comprehensive solutions.

All of these prove critical to solving some of the most serious problems we face, and I firmly believe that if it can be done at Paro, it can be done around the world . . . provided we come together with a common understanding that transcends our differences and disagreements.

A Razor's Edge

The Himalayan region is one of the most beautiful places on earth, but it is under serious threat. While Bhutan is rightly known as one of the happiest countries in the world, we have our share of problems, and like it is for people all over the world, our happiness is a choice rather than the result of favourable circumstances. It helps us maintain an attitude of joy and peace, which enables us to better confront the threats that do exist. But please do not confuse us with the mythical Shangri-La!

Just like the Arctic and Antarctica, the Himalayan glaciers have been melting for some time now due to climate change. They are receding at an alarming rate, and if this continues, glacier lake outbursts may lead to flooding, creating a dangerous and vicious chain of events. These glacial lakes are formed in the mountains by the glaciers melting, creating a large repository of water.

Unlike normal lakes at the bottom of valleys, glacial lakes are dangerous because they are not stable. First, they form on mountain slopes. Second, these lakes are made from unstable rocks. Big pieces of earth and sediment that are dislodged and carried downwards as a result of the movement of the ice, forming an accumulation of debris called a moraine. When glaciers melt, water moves down until it reaches the moraine, forming a natural dam.

Now, because of the way they are formed, these natural dams are certainly not stable. Any disturbance, such as an earthquake or enormous pressure, destabilizes the moraine. If the glacier continues to melt further, the dam cannot withstand the pressure, and it bursts. A moraine bursting is one of the most devastating natural disasters—the contained reservoir of water charges down into the valleys below, causing flash floods in the rivers downstream and triggering landslides. Rock, debris, branches, even entire trees are carried downstream, further creating another reservoir that collects water. When that happens, little water flows down and the rivers further downstream suddenly subside, becoming eerily quiet.

This is the calm before the deluge because we know that the river is being blocked upstream. Once the dams upstream burst, water cascades down into the valleys causing further flash floods and massive destruction. When this occurs, farms, villages, and livelihoods are destroyed. This has happened several times in Bhutan's recent history—in 1994, there were two glacial lake outburst flood (GLOF), resulting in the deaths of twenty-one people. On one occasion, a GLOF even swept away an ancient temple!

In 2019, we received a scare when two lakes burst. We were lucky that time because the lakes were small and slightly downstream. But in a country of over 2,000 glacial lakes with twenty-two at risk of flooding, we may not be so lucky next time. It is not just Bhutan but the entire Himalayan region, and the lives of one-fifth of humanity, that are effectively on a razor's edge.

Armed with this information, I headed to the TED Summit in Edinburgh in 2019 to call for the establishment of an inter-governmental 'Third Pole Council' by countries into which the ten major rivers flow: Afghanistan, Pakistan, India, China, Nepal, Bhutan, Bangladesh, and Myanmar. Such a council would be tasked with the singular responsibility of protecting the water repository in the Himalayas. This would involve closely monitoring the health of our glaciers and preventing them from melting. With the water towers of Asia under strain, 240 million people in the region can be directly affected, but more than 1.6 billion people who rely on these major rivers can be hit hard.

From the plains of Pakistan and northern India to the famed Yangtze in China and Southeast Asia's Mekong, people who rely on these waters may face disastrous consequences of floods or droughts. This destabilization may potentially result in tens of millions of climate change refugees who may be forced to move. Another scenario is potential political conflict over water in a region with three nuclear powers: China, India, and Pakistan. What makes the water situation even more complicated is that there are many countries in the region that do not get along. It is a troubled and volatile neighbourhood, yet the Third Pole must be protected for the sake of one-fifth of humanity. This was my appeal in Edinburgh.

While we cannot prevent an earthquake from occurring with the cascading effect of causing flash floods, what is within our control is global warming. In Bhutan, we have taken ownership and made immense sacrifices to protect our environment, not only for ourselves but also for the world and the collective future of humanity. We have done an outstanding job in environmental conservation, yet we bear the brunt of climate change even though we have done very little to contribute to it.

This is the paradox that we are faced with. When you live in a country surrounded by nature and with half its people surviving on subsistence farming, climate change is a constant reality, as opposed to those who live in a city, shielded from the harsh realities of the environment. We, in Bhutan, are more vulnerable to climate change, and probably suffer more from it too. Climate change impacts our agriculture and it is shrinking our glaciers. There have been more landslides during rainy seasons and visibly less snow when we climb up the mountains, as well as higher incidences of diseases spread by mosquitoes.

The proof of climate change is clear. Scientific evidence points to a warmer planet and rising sea levels. Since pre-industrial levels, global temperatures have already increased past the 1.5 degree mark. As we reflect on the year, it is evident that 2023 has set a worrying precedent in terms of climate change. It has officially been the hottest year since global records began.[1] July stands out as the single hottest month.[2] This is not an isolated incident either. Since records began in 1880, the ten warmest years on record have all occurred since 2010.[3] These sobering statistics highlight the escalating impacts of global warming and emphasize the urgent need for comprehensive climate action.

Even when governments shut down much of the world's activity during the 2020 Covid-19 pandemic, this did not do much to help with global warming. Although carbon emissions fell a record 7 per cent that year because of lockdowns and travel restrictions, the planet is still heading towards a global temperature rise in excess of 3 degrees Celsius this century.

Although Bhutan is a landlocked country, the rising sea levels have both direct and indirect effects on us. The immediate consequence is more frequent and deadly storms from the Bay of Bengal—the ocean east of the Indian subcontinent. The downstream effect is that as coastlines submerge, people in India and Bangladesh are displaced and climate refugees make their way inland.

This means, even without the direct risk of ocean levels rising and flooding vulnerable land masses, climate change poses an existential threat for Bhutan. We are effectively at the mercy of larger powers like India and China.

I want to make it clear that while I have been labelled an 'environmentalist' by many people, I have never claimed to be one. I see myself, instead, as an ordinary citizen of the world. I care for

---

[1] '2023 to be hottest year on record, EU scientists say,' *Reuters*, 6 December 2023, at https://www.reuters.com/business/environment/climate-change-2023-will-be-warmest-year-record-eus-copernicus-2023-12-06.

[2] Claire A O'Shea, 'NASA Clocks July 2023 as Hottest Month on Record Ever Since 1880,' *NASA*, 14 August 2023, at https://www.nasa.gov/news-release/nasa-clocks-july-2023-as-hottest-month-on-record-ever-since-1880.

[3] Rebecca Lindsey and Luann Dahlman, 'Climate Change: Global Temperature,' *Climate.gov*, 18 January 2023, at https://www.climate.gov/news-features/understanding-climate/climate-change-global-temperature.

the environment, but not necessarily more than the average person. Most people I meet are genuinely concerned and aware about climate change and about protecting the environment.

But whether we act on it is a different thing altogether. I believe that everyone in the world has a duty and a responsibility to look after the planet, which makes *all* of us environmentalists in one way or another. Personally, I balk at the term because it implies some people deserve the title and others do not. If this is the case, I have not done anything worthy to be called one yet!

An Agnostic Approach

I consider environmentalism a core part of our responsibility as human beings on this planet. Even more so than being religious, and I say this as a devout Buddhist.

Why? Because being religious means extending compassion to other people, which naturally must extend to all sentient beings. This can logically be extended to include the ecosystem that all of us rely on for sustenance, including animals and even plants. Being religious also provides an incentive to treat others well, as we innately believe doing good to others should be rewarded and doing evil punished. This takes the form of heaven or hell, as it does in Abrahamic religions, or good or bad karma.

Abrahamic religions believe that the earth is the creation of the same God who made us all. Therefore, we have the sacred responsibility to protect the environment for future generations, as they are also created by God. Eastern faiths, like Buddhism and Hinduism, teach that we are reincarnated until we achieve nirvana, so it behoves us to look after the environment, so we can be reborn into a better world.

Indigenous spiritualities from around the world, too, offer profound insights on environmental stewardship. For instance, many Native American tribes believe in a deep, spiritual connection between humans and the natural world, emphasizing respect for the earth as a living entity. Similarly, Australia's Aboriginal cultures view land as inseparable from their identity and spiritual well-being, leading to a strong focus on caring for the environment. In African traditional religions, reverence for ancestors and nature spirits fosters a sense of responsibility towards the natural world.

These perspectives, although outside the Eastern and Abrahamic paradigm, also underline the importance of environmental conservation for the well-being of current and future generations. I am merely extending these common concepts to the acts of doing good, beyond human beings, by animals and even nature. From an ant in the rainforest to a rhino in the plains to a whale in the ocean, they all need the environment to thrive. Many valuable species could disappear (and many have, indeed, disappeared) if we do not take care of this planet.

But we do not necessarily get rewarded for doing that, at least not directly. Protecting the environment *adds* to the honour that rightly comes from serving other people as a religious person, as both involve acting for a cause much larger than yourself. So, in this sense, I do aspire to be an environmentalist, because I have seen the effects of climate change on my country. This is also partly the reason why I have written this book on Bhutan's role in environmental conservation, how we have managed the sweeping change needed, and what societies around the world can do.

Note that because concerted action is so important, I have deliberately designed the principles I highlight in this book to be applicable to people of *any* political philosophy or religious belief system—hence my use of the term *agnostic*. I am not referring to agnosticism as the belief that we cannot know whether there is a god, but the adaptation of Bhutan's successes and the ideas we draw from it as suitable for people all over the world, regardless of political or religious background. I want to draw up ideas, lessons, and actionable steps that everyone can agree on and execute, without necessarily needing full intellectual, political, or religious agreement.

After all, in a diverse world, full consensus is by definition impossible! I have had the pleasure of meeting people and intellectuals from all over the planet, and I know first-hand how hard it is to get everyone to agree on what to have for lunch, never mind the best way of dealing with existential threats to our way of life, which are multi-faceted and require input from a vast number of interconnected disciplines and cultures.

Instead, I have written this book for leaders from all backgrounds and at all levels who want to change for the better and are looking for a comprehensive philosophy to bring the right people together in consensus rather than conflict. In practical terms, this means that if you are not a Buddhist, it would be nice if you became one, but I do not require it. If you do not believe in the ideals that make Bhutan's control over the development process possible, there is still concrete action you can take to help the planet and our people.

Even if you do not believe in the existential threat of man-made climate change or do not support the Paris Accord, I strongly hope you do and will argue for it, but I do not demand your conformity. Rather, I hope you accept the ideas I share in the spirit of wisdom, cooperation, and jointly working on the problems that we can all see before us in one way or another.

'Because It is There'

I wrote earlier about the value we Bhutanese attach to our mountains, and thankfully, laws have been put in place to protect them and the deities that reside there. This may sound as though we are romanticizing our mountains, but it is significant and symbolic to be able to still consider certain things as sacred in this modernizing world.

The sacred Himalayan mountain known to Tibetans as Chomolungma ('The Holy Mother') and to Nepalese as Sagarmāthā ('Goddess of the Sky') was given the name Mount Everest by British surveyors, after Surveyor-General George Everest. It is the tallest mountain in the world, and when the English mountaineer George Mallory was asked in the 1920s why he wanted to reach its summit, he famously replied, 'Because it is there.'

Mallory himself would die in the attempt, but that only intensified efforts to successfully reach the top. Chomolungma has been summitted thousands of times since the first success by Edmund Hillary and Tenzing Norgay in 1953, accumulating climbers' litter (and bodies) over the years.

Humanity should not be allowed to conquer everything. Indeed, Bhutan's own Gangkhar Puensum (Dzongkha, The White Peak of the Three Spiritual Brothers) stands slightly shorter than Chomolungma, but due to a fortunate 1994 change in Bhutanese law that banned climbing permits for mountains higher than 6,000 metres, it has never been successfully climbed.

At 7,570 metres, Gangkhar Puensum remains the tallest unclimbed mountain in the world. In 2003, the ban was extended to all mountaineering in Bhutan, so it will rightfully stay that way. We are a mountain people, after all, and know how best to treat our sacred peaks.

Of course, we in the Himalayas are aware of the benefits of mountaineering visits, but Bhutan has weighed these and found preserving our spirituality more necessary. After all, people have been to the moon and are planning to get to Mars, so there is no doubt that our mountains can be relatively easily conquered. Yet, there's something respectful and profound about disallowing attempts to summit the mountains. To leave the mountains in peace and not trample them is akin to letting go of our own ego as well. We should not have to dominate everything. Are we not already the dominant species of this planet? Do we not already know we are resilient and intelligent enough to tackle nearly any challenge? Is there really a need to conquer every square inch of land on earth?

Western governments are realizing this as well, and I can only hope their people will follow suit. In October 2019, the Australian government banned the climbing of the monolithic sandstone formation known as Uluru. It is a UNESCO World Heritage site, and the indigenous Anangu community had been fighting for years to prohibit climbers from scaling it due to its deep spiritual significance. Some of its stories are similar to the stories of deities that we have in Bhutan, speaking of spirit ancestors that shaped the land and of great serpents waging war around Uluru. It is also believed that those who take rocks from the formation will be cursed and suffer from misfortune.

In 1873, Uluru was given the name Ayers Rock after surveyor William Gosse sighted the landmark and named it after Sir Henry Ayers, the chief secretary of South Australia. The first tourists arrived in 1936. In 1983, against the locals' wishes, visitors were allowed to climb Uluru. Even more shockingly, a chain handhold was hammered into the rock so that visitors could make the steep 800-metre climb more easily.

But progress was made in the right direction, slow as it was. In 1993, it was officially given the dual name of Uluru/Ayers Rock. The colonial name has never been dropped, but more importantly, most Australians now refer to it simply as Uluru.

While the 2019 announcement of the permanent ban on climbing Uluru came as a pleasant relief, what truly surprised me was the hundreds of climbers who had queued up to ascend Uluru, just one day before its closure! Instead of respecting the decision to close the climb and perhaps view Uluru from a distance, hundreds lined up to 'conquer' the formation one last time. It was as though they did not get the point of the ban in the first place. Many people only understand the letter rather than the spirit of laws and are driven by personal motive and desire, not spiritual respect.

That said, even if we disagree about the sentiment that led Mallory and other mountaineers to Chomolungma, there is much to admire about the spirit and adventurous nature of explorers like him. It is a quality very few people have, and we hope it can be turned towards solving the problems a changing climate poses to people around the world.

The Right Ideas

Spirituality forms a big part of how we conserve sacred areas around the world. However, to get us very far, it must inform policies, legislations and plans that directly play a large part in protecting our forests and environment as well.

For decades, Bhutan has prioritized environmental protection as a national policy, way before it was even fashionable to do so. Therefore, it is not surprising that environmental conservation is one of the four pillars of GNH, a development policy that balances economic growth with sustainable development, preservation of culture, good governance, and environmental conservation.

While Bhutan is often perceived as a small and culturally cohesive society, it is not entirely homogeneous. The country is home to a diverse mix of ethnic groups, including the Ngalops, Sharchops, and Lhotshampas, each with their own languages, traditions, and customs. Despite this diversity, Bhutan has been successful in balancing happiness, environmental protection, and spirituality, a model that could be adapted to the West and cosmopolitan parts of Asia.

Emphasizing the exchange of ideas and mutual understanding, the preservation of harmony through dialogue and respect for culture and tradition is crucial. By sharing Bhutan's unique approach, we can contribute to a global conversation on sustainable development and well-being.

Perhaps one of Bhutan's greatest legislative achievements in history was the voluntary handing of power over from our King to a parliament elected by the people, which I was honoured to be personally involved in. Throughout this book, I'll share more about the processes that enabled this to come to pass quickly and peacefully.

Bhutan is still changing, and among our greatest projects has been the establishment of a reliable, clean source of hydroelectric power. Changes are deliberately slow and managed carefully, but even as we continue to evolve, we remain steadfast in our commitment to preserving our unique cultural and environmental heritage, and prioritizing the happiness and well-being of our people.

I invite you to explore with me the delicate balance between embracing progress and honouring tradition, as well as the innovative strategies and policies that have guided Bhutan's journey thus far. As we embark on this enlightening voyage, I hope you'll find inspiration and motivation to create positive change in your own life and community. Together, we can learn from one another's experiences, and work towards a more sustainable, harmonious world that benefits both ourselves and future generations.

Part One

My Life and Country

Chapter One

Growing Up Bhutanese

I promise you that if somebody had caught me by the shoulder at that moment and said to me, 'What is your greatest wish in life, little boy? What is your absolute ambition? To be a doctor? A fine musician? A painter? A writer? Or the Lord Chancellor?' I would have answered without hesitation that my only ambition, my hope, my longing was to have a bike like that and to go whizzing down the hill with no hands on the handlebars. It would be fabulous. It made me tremble just to think about it.

—Roald Dahl, *Boy: Tales of Childhood*

On the slopes of the Deolo Hills in east Kalimpong, India, lies a cluster of colonial buildings built over 100 years ago. These modest yellow cottages with rust-red zinc roofs form a small compound atop an open space among lush forests. One of the buildings is a hospital, another a bakery. A distance away sits a small farm with cows, pigs, and chickens roaming freely. A single church spire sticks out visibly from the cluster of buildings and sports fields.

At first glance, the entire compound looks like a small European settlement—but, in fact, it is a boarding school, and the site of some of my fondest memories.

Spanning 500 acres, Dr Graham's Homes is a safe haven for destitute children, most of whom are orphans. This place was where I grew up during my formative years and well into my teens. At the tender age of five, I was bundled off to Kalimpong to begin my education. It was the early 1970s, and Bhutan lacked schools. In an effort to encourage free education for all its people, the Bhutanese government sent hundreds of Bhutanese children to study in the schools located in the hill stations of India, particularly around the Darjeeling region. I was one of those children, and I was sent to Dr Graham's Homes, where I would spend eleven years.

Dr Graham's Homes is not strictly an orphanage, despite its being designed with abandoned children in mind. In 1900, Reverend Dr John Anderson Graham (who was affectionately known by us as 'Daddy Graham') founded the school to provide a home for abandoned Anglo-Indian children. After a visit to a tea garden in Darjeeling, Reverend Graham noticed the plight of the children there. The entire community suffered from great hardship and terrible deprivation. Most of the children in the Homes were offspring of British tea planters who settled in the region and later fathered children with local Nepalese, Lepcha, and Assamese mothers. Such liaisons were not unheard of.

But as the tea planters took on managerial positions at the plantations, they were allowed to invite their European brides to the land. As the foreign women sailed over, the local women and children in India were cast aside. The local women were no longer able to provide for their children, and many were sold or simply abandoned. Often, the women themselves were left destitute. Daddy Graham took it upon himself to look after these children by setting up a caring home and environment, where they could have the opportunity to lead a life of dignity.

Most of the Indian children in Dr Graham's Homes were from poor families. The Bhutanese children who arrived here were also from simple families, mostly farmers. But, somehow, the Bhutanese children always seemed to have a little bit more money, one way or another. They had more clothes, more *tuck* (snacks) and pocket money. I realized later that the Bhutanese parents probably could not bear the thought of sending their children to boarding school, that too in a foreign country. Those parents weren't particularly well-off either, but they gave their children everything they needed and more.

My own family was considered relatively well-off. My father, Nob Gyeltshen, was an officer in the Royal Bhutan Bodyguards and earned a decent wage. My mother Rinchen Zam raised six sons (of whom I am the eldest), weaving textiles in her spare time to make some money. We were not poor, but neither were we rich. However, we were frugal because my parents had to support us as well as their respective families. In fact, they even helped develop their villages, working hard to ensure a better life for others.

This meant they were very careful with their finances, even when sending us to a boarding school far away. So, unlike my fellow Bhutanese students, I rarely got extra pocket money. I was also much smaller in size and height compared to them, since most of the Bhutanese kids were already eight or nine years old when they were sent to Kalimpong.

My mother told me later that when I had left Bhutan for school, she was extremely concerned because I had barely learned to chew and was still sucking on my food. I must have developed slowly, and this was probably one of the reasons why I often felt inadequate. Seeing other Bhutanese children who were better off, bigger, and stronger didn't help either.

My younger brother Singye Dorji, who also attended school with me, didn't seem to be affected by all this. He was getting all the attention from everyone who met him. He also had a disarming smile that could charm anyone who came in contact with him. Singye is one year younger than me, and I remember senior girls talking to him as though he was their baby brother. They would pinch his cheeks and take him around. In turn, he would have plenty of jokes and stories to tell others. As a result, Singye grew up with a wider circle of friends, both boys and girls, and even teachers.

The six of us brothers seem to be evenly split between sociable extroverts and reserved introverts. Brother three, Tshering Wangchuk, and brother four, Tashi Tshering, are the former, and they know practically everyone in our town and village to this day. But brothers five and six, Tshewang Tobgay and Sangay Yeshi, respectively, are like me, reserved and quiet.

Perhaps I was acting too seriously for my age, but as the eldest of six sons, I felt compelled to take my responsibilities seriously. Somehow, I thought I needed to be definite and clear in whatever duties I had to shoulder, since I was the eldest, hence my mother and others always said that I was the more solemn and pensive one. Looking back, I realize it was something else: I was private and introverted because I lacked confidence.

In contrast to my social butterfly brother, I was pretty much a loner for the first few years at Dr Graham's Homes. I preferred my books to friends and alone time to football time. Rather than being lonely, I relished being alone and away from people, to the point I wished I was invisible!

In hindsight, this did nothing for my self-confidence. I never took part in any sports or extracurricular activities outside of my classes. Many Bhutanese excel in football, basketball, athletics, and swimming. But I refused to participate in any of these, unless it was compulsory. As a result, I never won a single certificate or award for such activities. Beyond physical activities, in my early years at school, I never took up responsibilities such as being class captain or monitor. If I could avoid people, I would. That is hardly a good start for a politician, but I am living proof that people can change and grow later in life.

Of course, I fully realize that while my introversion wasn't beneficial to me as a child, it didn't cripple me or keep me from excelling. This was how I plodded through my first few years at school. I didn't need to crack jokes, spar or compete with my classmates, or hang out with them, and I didn't feel the need to fit in. That said, giving up on a social life gave me ample time to bury myself in my books. My grades soared, thanks to that.

There was a turning point, though. In grade four, our English teacher read us Rudyard Kipling's 'Rikki-Tikki-Tavi', a story of a brave mongoose who defends his human family from a cobra. I enjoyed the story as well as our next assignment—recounting it in an essay—thoroughly. To my surprise, I won first prize for it, and it was the first time I had ever won an award in my life. This filled me with a new confidence I have never experienced before, and the sense I could manage whatever school threw at me.

Since that moment, I paid more attention in class and pored over my studies. From someone who preferred the safety of invisibility, I gradually became one of the top students. I was in tenth place in grade five, and in the top three in grade six. I put my entire heart into my academic performance and topped the class in grade seven. People started calling me 'mugpot', but it never put me off. I do not say this to boast, only to point out what's possible when you discover something worth doing with all your heart.

Despite doing well in class, I never really stopped being 'invisible'. It was too much of a 'superpower', and three decades later, old schoolmates were coming up to me saying they did not remember me from our days at Dr Graham's Homes. My fellow Old Boys and Girls (OBGs, as we call the Homes' alumni) maintain this was a joke, but I'm not fully convinced! One Bhutanese classmate only realized I was in her class when we reached grade seven, after I displaced her friend and fellow Bhutanese from first position, and she told me this thirty years later.

The teachers at Dr Graham's Homes were always kind to and supportive of me. My biology teacher even invited me to the biology lab on weekends to dissect frogs. I had told him that I wanted to be a doctor, and he kindly offered to show me how to examine and identify the nervous system of the amphibian, something that was outside of my curriculum. Dissecting frogs when my classmates were having fun or dating sounds geeky or just not what children might be doing in their leisure time, but it did make me feel special. I felt important and capable, and thoroughly enjoyed my studies as I maintained my class position.

A Love for Drama

It was also in my early years at school that I discovered a new passion: drama. I was given a role in a play called *Romany Roff* and got comfortable speaking on stage quite quickly. I put my thespian talents to great use and participated in a few more plays, thereafter, even acting in a Shakespeare play. I enjoyed learning my lines and dressing up. Although I was a young adolescent with very few friends and even less confidence, somehow drama managed to open up a different side of me. It was my safe haven, the only time when I felt I was finally adequate.

Being a 'mugpot' helped here, as I could memorize entire pages in a day or two. (Incidentally, I still do my best to memorize my speeches even today.) Suddenly, I was propelled from my solitude into the colourful lives of imaginary characters, far removed from my mundane one.

My newfound passion for drama has stayed with me throughout my school life, into my college years, and even now that I serve as prime minister. I have always believed in the power and importance of drama. It helps cultivate the mind and confidence, especially in children who, like me, are shy, introverted and have difficulty coming out of their shells. Drama did that for me. It gave me a sense of what it feels like to be part of a team.

As I refused to participate in sports and was a 'mugpot', I was never involved in any team-building or bonding activities at school. But being in a play forced me to be a team player. It also provided a good foundation for public speaking without the anxiety and fear that often comes with it. (Those who know me as a TED speaker might be surprised to learn I still feel stage fright even today!)

But in a play, you are not yourself. You are playing someone else and interacting with another character. This is liberating, especially if you have memorized your lines, your body language, and your tone. You know what to say and how to act. I realized later in life that these are some of the integral attributes that all public speakers must adopt in order to deliver a talk. Committing things, such as lines from a play, to memory is also a useful academic exercise for me.

* * *

Policy Brief: Reviving Drama and Imagination

During my tenure as prime minister, we reintroduced Shakespeare as part of the curriculum of Bhutan's schools, so that children may benefit from participating in drama, which had been losing its importance in schools for many years.

To kick things off, I even participated by performing a monologue as Shylock from Shakespeare's *The Merchant of Venice*, and also took part in slam poetry to appeal to the youth. For three months in 2017, fifty schools came to Thimphu and each staged a play every day at the first fifty-days-long National Drama Festival. A mix of plays was chosen, some from Shakespeare and most others from Bhutanese culture and in Bhutan's national language, Dzongkha.

Drama competitions were also held at the district level, where schools from twenty districts staged plays to vie for a chance to perform in the capital. I wonder if any other country has ever staged so many plays consecutively across such a short period!

* * *

Drama opened up doors for me. By the time I was in grade ten, I was known as a public speaker and was entrusted with delivering a sermon during church on Sunday. Every hostel at Dr Graham's Homes took turns to coordinate the activities for Sunday church services and sometimes, students were made to deliver a talk. My classmates seemed to have enough faith in me to take the stand on such a crucial day of the week. So, I took it upon myself and worked hard to write my speech and memorize it.

When the fateful Sunday came, I took to the pulpit and preached about honesty. While I have long forgotten what I said that day, I do remember ending my speech with a quote by the French philosopher Michel de Montaigne: 'A liar would be brave toward God, while he is a coward toward men.' I repeated this last line for dramatic effect. I have forgotten the rest of the sermon, but the powerful message in this line has served me well. Deception is effectively shaking your fist at all-knowing divinity, while simultaneously being too afraid of your fellow human beings to be honest with them.

Around this time, I was also made a prefect, a nice surprise I must say. Prefects in my school were somewhat like class monitors or school captains. There were about a dozen prefects, and they were given extra responsibilities along with being groomed for leadership. The teachers probably saw that I took my responsibilities seriously, topped my classes, did well in drama, and never got into trouble. This appointment helped further boost my confidence, which had slowly started to increase over the years.

With my improving grades, support from teachers, and budding acting career, there was so much going on in school. I got fully immersed in it, but it did not take away my yearning for family and home, especially for my parents. From the first day I was sent to Dr Graham's Homes till the day I graduated, I had pined for home, the warmth and love of my parents, and just being around them. I grew up not with the care and attention that parents often shower upon their children, but under the supervision and in the custody of a school.

I am grateful for Dr Graham's Homes' work, but it could never replace the intimacy of one's family. I don't think I ever got over this.

A Second Home

Despite missing my parents and longing to be at home in Bhutan, my time at Dr Graham's Homes was one of the best memories I have of my childhood. This was not just a boarding school; it was a second home, a place that shaped my memories, instilled invaluable skills, and honed the leadership qualities that would serve me later in life.

Although I lacked immediate attention from my parents because they were so far away, we had wardens whom we called 'aunties' and 'uncles', who would look after us. Each one was in charge of thirty children between the ages of five and fifteen. They were much more than just school staff—they were surrogate parents to us, many of whom were orphans experiencing care from an adult for the first time. We were really like a family, with the wardens caring for our every need, from our hygiene to homework and food (even if we were always hungry). Their care even extended to counselling us, when we needed it. They looked after us as if we were their own children.

Childhood at Dr Graham's Homes was filled with laughter, games, and camaraderie, but an underlying bond among us was our shared experience of hunger. The school provided us three basic meals a day, but our young, growing bodies craved more. In my last few years there, the school centralized its cooking system and we were fed more, and though, early on, we were hungry most of the time, the diet must have been quite balanced since we all grew up fit and healthy.

Most importantly, what the school taught us was how to survive, how to be independent and also self-sufficient. Since the majority of the pupils were homeless or parentless, Dr Graham's Homes taught us life skills that went beyond academics.

The school was our training ground. We cared for our hostels, which we fondly referred to as 'cottages'. From cleaning rooms, polishing their floors, and tending gardens to doing dishes and cleaning toilets, we learned that independence meant taking responsibility. We became a self-reliant family, finding joy in tasks like cleaning pots and pans, where the reward was leftover food. There were no cleaners and it was up to us as a 'family' to care for the facilities.

We grew up to be an independent bunch of children, as was intended by the school. There was a tailor to mend our clothes, a cobbler to fix our shoes, a bakery for fresh bread, even a workshop for mechanical repairs. Vocational training was available for those interested, providing a pathway to become seamstresses, cobblers, farmers, or mechanics. The school even housed a hospital for students to learn nursing, and a secretariat for students learning secretarial skills such as shorthand and typing.

Besides the main school, Dr Graham's Homes also had a department to look after babies and toddlers, who were mostly orphans. This department trained students as nannies, and many went on to work as au pairs abroad. This holistic approach ensured that every child had the tools to thrive in life, regardless of their academic prowess.

This meant the school instilled leadership qualities in most of us at a very early stage. Despite there being more prestigious schools in and around Kalimpong, many Dr Graham's Homes' alumni have gone on to hold significant positions in Bhutan's government. These have included the first democratically-elected prime minister, Jigme Y Thinley; Chief Justice Sonam Tobgye, who was the chairperson of the drafting committee of the Constitution; his successor as Chief Justice Tshering Wangchuk; and me, the first opposition leader and eventual prime minister. A coincidence? I think not!

Despite my minimal participation in extracurricular activities (except for drama), my education was well-rounded. I believe sending children to boarding schools at a very young age may not be ideal, but for parents lacking resources, knowledge, or experience to support school-going children, it can be an effective alternative. A farmer with no formal education might struggle to guide his child through school, oversee homework, organize extracurricular activities, or provide a balanced diet. Under such circumstances, a boarding school like Dr Graham's Homes becomes a beacon of hope, ensuring every child gets a fair chance at having a successful future.

* * *

Policy Brief: The Central Schools

After forming the ruling party post the 2013 election, one of the first few things I did was touring the country. I spoke to local governments to find out more about their school systems, encouraging them to set up boarding schools in their locality. This would enable them to better meet the educational needs of their children.

These schools were ideally meant for children who would be twelve and above, but if needed, even children as young as six could enrol—otherwise, they would be at risk of losing out on building strong educational foundations. These schools, known as central schools, provide hostel services to reduce the travelling time required to just receive education. Central schools are also located in large population catchment areas and provide meals, free uniforms, bedding, and sportswear—items that are often unaffordable for many villagers. Today, there are more than sixty central schools, developed mostly with financial assistance from the Government of India, across the country. They largely benefit villagers from remote areas and ease the financial burden of parents. They also enable children to spend more time on academic pursuits, sports, and extracurricular activities, allowing them to form closer bonds with their teachers and with one another.

Generally, children are much better off under the direct care and supervision of their parents, although this was a part of childhood I never got to enjoy. I cannot emphasize enough that a boarding school is only a better alternative for children if their parents are not able to support them in their education and school activities.

* * *

I always looked forward to the winter breaks, when I would be reunited with my family. During my first few years in school, Mother would travel all the way to Kalimpong to escort Singye and me back to Bhutan. My father was often on duty with the Royal Bodyguards of Bhutan, which was the unit responsible for the security of the royal family.

Father had been a sergeant in the regular army, but in 1964, he happened to be in Phuentsholing when he heard that then-Prime Minister Jigme Palden Dorji (elder brother to the Royal Grandmother

Ashi Kesang Choden) had been assassinated. He quickly went to the guest house, the scene of the crime, made some enquiries, and went after the suspect. Two days later, he apprehended the assassin, single-handedly capturing him alive as ordered. (Despite the danger he must have faced, Father never boasted about his accomplishment or even talked about it much. To my knowledge, he only told me the story once.) For his bravery and success, Father was commissioned as an officer and transferred to the Royal Bodyguards. He would eventually join the Queen's protection detail.

With Father on duty most of the time, Mother would make the arduous journey to Kalimpong to pick my second brother and me up from the Homes. Later, she would bring our two younger brothers along, having recently given birth to them. My third brother would ride on her back, harnessed and strapped to her body with a long shawl, and my fourth brother would be nursing on her lap.

When the school would reopen, she would send us back, making four trips in total. It must have been hard on her, especially as someone in a foreign land having to navigate the route to my school, but never once did I hear her complain. It was a Herculean effort for her to make these trips back and forth, but she never saw it as a sacrifice. Her immense toughness and resilience still amaze me today, and indeed these were once traits common to all Bhutanese. As the world changes, I hope that same spirit lives on in future generations and that they resist the pressure to be softer and more entitled as they prosper.

Mother had known hard work since her teenage years. In the 1960s, as Bhutan opened up to modernization, infrastructure had to be built. Young people were conscripted from every village to build Bhutan's first motor road and every family had to send at least one able-bodied person as a labourer.

Despite having able-bodied older siblings, Mother volunteered to go and ended up leaving her family, her home, and her village in Zhemgang (in central Bhutan) on three occasions to work for months on end. She wouldn't have been totally alone, as some people from her village were conscripted as well.

This road, which was completed in 1961, stretches from the border town of Phuentsholing in the south towards Paro. It was the first motor road in Bhutan, representing the start of modern development. I am immensely proud that Mother was among the many Bhutanese who toiled for years to construct it—and still think of her hard labour and sacrifices every time I travel on the highway. Mother herself recounts how difficult the work on the road was but is grateful for the increased convenience of travelling across the country. She does feel bad for her work-mates who returned to their villages permanently, and never got to see the completed road or benefit from it.

* * *

Policy Brief: The East-West Highway

During my term in office, I have prioritized the development of road infrastructure, recognizing it as the lifeline of progress in Bhutan. Our primary focus has been on expanding and upgrading the East-West highway, because it connected the remote eastern regions of Bhutan to central Bhutan and Thimphu, the capital city located in the west.

We have also highly prioritized constructing and upgrading roads leading to the *gewog* centres. Beyond this, we have extended our road-building initiatives to numerous villages. In Bhutan, villages have experienced significant development only after roads were built in their vicinities. Thus, our goal now is to replicate the success of our initial project across all villages, connecting them all by road.

Our work to expand and improve the East-West Highway cost around Nu 10 billion, financed entirely by development assistance from the Government of India. This project created work for more than forty contractors. To ensure they would be duly completed, the improvements were made in a single round of upgrades, causing a lot of inconvenience to travellers and drawing some criticism. I am glad to have helped carry on the work that pioneers like Mother started, and my vision is to make this road, with its incredible scenic beauty, one of the top 'must-drive' destinations in the world.

* * *

I have sometimes wondered why Mother's older siblings sent her to build the road instead of going themselves. She has done well in life and raised the six of us . . . yet this might not have happened had she not left her village. After the road was completed and she was able to go on vacation, she went to Kalimpong to hear the teachings of Tibetan lama Dudjom Rinpoche. It so happened that my father, who was a soldier then, was stationed in Kalimpong at the same time. He, too, had previously volunteered his service to the country as a conscript of the Royal Bhutan Army, as every village had to send someone to join.

Brought together by the circumstances of Bhutan's modern development (and a huge dose of fate as well) my parents met in Kalimpong and fell in love. Mother gave birth to me in Kalimpong in 1965. Five years later, as destiny would have it, I would return to the same place they first met, to be admitted as a student under the care of Dr Graham's Homes!

Walks to Remember

In my childhood, winter breaks were a time of adventure and bonding with my family. We'd embark on an annual migration, a tradition rooted in my father's semi-nomadic pastoralist heritage from the village of Dorithasa in the Haa district of Bhutan. Each year, as the cold set in, we'd accompany our cattle southwards, following their instinctual journey to warmer pastures. This tradition was not unique to us; many Bhutanese villagers share similar nomadic practices, moving in sync with their herds of cattle or yak.

Our summer camps, located 3,500 to 4,000 metres above sea level, were lush with fresh grass, herbs, and flowers. Our cattle grazed freely, while we gathered fodder for the milking cows and calves. As autumn drew to a close, we descended to the lower regions of the Samtse district, guided by the cows' instincts and our astrological calendars.

Our accommodations were rudimentary yet magical: open sheds with roofs made of wild banana leaves, divided by sticks into two sections—one for the tethered calves, the other for us. (Indeed, Father's birthplace was one such shed!) Above the calves, a shelf held our belongings: blankets, saddles, pots, and pans. Staying in this 10-metre-long shelter, filled with animals, milk, and cottage cheese, felt like a never-ending camping trip. It was a cherished time spent with my family, a beautiful end to my winter break before I returned to Kalimpong.

Such migrations usually involve gruelling hours of walking. But I found these long and arduous treks enjoyable. Even as a child, I loved to walk like many other Bhutanese do. In grade six, when I was about twelve years old, I even took part in a cross-country fundraising walkathon that took us from Kalimpong to Darjeeling, a good 55 kilometres, in a single day!

Every few years, my school would hold this sponsored walk. Sponsors from America or Europe would fund a student for every kilometre walked. I did not manage to get any sponsors, but the school allowed me to participate in the walk anyway. On the day of the walk, I felt such anticipation that I woke up at 2 a.m., ate an early breakfast with my schoolmates and took off on our walking adventure. It was a killer of a walk. The first 15 kilometres were all downhill, but the remainder was entirely uphill. We started off singing in the cool morning breeze while walking on the tarmac road. The original large, spirited group thinned into small gatherings of two to three children, and eventually we grew quiet, sweaty, and breathless when the heat of the afternoon sun started wearing us down. By the time we reached Darjeeling, we were all aching and had sores on our feet, knees, thighs and lower backs. But I would do it again, of course!

I enjoy walking even today, especially in my country. I believe many Bhutanese still do, despite the ever-growing number of vehicles imported into the country. Bhutanese are extremely adept at walking uphill, downhill, on rocky and steep terrain, and even on slippery ice or deep snow. Almost every one of us, women included, have strong thigh and calf muscles, and are able to navigate the most challenging paths without breaking a sweat. Walking is part and parcel of our daily lives, a form of meditation and a chance to immerse ourselves in our pristine surroundings.

I have walked through many parts of my country, from the remotest villages to tourist trails and even to border areas. Those near India are hot and humid, while regions near the Chinese border are frigid and cold. I also did a sixteen-day Move for Health walk to raise funds for the Health Trust Fund. (The Fund, established by former Health Minister Lyonpo Sangay Ngedup, finances the procurement of all essential drugs in the country to ensure that healthcare remains free.) It took me across a distance of 500 kilometres, from the east of Bhutan, in Trashigang, all the way to our capital, Thimphu, in the west.

There is always something to see in Bhutan if you take the time to walk. In addition to the beautiful countryside and magnificent mountains, the other thing that entices me to walk is the clean and oxygen-rich air, as well as the mixed smells of the natural mulch of the forest, flowers blooming, pine needles, and fresh tree leaves that inevitably fill my lungs each time I take a breath. I get immersed as I walk further into the forest, listening to birdsong and deer barking, half expecting to spot a beautiful bird or wild animal during a hike. Walking and jogging have a beautiful meditative quality to them that clears the mind, especially on our nature trails. It allows me to think deeply—indeed, many of my ideas and plans have been born on walks.

Of course, practical realities matter too. My village of Dorithasa in western Bhutan is a three-day trek from Samtse, the nearest town along the highway. Even buying basic supplies or groceries requires an immense amount of effort, something many in developed areas don't realize. Going to town, or 'going to the bazaar' as most Bhutanese would say, means making the three-day journey to Samtse, followed by another three days on the return trip when we were not migrating.

So, going shopping for provisions was a week-long affair that, when I was a kid, I would be extremely excited about. Villagers would get the horses ready and prepare supplies for night halts. Perhaps, in an attempt to keep me distracted, my parents would feed me rock sugar and sometimes, as a special treat, they would give me balls of jaggery, which I loved. There would be an air of excitement and adventure every time we went shopping in Samtse. My family and other villagers would buy necessities like hammers, nails, tea leaves, slippers, some clothes, sugar, salt, kerosene, and even swords. The adults would pack all these provisions onto their horses, and we'd walk all the way back to our village.

As I grew older, I could tell that the excitement had waned and I saw the drudgery in the preparation that had to be done beforehand just to shop for some household items. The trek was also sometimes unpredictable due to bad weather or other unforeseen circumstances. It was no longer as fun as I used to think it was.

As an adult, this experience made me realize the importance of roads. Even dirt roads connecting remote villages would cut down on the time and hassle of travelling. Many years later, the moment I got the opportunity to serve in government, we expanded the farm road network. By the time our government completed its tenure, almost every village was connected by road. Dorithasa was one of the last villages to be connected. These were not hardy, all-weather roads, mind you. They were basic tracks—bumpy and uncomfortable—but there is much appreciation of the fact that there is a road at all!

The arrival of a road in a village signifies the arrival of modern development. Electricity, water, telephone lines, a school, and a canteen are all important. But it is ultimately the construction of a road that seals the villagers' confidence that modernization has arrived.

* * *

Policy Brief: The Gewog Shops

To lessen the hassle of spending a week to 'go to the bazaar', the government urgently established farm shops in every gewog (county). The idea was to offer household items, produce, and necessities to the villages so that residents need not travel long distances to get basic necessities. I personally did not want any farmer to have to walk for days just to purchase simple items, such as salt, sugar, or cooking oil.

Now, shops along the way may sell those goods, but they do so at exorbitant prices—almost twice or thrice what urban people pay in Thimphu. I have been aware of these economic realities, but both the long travels and high prices are unacceptable to me. I know that this strong commitment to farm shops is influenced by my own experiences growing up. As it is, our villagers are among the poorest people in the country. They barely have access to income and earnings, and to see them pay that much more for essential goods weighs on my conscience.

While the farm shops sell these goods for about the same price as in Thimphu, I think they should be subsidized even further. When we established them, critics (all of whom lived in Thimphu and did not have to pay exorbitant prices for basic goods) said we were 'destroying the private sector'!

The hypocrisy was not lost on me. These very people were the first to complain loudly when the prices of goods in their neighbourhood shops increased even slightly. To me, the welfare of the villagers comes first, and we have continued to implement our plans despite what our detractors said. The better lives of the villagers, and the results we have obtained, speak louder than any argument we could have made.

* * *

Preparing for My Career

I was very distracted during my high school years at Sherubtse College in the eastern Bhutanese town of Kanglung. Compared to being in a boarding school, where there were so many responsibilities on top of chores and other menial tasks, years eleven and twelve of high school meant I was suddenly given a lot of freedom to come and go as I wished, which I totally exploited at first. I drank too much cheap alcohol. I now think this was a form of escapism to avoid dealing with a new environment, with new people, and a new system.

Instead of going to class, I would head over to my cousin's place in Yongphula. It was a great place for free booze or a hearty meal, and I loved hearing him talk about his experience as an officer in the Royal Bhutan Army. Like most boys, I have always been fascinated by the military, especially since my father was a soldier. It is indeed a place of honour, duty, and camaraderie, and I was drawn to how structured and disciplined it is. Every role is defined, each person's duty is regimented and almost everyone is on equal standing.

So, one day, I wrote in to the Royal Bhutan Army headquarters and applied to be admitted to officer training. I was so determined to join that I dropped out of high school even before my year eleven examinations! That was very irresponsible of me, and I had not discussed this with anyone, including my father.

Somehow, Father was aware of it—he must have also been informed about my absence from school and me not appearing for my examinations. One day, while we were at home, I finally plucked up the courage to let him know of my decision to join the army.

'Look, Son. I am in the army, your cousins are in the army and you have a few uncles in the army, too,' he replied. 'But there is no one in our family or even our village who is in the civil service. We need people there as well, and I'd like you to join the civil service.'

That was the first time my father requested something of me. He had never interfered in my personal life before, so for him to make such an appeal, it must have meant something to him. (My fifth and sixth brothers eventually joined the army a decade later, with his blessings).

I agreed to his request, but I admitted that I had discontinued my studies. 'Do not worry, you'll be fine,' he said. I immediately felt reassured because he had so much trust in me, yet I was also suddenly feeling the weight of my responsibility as the eldest among six brothers.

True enough, the principal of Sherubtse College, Father Leclaire, graciously allowed me to repeat year eleven in the same stream of science that I had left, despite this not being normally allowed. (High school then was divided into arts, commerce, and

science streams.) Father Leclaire listened to me carefully and made
an exception for me.

* * *

Father William Mackey and the Jesuit Schools in Bhutan

Father Gerald E Leclaire was Sherubtse College's first principal. It had
been established as a public school in 1968. The first principal of the
school was Canadian-born Father William Mackey, a Jesuit priest
who was invited by the Third King, Jigme Dorji Wangchuck, in 1963 to
become an educator as part of Bhutan's modernization efforts.

Father Mackey went on to live in Bhutan for thirty-two years,
transforming and modernizing a handful of primary schools into an
integrated system of primary and high schools, technical schools,
teacher training institutes, and a college. He was awarded with the
highest honours for his lifelong contributions to education.

Despite technically being a missionary priest, he never converted
a single Bhutanese person—believing it more important to focus on
providing the people with a strong educational foundation.

Those Jesuit educators in Bhutan were not the first to have set
foot in our nation. As early as 1627, Portuguese Jesuits Estevao Cacella
and Joao Cabral were the first Europeans to visit Bhutan. They even
met our founding father Zhabdrung Ngawang Namgyal and spent a
few months in his court. They were also granted land in Paro to build
a church, but having no success in conversion, the Jesuits eventually
left for Tibet.

* * *

The rare opportunity to repeat year eleven was a defining moment
that I couldn't afford to screw up. Aiming for a scholarship and
a bachelor's degree, I studied hard to not let my parents down—
especially not Father, who worked very hard to support us brothers.
I wanted to make him happy and proud, and thankfully, he had a
lot of confidence in me too, though I never could figure out why.

I got serious about my studies while pursuing my passion in drama by taking part in some plays in high school. I played a part in *Julius Caesar*, *Macbeth*, and even in Oscar Wilde's *The Importance of Being Earnest*. These plays were directed by our English teacher, Mr Fanthome, who became somewhat like a mentor to me and allowed me to spend a lot of time in his home. Like Father, he too had confidence in me. (Some of my friends say they overheard him telling his wife about me: 'Mark my words, he will be somebody someday.') Indeed, he was the one who instilled in me the importance of public service and nurtured my passion for it.

I obviously did not want to disappoint the people who placed so much faith in me, so I once more became the mugpot that I had been in primary school, pulling all-nighters, taking detailed notes, studying earlier and not leaving it to the last minute. But I wasn't just mugging—I ensured that I understood what was being taught and could even predict the exam questions based on past papers.

Eventually, my hard work paid off. The United Nations Development Programme (UNDP) in Bhutan offered scholarships to a university in the United States, which could only go to the top two scorers of my class. I scored the second highest in the class, which meant I was bound for America.

Why Pittsburgh?

Many people who have met me often express surprise when I say I studied at the University of Pittsburgh, given it is not often a university of choice for students with scholarships. 'Why Pittsburgh?' I have often been asked.

In the interests of pre-empting this question, allow me to tell the story here. Upon accepting the UNDP scholarship, I had to decide what to study and consulted with the Royal Civil Service Commission, which administered the UN scholarship in Bhutan. The plan was for the commission to send students abroad, enabling them to return with degrees and serve in the civil service after.

I was deeply interested in architecture and discussed it with then-Royal Civil Service Commission chairman Jigme Thinley. He would later become Bhutan's first democratically elected prime minister, at the same time when I became the first opposition leader of the country.

'Why do you want to study architecture?' he asked.

'I want to blend the beautiful form of Bhutanese architecture with the functionality of Western architecture,' I replied.

'Well, we have a few students doing architecture already,' he said. 'We need more engineers, which we do not have. Why not do mechanical engineering?'

So I researched the best mechanical engineering courses available then. According to a book on 'The 250 Best Colleges in the USA', they were offered at the Massachusetts Institute of Technology (MIT), Stanford University, and the University of California at Berkeley. I wrote to all of them, but every one of them came back to me saying it was too late for the current intake, but they would consider me for the following year. Around the same time as my university applications, I chanced upon a *TIME* magazine article that declared Pittsburgh in Pennsylvania as the most liveable city in the United States. I suppose I am someone who is easily convinced! Because of that one article, I decided to write to the University of Pittsburgh as well. They accepted me for the current intake.

As I was about to pack my bags for America, I received news from UNDP that my scholarship had been postponed due to budgeting issues. It was going to be a two-year wait for me before I could continue my studies. It was, somewhat, a letdown, but this also meant I had sufficient time to reapply to MIT and Stanford.

But I didn't. Perhaps it was some sense of loyalty to the university. Perhaps also because the University of Pittsburgh had accepted me when other had not, I felt a sense of responsibility and obligation to follow through on my application with them. That was how I ended up in Pittsburgh, doing a bachelor's degree in mechanical engineering.

Of course, I had a two-year wait ahead of me. It was, somewhat, a 'gap year' for me in the days before gap years even existed!

During those two years, I helped my parents build a house on our land in Thimphu. I designed the place myself (this was before strict building regulations were in place), sourced material for it, and even worked with contractors, suppliers, and workers on the construction site every day. We managed to build two small, pine-panelled cottages, which I was very proud of, as I had convinced my parents to embark on the project. The total expenses amounted to about Nu 700,000 (US$9,600) per house, which was a bargain even for 1987. The construction materials were also of good quality, and we earned some income renting the houses out to expatriates. (Later, my wife Tashi and I would live in one of them for many years, raising our family there. Today, that house has been converted into Phang-Guu, a restaurant serving traditional Bhutanese food, started by my son Gyamtsho. Tashi built our present home, and she's proven that she's a much better builder than me!)

I also worked as a chauffeur during this time, driving tourists and even international guests and experts invited by the Bhutanese government around. I enjoyed all of my conversations with them.

* * *

Policy Brief: A Love for Nature

While working as a chauffeur, one of the few guests I had the honour of ferrying around was Sir Simon Bowes-Lyon (a first cousin of Queen Elizabeth II) and his wife, who toured Bhutan in 1986. They began at Thimphu in the west, moving on to Bumthang in central Bhutan, and all the way to the east to Trashigang. There, the couple went for a trek while I waited in town to drive them to the border of Bhutan and Guwahati in India, where they were to end their trip.

They returned from their trek with more things than when they had started. In their arms were stacks of plant presses used by naturalists collecting specimens for study. These bundles, consisting of layers of cardboard and blotting paper, were bound securely by straps. Within the layers of blotting paper were multiple flowers, leaves, stems and seeds of the many flora species that they had encountered during their trek.

It did not occur to me then to ask them what the specimens were for. It never once crossed my mind that one day, it would be illegal to pluck flowers or plants from their native habitats and transport them all the way to England or that someone might want to do so with the plants and flowers that I encountered regularly. Some botanists and horticulturalists were permitted to do so in Bhutan from 1914, amassing a comprehensive record of more than 6,000 species.

In 1975, the Bhutanese government commissioned the Royal Botanic Garden of Edinburgh to produce the first-ever publication about the flora of Bhutan—perhaps the very project Sir Simon Bowles-Lyon had been collecting samples for. Titled *Flora of Bhutan*, the collection spans nine volumes, with in-depth information on trees, herbs, plants, seeds, and flowers.

Today, the Bhutanese government is much stricter, with legislation drawn up to protect rare and valuable flora. Our rich, pristine biodiversity may indeed hold many medicinally important secrets, but any exploration and research must be led by Bhutanese. I'll say more about these efforts in chapter seven of this book.

* * *

My gap year was a rather carefree period for me, which allowed me to learn much from books and try my hand at architecture, construction, chauffeuring, and tour guiding. But, towards the end of the two-year wait, I started becoming frustrated and hoped to be packed off to America as soon as possible.

September of 1987 came not a day too soon and, finally, I was aboard a plane for the very first time, flying out of Bhutan towards an entirely new landscape and way of life.

Chapter Two

Culture Shock, Two Ways

Love is that condition in which the happiness of another person is essential to your own.

—Robert A Heinlein, *Stranger in a Strange Land*

I would be lying if I said I did not face a culture shock when I arrived in America. Although I had seen how the United States looked and expected it to be similar to what I saw in films and photos, the city of New York (where I stayed briefly before heading to Pennsylvania) was larger than life. I was immediately hit by the prosperity. The skyscrapers with glistening glass windows, large modern cars (so many of them!), and big, fancy restaurants that dished out huge portions of food—there was just so much to take in. It seemed like a booming metropolis where everyone was well off.

Like many, I had held two contrasting images of America before my first visit. The first image painted a picture of opulence and abundance, a veritable land of plenty. I imagined streets lined with shops overflowing with clothes, food, shoes—essentially everything one could desire. I even fancied that Americans, with their excess of belongings, would simply discard their unused items, which I could acquire at a bargain.

Yet, the second image starkly contrasted with the first. It was a portrait of destitution, of an America plagued by poverty. I am not exactly sure how this notion first took root in my mind.

Perhaps, it was a movie scene or a book passage. Or maybe Elvis Presley's haunting tune 'In the Ghetto' had etched this vivid image of dilapidated neighbourhoods, gang-ridden streets, and broken families neglecting their children. This bleak vision of America was potent, yet oddly, I never recognized its contradiction to my other image of a prosperous America until I visited Pittsburgh myself.

The mention of a housing project piqued my curiosity, prompting me to explore it first-hand. So, one day, I ventured alone into one of Pittsburgh's impoverished regions. Admittedly, it might not have been the wisest decision. As I navigated the streets, the grim reality of my second image of America came alive before my eyes. Vandalised walls stood as silent witnesses to the neighbourhood's struggle and trash-littered roads were a testament of neglect. Plywood-covered windows stared back blankly, hiding the lives of the predominantly Black families within. Unsupervised children played among loitering men, painting a picture of a social fabric worn thin. I do not remember seeing any white Americans there.

Fear crept in, replacing my initial curiosity, and I quickly left. But the stark image of this other America, so far removed from the land of plenty I'd once envisioned, lingered long after.

Yet, both images were accurate. How is it that such wealth and prosperity can exist alongside poverty in the same neighbourhood or country or even in the world? I could not reconcile this paradox. The experience left such a lasting impression on me that I have become an ardent supporter of eradicating poverty in all its forms and of reducing the wealth gap. The pent-up frustration of many Black communities in America is real, and even back then, when I was studying there, I got a good understanding of what they were (and still are) fighting for. It seems like there is still a lot of work to do in this area—not just in the US, but across the world, especially in many developed countries.

To this day, I dream of making Bhutan prosperous and making sure that no one is left behind or is destitute. I saw what prosperity could bring to people: a job, a house, a car. If there's a country where everybody can have these, it is Bhutan—we have the blessings of enlightened kings and, with just over 700,000 people, we are ultimately a very small country.

Of course, this must happen keeping our emphasis on the environment and happiness in mind. Poverty and want should have no place anywhere. Thus, this aim has become one of our government's focuses for the future.

* * *

Policy Brief: Poverty Reduction Efforts

During my time in government, I have overseen a host of measures aimed at improving the quality of life for citizens and reducing poverty levels. Recognizing the crucial role of education and health in poverty reduction, we enhanced the country's already free access to both and improved the quality of the services provided. This initiative has resulted in higher literacy rates and improved health outcomes, contributing significantly to poverty reduction.[4]

Life can also be unpredictable, so, to safeguard citizens from financial hardships arising from unforeseen incidents, our government has subsidized and enhanced life and home insurance schemes. These initiatives have provided a safety net for many Bhutanese families and helped them maintain their livelihoods during challenging times. There is also a crop compensation scheme, which compensates farmers for crop damage caused by wildlife or storms, protecting them from income loss and aiding the reduction of rural poverty.

In an innovative approach to poverty reduction, I helped commission a detailed survey of the poorest families. This initiative helped identify every family struggling to escape poverty. Accompanied by photos and recommendations for support, this

---

[4] 'Bhutan has achieved significant reduction in poverty levels, says new World Bank report,' *The World Bank*, 17 September 2014, at https://www.worldbank.org/en/news/press-release/2014/09/17/bhutan-poverty-report.

personalized approach has allowed for more targeted and effective poverty reduction efforts.

* * *

University Life

Adjusting to university life came naturally to me, with one glaring exception—the seemingly disrespectful behaviour of some classmates. They would unceremoniously prop their feet on tables, exude rudeness, and sometimes even smoke at the back of the class. This was a jarring contrast to my experiences in Bhutan, where such conduct would be unthinkable. I later discovered, to my relief, that this was not a typical class but a relief session led by a student. Still, the cultural disparity left me bewildered.

A second incident that underscored my cultural disorientation came after I befriended an American classmate. One day, while walking to school, I decided to stop by his off-campus rental house and accompany him there. As I approached, I noticed the door was slightly open. In Bhutan, this is an open invitation to enter, so I walked right in without knocking. Was he furious!

Back home, our doors are often left unlocked, even open, welcoming neighbours, relatives, or community members to walk in freely. The concept of locked doors was foreign to me, as was the idea of knocking before entering. In Bhutan, privacy is a fluid concept, with people regularly walking into others' homes, rooms, or offices. So, the idea that I had unknowingly violated a norm by not knocking left me both perplexed and embarrassed.

I enjoyed my mechanical engineering classes. My high school years had provided a strong foundation in calculus and physics. A few of my classmates picked up on this because they would invite me to their homes, where I'd give them tuition and, in exchange, they would offer me some food or beer. In my four years there, I did modules such as aerodynamics and thermodynamics. But out of the many subjects I had to learn, there was one I was truly enthralled by: computing.

Those were the early days of computing technology, when its foundations were still being laid. It may seem rudimentary now, but in the late 80s, it was state-of-art technology. We used the latest computers, from the IBM XT with an impressive 128 KB RAM to its successor the PC AT with a whopping 256 KB RAM. I was astounded by how quick it was (at that time). There were multiple computer labs on campus where I would spend many hours. I marvelled at the technology, much of which I had never heard of in Bhutan. Now, I was seeing it with my own eyes.

For me, computer programming was the epitome of enjoyment. We used to boot up PCs using 5 ¼-inch floppy disks—a concept that might baffle today's tech-savvy generation. The sound of the machine whirring to life was like an orchestral symphony to my ears. My passion for computing was so intense that I once spent thirty-six hours in a lab to finish a project, subsisting solely on snacks from campus vending machines! While my classmates grappled with bugs in extensive programs that spanned hundreds of pages, I distilled mine into a concise, flawless fifteen pages.

The output of the program was a diagram of a simple machine that was printed on an A0-sized paper, depending on values that were assigned to variables. I wrote my program to generate accurate and attractive results, which my professor hung on his office wall! I was honoured, even more so, when eighteen months later, during my last month in college, he called me to his office, removed my chart from the wall and returned it to me.

Before university, I had never seen a computer in Bhutan. The most advanced technology I had encountered was an electronic typewriter at the UNDP office, which I used to type my scholarship applications. Given the absence of PCs or mainframes back home, I relished subjects that involved computer programming. However, I struggled to see how mechanical engineering concepts like thermodynamics, aerodynamics and fluid mechanics would be applicable in Bhutan.

During my studies, I once wrote to the Royal Civil Service Commission suggesting a shift to civil engineering, as it seemed more relevant for Bhutan's developmental stage. I never received a response, so I continued my journey in mechanical engineering.

I had a fantastic time in America, and spent it soaking up everything, from studies to computing and sports such as football, basketball, and baseball (which I still enjoy and follow). Some of my fondest memories are of window shopping in the city or drinking at the bars, watching television programmes like *Jeopardy!* and holiday seasons like Thanksgiving.

Calling Home

Despite my enjoyment of the four years in America, the worst part was that I never returned to Bhutan once during that period. As a student on a J1 visa, I was not permitted to take on any part-time jobs, so there was barely any income for me. The UN did give me a stipend, which I saved up. But it was not enough for a plane ticket home.

So, I got by through making calls home. International calls then were not the easy processes they are today, but a complex, cumbersome, and expensive game of connecting the dots. From Pittsburgh, I would have to connect to an international operator, who would then connect to an operator somewhere in Delhi, who would have to find a way to connect to a telephone in Bhutan. Sometimes, the calls just wouldn't connect to the next node, and I remember requesting the operator to try again.

The other problem we faced was that my parents didn't own a telephone, so they would have to use our neighbour's phone. This meant that each time I wanted to call in, I would have to ring my neighbour and ask her to being my parents over. I would hang up and call back in another fifteen minutes to half an hour, putting myself through that near impossible task of connecting through the international operators twice. If I was lucky, I would get to speak to my parents on the phone, and each time I managed to, I was grateful to be able to hear their voice. That made all that trouble worth it!

In those days, such trunk calls were expensive, so we had to make our conversations quick and to the point. Sometimes, the call would just drop or there would be too much static noise to be able to hear each other properly. The high time, effort, and money meant I only managed to speak to them four times during my four years in America.

I also resorted to sending letters, postcards, and the occasional small package to them. My parents couldn't read, so one of my brothers would do so and write back to me on their behalf. While I was in college though, I tried not to worry too much about my parents because I didn't have a choice. Getting word to and from them was so difficult, I usually had no choice but to convince myself that everything was okay back home.

Email was just starting to exist—but sadly, while I could send them from school, no one in Bhutan had what was needed to receive them. That left me out of the initial excitement of my classmates sending their first emails to other friends in other universities across America! Email, then, was not an option, although I really wish I was one of the first few students to have used it.

Communications technology has evolved significantly today, making the world more connected than ever before. We've moved beyond the days of long-distance trunk calls and snail mail, as these have been replaced by instant online connectivity. Texting, video calling, and various other forms of digital communication are now at our fingertips.

My own family is separated by vast distances, but Tashi and I can effortlessly stay in touch with our children, especially our daughter Galek Yangzom. WhatsApp has proven a valuable tool for catching up, especially now that Galek is pursuing her Education studies in the US, and earlier when Gyamtsho was studying and working abroad.

Being so connected means I have the security of knowing that if Galek needs anything, I am only a text message or phone call away. Furthermore, like all families I know of, we have a family group chat where we share updates, articles, photos, and videos, and recommend movies or books. We do not have to be too worried about each other, because our lives have become so transparent and apparent online. We are close despite the physical distance, reducing worries and enhancing relationships.

On one occasion in 1990, I was troubled after learning what was happening to my parents on the phone. Bhutan may be known for its tranquillity, but it has had its share of protests and violence. I remember feeling a strong urge to return home and serve my country amidst the chaos. Tensions had broken out in Bhutan about the citizenship status of the Lhotshampas, an ethnic Nepalese group. A recent census had revealed many illegal immigrants in southern Bhutan. But the census results stirred unrest and, influenced by events in Nepal, some protesters aimed to overthrow the government, resulting in a heightened security situation.

Many protesters fled to Nepal, calling themselves refugees, and re-entered Bhutan to intimidate their fellow Lhotshampas, causing violence and fear. Their strategy was to make as many Lhotshampas as possible abandon their country, so that they could regroup in Nepal and return to Bhutan with numbers to forcefully overthrow the government. Consequently, many Lhotshampas sold their properties and renounced their citizenship. In 1991, UNHCR and Nepal opened refugee camps, where numbers swelled to over 100,000, though many were not Bhutanese.

The governments of Bhutan and Nepal agreed most camp inhabitants were not legitimate Bhutanese citizens. During a joint verification by the governments of Bhutan and Nepal, Bhutanese officials were attacked but escaped. An international coalition later accepted these refugees, recognizing the issue as illegal immigration rather than a typical refugee situation. All this happened while I was still a college student in Pittsburgh and only increased my desire to return to Bhutan, assist my King, and serve my country in any way I could.

To this day, I am deeply committed to fostering unity and mutual respect among our diverse communities, and my relationship with the Lhotshampas is one of profound friendship and mutual understanding. They form a significant part of my voter base, and over the years, I have made it my mission to learn their language and understand their culture better.

Our shared commitment to harmony is reflected in our religious practices. His Majesty the Fifth King has been instrumental in building bridges between the predominantly Hindu faith of the Lhotshampas and the traditional Vajrayana Buddhism of Bhutan. His active participation in constructing mandirs (Hindu temples) and involvement in Hindu ceremonies is a testament to the deep respect and appreciation we have for the Lhotshampa community. By celebrating our differences and embracing our diverse faiths, we are strengthening the fabric of our society and preventing others from exploiting its fault lines.

'I Just Had a Son!'

By the time I completed my degree, I was desperate to go home—after all, my parents and the Bhutanese government were both expecting it. (In those days, most Bhutanese overseas students returned home after completing their studies to quickly begin their service to the country. This, seemingly the most natural thing to do back then, would surprise many foreigners.)

What neither my parents nor the government expected, however, was my returning with a family in tow. A university schoolmate, my first wife Cera was a Korean–American orphan raised by an American couple. We met at university and hit it off immediately. Quite soon into our relationship, we found out that she was pregnant, so we tied the knot in a quick court marriage and a private dinner. In 1991, my son Gyamtsho was born at the UPMC Magee-Women's Hospital in Pittsburgh.[5]

---

[5] Interestingly, its name is hyphenated due it being formed in the 1962 merger of Magee Hospital and Pittsburgh Women's Hospital. The apostrophe normally used in 'Women's' is also left out.

The joy of being a new parent was beyond anything I had experienced so far, and the nurses celebrated with us in our private ward with a cake, flowers, and balloons. We were ecstatic, but sadly, neither of us had family or relatives present to share the moment with. I was so overjoyed that I yelled, 'I just had a son!' at a large African-American stranger while getting coffee at a vending machine! (He just gave me an amused look and replied, 'Congratulations!')

That said, Cera knew I had no intention of staying in America, and she was very supportive of us living together in Bhutan. As soon as the visas and paperwork were sorted out for Cera and Gyamtsho, we found ourselves on-board a flight home, via Delhi. I was so excited to be heading home that as soon as the plane landed in Delhi, I immediately changed into my bright orange and yellow *gho*, which coincided with the colours of Bhutan's national flag. Cera donned a *kira* (I have no idea how she got her hands on one) and we put baby Gyamtsho in a tiny gho as well. People at the Delhi airport who saw us must have thought we were nuts, but I couldn't think of a better outfit to return home in than my national costume.

When we finally landed in Paro, we were greeted by the clear blue skies, bright sunshine, and crisp air of home. Returning to Bhutan was such an emotional moment for me that I had a strong urge to just drop to the ground and kiss the tarmac! (I eventually decided against this overly dramatic gesture.) I do vividly remember that intense longing to be home . . . which I finally was.

However, the novelty wore off and Cera decided to leave me shortly after Gyamtsho turned one. I suppose she tried her best to adapt to a life in Bhutan, but it must have been truly challenging for her. Despite that, she generously gave me full custody of Gyamtsho, something that I am grateful for to this day.

Finding Work

Upon my return, I immediately reported back to the Royal Civil Service Commission to sign up as a civil servant. In those days, the screening process was less strict than it is today, although exams and interviews were still required. Those with professional experience or who held technical degrees like engineers, architects, and doctors were accepted immediately without screening due to a shortage of such qualified personnel. That would be unheard of today!

Such professionals also entered at a higher position and pay grade than other officers. I had essentially caught up with my classmates who had gone to India for college, returned, and joined the civil service, despite the three-year delay spent repeating my Year 11 and awaiting my scholarship from UNDP.

Of course, this would all only be applicable if I could find some place my skills were needed, and the Royal Civil Service Commission was unable to place me in a suitable job. Unlike today, with officers being deployed to relevant agencies by the commission, I ended up having to explore opportunities on my own.

My first visit was to Bondey Farm, a horticultural hub established in 1966, where I hoped to apply my skills to design agricultural tools. However, they had no need for new designs and handled only basic repairs. (Years later, as prime minister, I worked with them to establish manufacturing lines for ploughshares, which would, in turn, be used in rototillers from Japan, greatly improving the efficiency of our agricultural sector. Much more remains to be done, seeing that Bhutan remains a mostly agrarian society.)

Next, I approached the Department of Power's central maintenance unit. Here, I thought I could contribute by designing and manufacturing micro-hydroelectric units. My proposition was met with enthusiasm, but it soon became evident there was no one to mentor me. They offered me a management role instead, which I turned down, citing my lack of experience and incomplete engineering training.

Finally, I considered Druk Air, the national carrier, which was looking for technicians to fix planes. Despite some aeronautics design knowledge from university, I lacked practical experience in aircraft maintenance and would need further training. So, this option also fell through.

In the midst of my relentless job search, I found myself reflecting on the letter I had sent during my college years to the Royal Civil Service Commission, requesting a change of course. My intuition about the irrelevance of my current field was proving accurate. I wished I had been allowed to switch to civil engineering, given Bhutan's ongoing construction boom, including schools, hospitals, bridges, roads, and offices. Such a skillset could have been more beneficial for my country.

Finally, a glimmer of hope appeared when the Department of Education announced they were seeking engineers. I joined their technical education cell, a small team consisting only of a unit head and one support staff member. Recognizing that if I couldn't pursue an engineering career, I could at least train others to do so, I invested myself in developing vocational training across Bhutan.

With the assistance of various international organizations such as the World Bank, Asian Development Bank, UN, German Technical Cooperation, and the Indian and Japanese governments, we enhanced existing institutes and established new ones. Our efforts led to the creation of the National Technical Training Authority, an autonomous agency focused on vocational training, which later merged with the Department of Labour to form the Ministry of Labour and Human Resources. I continued my journey there until 2007, contributing to the development of my beloved country in my own unique way.

Cultural Immersion

If I was to serve my people, I would have to better understand local culture. Having spent eleven years in India and four years in the US, I had mostly grown up away from Bhutan and only had a weak grasp of the Dzongkha language, which I had rarely been exposed to! Now that I was back in Bhutan, I had to relearn the language almost from scratch.

I engaged a teacher to help with the process. Every day, he would help me to read and write it, and in my spare time, I read the local newspapers to expose myself further. Gradually, after putting in a lot of hard work over several years, I managed to master the language to a degree that I was happy with. I am still learning but at least I know enough not to be ashamed of myself!

But my learning went beyond Dzongkha. I even made an effort to learn our traditional folk dances, which most students learn in school from a young age. Bhutanese dances are a social event performed on all occasions. Guests typically join the dancers by forming a circle, singing praises to our country, our lamas, and our spirituality, though romantic love is sometimes a topic as well.

The folk dances are not complex and mainly involve simple, repetitive steps where you move from side to side, or to the front and back, occasionally spinning around. Most people join in the fun and learn spontaneously. They start simple but do not always stay that way, especially during lively parties or archery games where alcohol is flowing!

The point is that practically every Bhutanese person grows up knowing the traditional dances. However, for me, joining a crowd or participating in these dances had always felt like an insurmountable challenge. I have always been somewhat awkward and uncoordinated, even in relaxed environments.

My limited exposure to folk dances during school, coupled with my introverted nature, made me shy away from such activities. Even after stepping into professional life, my self-confidence remained low. To truly immerse myself in a *boedra* dance and enjoy it, I had to overcome significant personal barriers.

In the same period as my language lessons, I sought help from the Royal Academy of Performing Arts. They tutored me in the traditional boedra songs and steps. After several months of dedicated effort, I managed to memorize some songs and learn the associated dances. Today, I can join in the dance, albeit with a conscious effort.

Immersing myself in my culture also meant I had to learn our national sport—archery. In rural Bhutan, all children grow up practising archery. As a child in Dorithasa, I remember playing with other children, making our own bows from bamboo in the forests and our own arrows with feathers we gathered to use as fletch.

Archery in Bhutan is unlike any other way to practice the sport around the world. You have to hit a target as small as 3 feet tall by 1 foot wide (90 cm by 27 cm) from an incredible 145 metres away! For reference, the Olympic standard is to shoot from less than half that distance, just 70 metres.

Two teams of eleven archers each compete against each other, situated on each end of the targets. Each person shoots two arrows with a counterpart from the opposing team. This goes on till everyone from both teams finishes shooting. Then, they tally the points scored and switch the side of the target they are on. The fun comes from the hollering, teasing, and cheering, which is not just allowed but encouraged! When you hear a commotion, you know there is an archery match going on.

Each team even has its group of singers and dancers to cheer them on. The most vocal cheerleaders are the archers themselves. Not only do they cheer for their own team but they also distract the opposing team with songs and dances or by standing near the target and teasing their opponents. A good amount of alcohol is also present at every archery match in Bhutan and drinking is, once more, allowed and even encouraged.

Although it is a serious game, as a good archer will have bragging rights in his village, it is also a community event where families and friends all get together and have a party that lasts for two or even three days. If I hadn't learned Dzongkha and traditional dances, it would have been almost impossible for me to take part in these archery matches.

The Projector of Fate

I enjoyed my work, whether it was at the Department of Education or the Ministry of Labour and Human Resources. Vocational training, to me, was something I had fond memories of, perhaps due to my time at Dr Graham's Homes, which had been designed around it. My time there, however, was most marked by me meeting my current wife, Tashi Doma.

After Cera left and I continued to work as a civil servant, I had no plans of getting married again. I had girlfriends but wasn't ready to settle down. In fact, I even contemplated not marrying at all! Plus, I couldn't bear even the possibility that a stepmother might mistreat Gyamtsho, who was very close to me. He was growing up well and spending a lot of time with his grandparents.

Meeting Tashi at a conference for teachers changed all that. She was making a presentation and although we had never crossed paths before, when I laid eyes on her, it was love at first sight . . . at least for me! (I do not think she even noticed me at the time.)

I was so besotted that I started asking teachers who this person was. I soon found out that she was with the World Food Programme, a counterpart of the Department of Education. Naturally, I started racking my brain to find ways to meet her in person. Our respective job scopes were independent of each other, and the chances of meeting were almost nil.

But as luck or fate would have it, she came looking for me one afternoon. Tashi had been sent by her boss to find a projector but had picked up a broken one. Someone had told her to look for the tech geek (me) who might be able to fix it.

When she walked through my office door that day, I was flabbergasted. It was like a dream come true!

We managed to fix the projector together and that was really the beginning of my courtship. Next thing we knew, we were constantly chatting on the phone, and she would be talking about her work. This was something that drew me to her: her zeal and passion for her work, which had to do with feeding poor children so that they could attend school.

Tashi would tell me many stories about her trips to remote villages across the country, which she had to walk for weeks just to reach. As part of the World Food Programme, she would visit these remote schools to monitor school feeding, including food storage, kitchen hygiene, and quality and nutrition of the food itself.

These villages had never seen a woman in her capacity, an officer from the capital who held a certain amount of authority. Most teachers, local officials, and support staff were men, and the children in one village even called her 'sir', because no feminine equivalent even existed for them!

Ever the perceptive one, Tashi told me that this was an indication of how little regard women received in national development, which she reckoned had to change. Perhaps it was her strength and energy that rubbed off on me because I decided that this was the person who I wanted to be with. By 1998, I knew that we were made for each other and proposed.

Tashi has been (and still is) my biggest supporter, guide, and mentor in everything that I do in my life. I owe much to her, as she has always been there for me, forcing me to grow both as an individual and a husband. After twenty-five years of marriage as I write this, we are still behaving like the young adults we were: going to the gym together (which I never had the confidence to do in the past) and learning yoga together. While in Bangkok, we took up swimming too. We also intend to pick up some ballroom dancing when we have the opportunity.

A New Daughter

A year after we were married, our daughter Galek was born in 1999 at the Jigme Dorji Wangchuck National Referral Hospital in Thimphu. The experience at its maternity ward was a study in contrast to Magee-Women's—instead of having our own private space, Tashi delivered our baby in a delivery room where three other women were also delivering at the same time, separated only by a thin screen curtain. Childbirth is a painful and messy process, and there was no privacy or peace to speak of.

Moreover, nurses and doctors could rarely be found while Tashi was in labour. When the nurses did come, they were kind to us and helpful—but I could see they were also overworked and could not stay for more than a few minutes.

To help Tashi cope, I delved into some skills that I had picked up from prenatal classes that I attended with Cera in Pittsburgh. This included coaching Tashi to breathe, giving her ice and lollipops, and getting a tennis ball to rub her back. When I thought her contractions were coming, I would coach her to take slow, deep breaths in and out. These techniques worked like a charm and soon after, we were carrying our baby daughter in our arms.

After delivery, Tashi recuperated in a maternity ward alongside some twenty other mothers. We have vivid memories of the groans, swearing, and yelling that filled the ward. I will also never forget the metallic stench of blood, sweat, and other fluids, which a lack of good air circulation kept trapped in the room. It was a lot to bear, but I remained by Tashi's side throughout, even sleeping with her in her bed!

On one occasion, I had to bring Tashi to the toilet, and I remember fearing she would slip on the wet floor. After I put her back to bed, I washed her cloth diapers with a sense of dissatisfaction about the whole ordeal.

One thing that was blessedly different was the presence of family and relatives there with us to celebrate the birth of Galek, enabling me to express my joy openly. Thankfully, Tashi recovered quickly and was discharged the following day.

* * *

Policy Brief: The Gyaltsuen Jetsun Pema Mother and Child Hospital

The birth of my firstborn Gyamtsho in Pittsburgh was a revelation, highlighting the importance of a supportive environment and quality facilities for expecting mothers. However, on Galek's birth in Thimphu,

I confronted stark realities: lack of workforce, bed shortages, outdated equipment, and subpar services. The staff did their best but were seriously limited in their ability to serve patients. While I yearned to replicate the world-class medical experience I had abroad, I knew it was a tall order for Bhutan at that time.

Healthcare in Bhutan is free, a fact that might seem wonderful on the surface, but it comes with its own set of challenges. Catering to diverse needs without charging a penny can strain any system.

The contrast between the birth experiences of my two children was so profound that it propelled a significant change. Fifteen years later, while serving in the government, I helped oversee the construction of the Gyaltsuen Jetsun Pema Mother and Child Hospital, named after our beloved Queen Jetsun Pema. This 150-bed maternity hospital aims to alleviate the load on the main hospital and enhance the birthing experience for Bhutanese mothers.

Half of this hospital caters to obstetrics and gynaecology, including wards and delivery rooms. The other half has been designed as a community health centre, offering comprehensive care for women, from check-ups to medication and counselling.

By the end of my first tenure, the first half of the hospital has become operational, offering services such as prenatal classes and even prenatal yoga—as I found out during consulting visits with Tashi.

However, despite these strides, more can still be done. Our services remain inadequate compared to international standards, evidenced by the scores of Bhutanese mothers traveling to Bangkok and Thailand annually for childbirth. This trend underscores the need for improvement.

Childbirth is a momentous occasion filled with joy, but it can also evoke fear and anxiety. Some couples resort to loans to ensure a safe and comfortable childbirth experience in overseas hospitals. But it is not feasible for every Bhutanese family.

Therefore, it is crucial for the new hospital to provide high-quality, comprehensive services to all expectant mothers in Bhutan, ensuring they feel secure and cared for during this significant life event.

* * *

Back to America

Three years after the birth of my daughter, I found myself packing our bags again. I was heading back to America, this time to Cambridge, Massachusetts, and bringing my entire family with me. There, I was set to do a master's in public administration at the John F. Kennedy School of Government, a public policy school of Harvard University. It boasts an illustrious group of alumni, including Canadian Prime Minister Justin Trudeau, former Singaporean Prime Minister Lee Hsien Loong, Colombian President Juan Manuel Santos, and former UN Secretary-General Ban Ki-moon, among others. One of my classmates from the time is the present-day Prime Minister of Singapore Lawrence Wong, who took office in May 2024 and remains a close friend of mine.

It had not crossed my mind to do a master's degree, since my career had been smooth sailing until then, and I was given a lot of opportunities. I had no thoughts then of making major changes, but the Royal Civil Service Commission had recently announced that civil servants above the age of forty would no longer be eligible to go for a master's degree under the government programme. I was thirty-eight at that time, and so, I decided to make use of the time I still had.

Every day of my year spent in Cambridge added immeasurably to my knowledge, not just of administration but also management, leadership, negotiation, economics, global affairs, international relations, and networking.

Vocational training is critical, but it can't create jobs on its own; it must provide skills required by the economy. Thus, I devoted a lot of time to studying economics, including micro- and macroeconomics, competitiveness, and so on.

Back then, I had no inkling that, in just a few years, Bhutan would transition to a democracy. If I had known, I would probably have attended some of the popular classes such as campaigning and politics. Politics looked very interesting, as did international relations, but I was determined to study economics, which I felt would have been more relevant to my work.

* * *

Policy Brief: Operation All Clear

History has a way of repeating itself because, once more, violence flared up in Bhutan while I was away. This time, it involved Indian insurgent groups that had united and, in the late 1990s, set up a large number of camps in southern Bhutan, near the Indian border. They chose their sites well, capturing strategic locations in uninhabited places that needed hard, days-long treks to reach. These included the United Liberation Front of Assam (ULFA), National Democratic Front of Bodoland (NDFB), Bodo Liberation Tigers Force (BLTF) and Kamtapur Liberation Organisation (KLO). For over six years, the militants refused to leave, despite the repeated personal requests by the Fourth King.

Finally in late December 2003, the Bhutanese government launched Operation All Clear, a by-any-means-necessary effort to evict them, using force if required. This was a great escalation, but the Fourth King was taking a calculated risk, and in the process would go on to vividly display the wisdom, courage, and compassion we rightly associate with Rigsum Gonpo (that is, the three Bodhisattvas representing those virtues, about which I will write more later).

The operation was an act of shrewd wisdom and great courage. Failure would have likely led to an unending conflict, with international forces stepping in to aid in the fight. The militants, deeply embedded within our lush, humid jungles, would have been able to launch relentless terrorist attacks on both India and Bhutan to this day.

Prior to this, the Royal Bhutan Army had begun enlisting volunteers to form a militia, each of which would undergo two months of rigorous military training. An impressive 634 patriots signed on the dotted line, ready to risk their lives to defend their nation's sovereignty.

The recruitment drive was underway when I departed for my graduate studies. A part of me yearned to join this noble cause, but I also realized that I could serve my country in multiple ways.

My plan was to acquire my master's degree first, and then enlist in the militia upon my return. After all, the ongoing negotiations and looming threat of conflict had been a slow-burning issue for years, so the need to join the militia didn't seem immediate, though its significance was not lost on me.

The news of the sudden escalation ignited a fierce determination within me to return to Bhutan and join the militia. Without wasting any time, I rushed to my counsellor and informed her of my urgent need to return home. She understood my situation and offered her full support.

I immediately began securing air tickets for my entire family to fly home. However, before I could even confirm our flights, Operation All Clear had concluded. In a swift and decisive two-day campaign, the Royal Bhutan Army, under the personal leadership of the Fourth King, dealt a devastating blow to the insurgents.

Over thirty insurgent strongholds were obliterated. Indian experts had projected that it would take no less than 30,000 troops and half a year to dislodge the insurgents. However, with barely 3,000 Bhutanese soldiers, the Fourth King's fearless leadership and a blend of astute tactics and deception, the operation triumphed in mere days. His wisdom and courage had turned a potential bloodbath into a resounding victory.

Yet, amidst the rigours of the operation, the Fourth King's compassion shone through as he ensured provisions—food and essential supplies—to the women and children of the captured insurgents' families. Despite the victorious outcome, there were no grand parades, and he ensured that everyone our troops captured was treated humanely. Any apprehended militants were eventually extradited to India.

With an immediate return no longer needed, I remained in America and completed my degree. I did feel disheartened once again at being away when my country needed me. The first time, there was nothing I could have done to help—but now, understanding the situation and actually being able to make a difference, I cannot help but regret not joining the militia and fighting for my country.

* * *

A National Day Bombshell

I returned to my job at the ministry after completing my master's degree. Just a year later, on National Day (17 December) of 2005, a bombshell announcement was made by the reigning Fourth King. He, as well as the Crown Prince (now the Fifth King), would usually travel to all *dzongkhags* (districts) to not only discuss and monitor national plans but also to celebrate National Day in a different dzongkhag each year. That particular year, National Day was held in Trashiyangtse, a remote dzongkhag in eastern Bhutan.

In a nationwide broadcast from Trashiyangtse, he announced that he would be abdicating the throne to make way for the Crown Prince to oversee a new, democratic Bhutan. The news of his abdication rocked the nation to its core.

Everyone was in shock. King Jigme Singye Wangchuck was only fifty-one years old then and at the height of his popularity. He had ruled for just thirty-three years, and everyone expected him to do so till a ripe old age, if not his death. Speaker of National Assembly Dasho Ugyen Dorje likened the announcement to 'darkness setting on a bright day'.[6]

This, and his subsequent actions to establish democratic rule by the people, may have been one of the most courageous things any monarch has ever done. In hindsight, this unprecedented move was one of the best examples of enlightened leadership and wisdom, courage, and compassion I have known—a demonstration of the Fourth King's sincere wish to establish democracy as quickly and smoothly as possible.

In his wisdom, he knew this would have been far more difficult with himself as a larger-than-life figure, and he was brave and compassionate enough to make the effort to persuade the people it was worth doing—to the point of abdicating himself. It was better, His Majesty believed, to sever ties completely and hand over the transition and imposition of democracy to a new king.

---

[6] King Jigme Singye Wangchuck with Mieko Nishimizu, *Portrait of a Leader: Through the Looking Glass of His Majesty's Decrees* (Centre for Bhutan Studies, 2008), 134.

Chapter Three

The Foundations of Bhutan

I love how the landscape gives the impression of vast space and intimacy at the same time: the thin brown line of a path wandering up an immense green mountainside, a plush hanging valley tucked between two steep hillsides, a village of three houses surrounded by dark forest, paddy fields flowing around an outcrop of rock, a white temple gleaming on a shadowy ridge. The human habitations nestle into the landscape; nothing is cut or cleared beyond what is required. Nothing is bigger than necessary. Every sign of human settlement repeats the mantra of contentment: 'This is just enough.'

—Jamie Zeppa, *Beyond the Sky and the Earth*[7]

In a most fitting display, the Parliament Hall of Bhutan has on its ceiling an elaborate mandala, like the ones we see in temples across the land. A cosmic diagram that represents the four cardinal directions, the mandala is a meditation aid in Vajrayana Buddhism.

This large and colourful square symbol hovered above us as we sat in the Parliament Hall. I was with other members of parliament, and we were all awaiting the arrival of the King.

It was 8 May 2008, a special occasion of many firsts: it was Bhutan's first sitting of the first session of the first multi-party

---

[7] Jamie Zeppa, *Beyond the Sky and the Earth: A Journey into Bhutan* (New York, NY: The Berkley Publishing Group, 1999).

parliament. It also marked the beginning of what I had come here to do—to speak on behalf of those who had voted us in during the National Assembly election of 2008.

Being here early allowed me ample time to soak in my surroundings. The hall is a feast for the eyes, and this was the first time I saw it from the inside. While the view from the visitors' gallery is like watching an elaborate painting, being in the 'well' is like seeing that painting as a hologram of incredible complexity from within.

Although it is not as magnificent as the *kuenreys*, or assembly halls, of our *dzongs*, I am convinced that our parliament chamber is among the world's most striking government buildings. Frescoes depicting traditional Bhutanese motifs, such as clouds and dragons, adorn the ceiling, walls, benches and viewing galleries. Royal yellow and gold embossed wallpaper lines the high walls from top to bottom. A large mandala painted on the ceiling looks down upon us as we sit in the semicircular seating area. Paintings of auspicious symbols—such as the endless knot, treasure vase, and so on—surround the mandala, filling up every inch of the ceiling. From its centre, Zhabdrung Ngawang Namgyal, the founding father of Bhutan himself, looks down upon us.

Every space in this hall is decorated down to the finest details. Whether it is the walls, benches, or balcony rails, detailed carvings embellish every fixture. The craftsmanship involved in detailing this hall is exceptional. Perhaps no parliament house in the world so embodies our love for our culture and the art that keeps it alive.

In the middle is a semicircular seating area where Bhutan's forty-seven-seat National Assembly (or lower house) is seated together with the twenty-five-member National Council (or upper house) during joint sessions. Facing the seats and the entire hall is a large stage containing the Golden Throne—it is large enough for one to imagine it seating two people. But it has always been for only one personality—the Dragon King. The presence of the throne is a reminder that while we sit here as elected members of parliament, we are there by authority of the king alone. He traditionally summons the first sitting of parliament and also sits in on the proceedings as and when he wishes.

According to the Constitution, he will preside over the opening and closing of each parliament session. Indeed, King Jigme has done so for each and every opening and closing session of parliament during his reign and has never missed one—he has always also ensured his availability by remaining in Thimphu when House is in session. The Parliament of Bhutan officially consists of the National Assembly, the National Council, and the king himself.

The decorations in the hall not only speak of Bhutan's traditions but also remind us of our history and the Zhabdrung continuously watching over his people. They remind us of our sacred duty to our king, country, and people. It is a reminder that we, the people, only hold power because the king has allowed it.

I heard someone announce the arrival of the King. The whole hall fell silent and with our heads bowed, we stood up to receive His Majesty . . . or rather, for him to receive us.

I watched as he walked up the steps onto the stage and prostrated himself thrice towards the dais, paying his respects to the Golden Throne. It is not just his seat but also a sacred artefact in its own right. Plated in pure gold, the throne itself has been consecrated and sanctified with holy scriptures that have been embedded into it. The sanctity of the throne therefore symbolizes the sacredness of the monarchy.

The monarchy, founded over one hundred years ago, is the most important institution in Bhutan. It is the symbol of our unity, protector of our people, and the fountainhead of our future. After 200 years of constant fighting, instability, and suffering, the emergence of the monarchy spearheaded unprecedented peace and stability. Each subsequent king has brought about more and more peace, prosperity, and happiness to the people over a century-long process of governance and modernization.

Bhutan has been blessed with enlightened monarchs. We revere them, looking up to them as Plato's ideal of a philosopher king, an extraordinary aspect rarely seen in the modern world today. All of us in Bhutan love our kings, and I am sure we are not unique in doing so.

What makes Bhutan's monarchy exceptional and different from other governments is that the First King of Bhutan did not conquer the country and install himself as its ruler. Instead, he was elected—and each successive King has wielded *less* power, by their own design. Bhutan's monarchy has been a unique example of a gradual transition of power from the monarchy to the people. This process of democratization was not sudden but rather a carefully planned and executed transition spanning generations.

The King prostrated himself before the Golden Throne, ascended to it, and gave the signal to start the day's proceedings. But first, an important ceremony had to happen. As with all public events in Bhutan, such as appointments of senior officials, weddings, festivals, and so on, the traditional *Zhugdrel Phunsum Tshogpa* ceremony is held to mark the beginning of the event. It is similar to a ribbon-cutting, except the zhugdrel ceremony is steeped in symbolism and tradition and is unique to Bhutan.

The zhugdrel ceremony, a hallmark of Bhutan's Drukpa tradition, is a meticulously choreographed ritual that weaves together the threads of celebration, inauguration, and veneration. It might appear time-consuming to an outsider, but each stage of the ceremony is profoundly significant.

In the ceremonial setting, participants are arranged in rows according to their rank and seniority, all facing the king, the dignitary of the event. The ceremony begins with offerings to the shrine—fragrant saffron water, saffron root, and tea accompanied by saffron rice.

Following this, a unique offering of *marchang*, a blend of alcohol and butter, is made. This is presented in a traditional, ornate vessel placed before the king. As the marchang is offered to guardian deities and sentient beings, an ancient incantation fills the air. A drop of this sacred brew is then offered to the king, who dabs it with his finger and places it on his tongue, signifying acceptance.

With the completion of the marchang ceremony, an array of food items and ceremonial money are distributed to everyone present. The distribution typically begins with *doma* (betel nut) and *paney* (betel leaf), followed by an assortment of fruits and sweets— melons, oranges, guava, sugarcane, dried fruits, peaches, pears, and more. A total of fifteen types of fruits are usually included, and the number of food items can range from nineteen to twenty-three, or even go up to thirty-four. The final item is always something hard, like a walnut or *chugo* (dried cheese). This symbolizes protection from malevolent spirits, indicating resilience and indestructibility.

As these food items are distributed in a specific order, prayers echo through the gathering. The ceremony concludes with a prayer for the health, prosperity, and well-being of every individual in attendance.

The roots of the zhugdrel ceremony can be traced back to the consecration of Punakha dzong in 1640 by the Zhabdrung himself. According to historical accounts, he was deeply moved by the vast and diverse gifts brought by people from all corners of the country. He arranged the attendees according to rank and status, and distributed these offerings while reciting prayers to his previous reincarnations, known as *Phunsum Tshogpa*. This marked the birth of the tradition of zhugdrel phunsum tshogpa, which continues to this day.

Today, the zhugdrel ceremony holds such an esteemed place in Bhutanese culture that it is mandated in the Constitution to open every parliament session with a zhugdrel phunsum tshogpa tendrel— an auspicious coincidence. It embodies the collective aspiration of the Bhutanese people for glory, grace, wealth and auspiciousness.

After the necessary rites had been completed, the King opened the session with a royal address that marked the first Parliament of democratic Bhutan. During the address, he paid tribute to his forefathers, including the Buddha, Guru Padmasambhava, and Zhabdrung Ngawang Namgyal. He also made it a point to remind us all who were there that constantly nurturing democracy has been the 'highest achievement of one hundred years of monarchy'.

His Majesty declared:

This has culminated today with the first sitting of Parliament
and the start of democracy, whereby my father the Fourth Druk
Gyalpo and I, hereby return to our People the powers that had
been vested in our kings by our forefathers one hundred years
ago. We do so with absolute faith and confidence, offer our
complete support and our prayers for the success of democracy.

As King, henceforth, it is my sacred duty to ensure the success
of our new democracy so that it will serve to fulfil the aspirations
of our people always.

But he also warned us:

Our new politicians must be mindful of the experiences of nations
where democracy has failed and hardship, disunity, internal strife,
and violence have plagued the people. We must never allow the
development of such conditions of Bhutan.

As democracy's first government, you have the responsibility
of setting the right examples, laying strong foundations and
promoting the best practices of democracy. We, the people and
King, have complete confidence and faith in the new government.
As long as you work to serve the country and people, you will
have our full support. If you should falter in your service to the
nation, then the duty to counsel you also rests with the people
and King.

To me, this was a strong indication that although democracy was
gifted to the people by our kings, the responsibility was now on
us to nurture this great treasure, ensuring that our governance was
well-founded and practised with the good of the people at the
forefront. I quietly pledged my allegiance and duty to this new
democracy, to our kings, and to the country in the revered presence
of the Triple Gem—the triad comprising the person of the Buddha,
his dharma (teachings) and the *sangha* (community) that spreads and
lives by them.

This historic day was witnessed by many who came to the Parliament Hall. Former ministers, civil servants, businessmen, expatriates, and people young and old filled the viewing galleries, eagerly participating in the momentous occasion.

I have often wondered what was on their minds that day. Were they feeling nervous about what this new democracy would spell for their country, which was to be in the hands of these politicians seated below? Or did they feel confident that with the King's blessings, democracy would flourish in Bhutan? It was hard to tell. We were navigating uncharted waters.

All I knew was that this was undoubtedly a significant step of our monarchs' selflessness, which I mentioned in my vote of thanks that day as the opposition leader. I concluded, 'I offer prayers for the success of democracy in the country and hope that the roots of democracy will further strengthen in the years ahead under the guidance and dynamic leadership of His Majesty the King and that the country and the people achieve the noble goals of Gross National Happiness.'

The striking Parliament Building is nestled in the heart of Thimphu. Merely a stone's throw from the grand Tashichho dzong, the Parliament Building radiates its architectural magnificence and historical significance. Once upon a time, the medieval fortified monastery of Tashichho dzong served as the nerve centre from where the Druk Desi (secular ruler) governed his district. Today, the Parliament Building holds equal prominence, ever since Bhutan transitioned to a democracy.

Perched on the opposite bank of the serene Thimphu river, the Parliament Building presents a captivating sight. At a distance, it mirrors the grandeur of the Tashichho dzong, albeit on a smaller scale. Much like the imposing towers that adorn the corners of the fortified monastery, the Parliament Building also boasts a tower at each corner. The stark white walls and tiered golden roofs may be less intimidating than the Tashichho dzong, but the events unfolding within its walls are of monumental importance.

The Parliament Building is a hub of national activity, housing the National Assembly hall, its secretariat, the Prime Minister's Office, and the Ministry of Foreign Affairs. Constructed in 1995 with assistance from the Government of India to host the South Asian Association for Regional Cooperation (SAARC) summit, it would later accommodate the Ministry of Foreign Affairs and the National Assembly.

The National Assembly was established before Bhutan's shift to democracy in 2008. Before that, it had been composed of representatives from the general population, government, monastic order, and armed forces, with the people's representatives being elected, and the rest being appointed. Even though political parties were absent, and the prime ministerial position—introduced only in 1998—rotated annually, this decentralized government was an early semblance of democracy. Since the advent of a multi-party democracy in 2008, National Assembly sessions are held in the Parliament Building at least biannually.

Before my formal induction as a parliamentarian, I had visited the Parliament Building seven years prior to observe the proceedings of the former National Assembly. Back then, the seating arrangement was markedly different. Elected representatives would sit on long, backless wooden benches facing the stage where the king would sit. This traditional layout, while respectful to the king, seemed quite uncomfortable, as royal etiquette required sitting with our backs upright in the king's presence. I used to wonder how challenging this might be for some, perhaps even for me.

Years have passed since I last stepped foot in the old National Assembly of Bhutan. It felt like a different epoch when I watched representatives, adorned in traditional Bhutanese attire, enter this esteemed hall. Now, as a member of the first democratically elected government, I find myself immersed in an environment that has undergone a tasteful transformation.

Where long benches once lined the room, plush wooden armchairs with rich brown faux leather upholstery have now taken their place. The desks, dark and curved, form a grand semicircle when arranged together. Each desk is equipped with knobs and switches controlling microphones and voting buttons. Four rows of such desks house today's parliament. Even the stage has been modernized, with large television screens broadcasting parliamentary proceedings. This arrangement mirrors many other parliament halls worldwide. Yet, the resemblance ends there. The vibrant hues, statues, ornate ceiling, and decorative hangings—all quintessentially Bhutanese—remain untouched.

Sitting among the seventy-two members that comprise the lower and upper houses (the upper house being the twenty-five-member non-partisan National Council), I found myself humbled. My gaze descended from the intricate ceiling to the stage, resplendent with religious iconography and vivid tapestries. The stage, the heart of the hall, is impossible to overlook. Flanking it are altars dedicated to Buddha and Guru Padmasambhava, revered as the Second Buddha.

Two large *thangkhas*, Tibetan Buddhist paintings on silk appliques, dominate the stage. Serving as meditation aids for Vajrayana Buddhism practitioners, these thangkhas are common in Bhutanese homes, offices, temples, and monasteries. In the Parliament Hall, at least fifteen smaller thangkhas grace the viewing gallery windows and the back of the hall. However, the most striking ones are the two large ones on stage. One depicts the eighth-century Buddhist master Guru Padmasambhava from India, and the other portrays Bhutan's founder, Zhabdrung Ngawang Namgyal, the Tibetan lama who unified Bhutan in the seventeenth century.

At its zenith, Vajrayana Buddhism, also known as Tibetan Buddhism, spread across Mongolia, much of China, and nearly the entire stretch of the Himalayas. Today, Bhutan stands as the last independent kingdom preserving the Vajrayana tradition. Despite this, Buddhism flourishes in Bhutan, experiencing a sort of spiritual renaissance. With more monks than soldiers, many spend years meditating in solitude in remote monasteries.

For a country as small as it, Bhutan boasts an impressive number of monasteries—around 2,500. Journey through Bhutan, and you'll encounter *chortens* (also known as *stupas*) near roads or river confluences. About 10,000 of them dot the mountains and valleys. Prayer flags flutter in the wind, prayer wheels are inscribed with mantras, and images of religious figures or symbols adorn cliffs, serving as constant reminders of our spiritual heritage. With ongoing construction of chortens and renovations of temples, monasteries and dzongs, Bhutan's Buddhism is being rejuvenated. The royal family, one of the largest patrons of the religion, generously supports many high-profile projects.

Vajrayana Buddhism permeates Bhutanese life, from birth to marriage, promotions, new homes, and everyday affairs. It not only influences our unique culture but defines it, shaping our worldview, social behaviour, and political mindset. Many Bhutanese devoutly practise the religion, making it their primary pursuit. They accumulate merit every day by chanting prayers, circumambulating religious monuments, and lighting butter lamps.

* * *

Policy Brief: The International Vajrayana Conference

During my time in government, I requested that the Centre for Bhutan & GNH Studies (CBS) convene an annual International Vajrayana Conference. It has gained immense popularity over the years, attracting scholars, practitioners, and enthusiasts from across the globe.

The conference serves as a vibrant platform for intellectual discourse and exchange of ideas on Vajrayana Buddhism. It is a place where the ancient wisdom of this tradition intersects with contemporary thought, fostering a deeper understanding and appreciation of its relevance in today's world.

Sadly, after three successful editions, the conference was halted due to the Covid-19 pandemic. However, this pause has not dampened the spirit of the organizers or participants. Instead, it has reinforced their commitment to preserve and propagate Vajrayana teachings and practices. The conference resumed in October 2022 with 400 attendees from more than thirty countries.

One significant resolution that emerged from these deliberations is the proposal to establish an International Vajrayana Centre in Bhutan. This centre would aim to serve as a global hub for Vajrayana studies, offering resources, conducting research, and organizing events that promote the understanding and practice of this profound tradition. It underscores Bhutan's role as a custodian of this rich spiritual heritage, and its commitment to sharing it with the world.

* * *

The Three Founders of Bhutan

Guru Padmasambhava and Zhabdrung Ngawang Namgyal, along with Buddha himself, form the 'holy trinity' in Bhutan's Vajrayana Buddhist belief system. Despite none of them being native Bhutanese, they are so ingrained in our cultural narrative that we do not consider them foreigners.

Though Buddha may never have graced Bhutan with his presence, the nation's spirit thrives under the tenets of Buddhism. Bhutan takes pride in being one of the few nations worldwide where Buddhism is revered as the state religion. But it does not stop there; Bhutan holds a unique position on the global stage as the sole country practising Vajrayana Buddhism. Delving deeper, the official state religion of Bhutan is Drukpa Kagyu, a distinct offshoot of the Kagyu school rooted in Vajrayana Buddhism. This spiritual affinity paints a vivid picture of Bhutan's cultural identity and religious devotion.

More than a millennium after Buddha attained nirvana and subsequent death (known as *parinirvana*), Buddhism found its way to Bhutan, thanks to the charismatic Indian tantric teacher, Guru Padmasambhava, also known as the Lotus Born. His portrait, etched in every corner of Bhutan, is unmistakable: a benevolent smile beneath a thin moustache, penetrating eyes under furrowed brows, and a *vajra* (thunderbolt) firmly held in his hand to signify indestructible power. This iconic figure graces every Bhutanese temple, shrine and home, either as a statue or a painting. (The vajra also gives Vajrayana, one of the three major schools of Buddhism, its name.)

Guru Rinpoche, as Padmasambhava is affectionately known, introduced Vajrayana Buddhism to Bhutan in the eighth century. His influence extends beyond Bhutan to regions like Tibet, Nepal and parts of the Indian Himalayan states, where he is revered as the 'Second Buddha'. As the founder of the Nyingma sect of Vajrayana Buddhism, he is celebrated for subduing demons and evil spirits during his travels.

What, one might ask, makes Bhutan so special? Why did Guru Rinpoche choose to invest considerable time traversing the harsh terrain of our land? Perhaps the reason lies not just in the physical attributes of the land but also in its spiritual and cultural riches. Bhutan, with its majestic mountains, dense forests, and serene valleys, has long been considered a sacred place, a spiritual sanctuary. It was here that Padmasambhava found fertile ground for his profound teachings.

Moreover, the people of Bhutan, deeply rooted in their cultural traditions and practices, were open to the transformative powers of Buddhism. Padmasambhava's teachings resonated with them, leading to the widespread acceptance of Vajrayana Buddhism. This spiritual alignment between the guru and the people contributed to Bhutan's unique religious culture, one that continues to thrive today.

His life, much of it steeped in mythology, is celebrated through vibrant religious festivals, or *tshechus*, which feature dance performances depicting tales of his supernatural abilities and various manifestations. His journeys across Bhutan have left an indelible mark on the country, with numerous landmarks, such as sacred water spots, caves and 'walking stick' trees, said to be blessed by him. In parts of the country he visited, his imprints have been left on rocks. These sites are still revered today and have become popular pilgrimage destinations.

* * *

What Happens at a Tshechu?

Tshechus are an absolute riot of colour, culture, and spirituality—true spectacles that encapsulate the essence of Bhutan. These religious festivals are held annually in various temples, monasteries, and dzongs throughout the country, and they are a sight to behold. If you have the opportunity to attend one, do it!

Imagine the scene: swarms of people dressed in their finest traditional attire, a kaleidoscope of richly embroidered ghos and kiras, all converging at the festival site. The air is filled with the scent of incense and the tantalizing aroma of local delicacies being prepared at nearby stalls. There's a tangible sense of anticipation as the crowd waits for the festivities to begin.

The central highlight of any tshechu are the *cham* dances. These are carefully choreographed masked dances that tell tales from Buddhist mythology, often featuring the life and deeds of Padmasambhava. The dancers, monks, and laymen don intricate silk costumes and beautifully crafted masks, transforming into wrathful and compassionate deities, heroes, demons and animals.

As the haunting rhythm of cymbals, drums, and horns fills the air, the dancers begin to move. They weave intricate patterns, their movements simultaneously graceful and powerful. Each step, each gesture is imbued with deep symbolic meaning, and it's said that witnessing these dances can cleanse one's soul of sin and bring blessings.

But tshechus are not just about the dances. There are also religious rituals and ceremonies, including the unveiling of a giant *thongdrel*, a sacred scroll painting, which is believed to bestow blessings upon all who gaze upon it. And let's not forget the social aspect—tshechus are a time for communities to come together, catch up with friends and family, enjoy good food, and share in collective merriment.

A favourite feature of tshechus are *atsaras*, the masked clowns who bring a mix of humour, wisdom, and cultural symbolism to the festivities. These vibrant figures, known for their exaggerated masks and lively antics, serve as both entertainers and protectors, blending playful mockery with profound teachings to ensure the sacred rituals are engaging and accessible to all.

Atsaras represent the balance between the sacred and the mundane, using humour to humble egos and impart moral lessons subtly. Their energy and comical interactions particularly appeal to children, making the spiritual and cultural elements of tshechus enjoyable and memorable for young audiences.

In short, a tshechu is a feast for the senses, a profound spiritual experience and a vibrant social event all rolled into one. It's an unforgettable spectacle that offers a glimpse into the rich tapestry of Bhutan's culture and spirituality.

* * *

Beyond his historical significance, Padmasambhava holds a central place in the spiritual consciousness of the Bhutanese people. He is prayed to for blessings in all aspects of life, from health and wealth to longevity and academic success. The story of his miraculous birth from a lotus flower and his subsequent life as a prince, ascetic, and monk further underscore his spiritual stature. His role in establishing Buddhism in Tibet and translating Buddhist scriptures into Tibetan has had a lasting impact on the region's spiritual landscape.

A legend of Padmasambhava with contemporary relevance is one of King Sindharaja of Bumthang, who fell gravely ill after antagonizing local deities. In desperation, Sindharaja invited Padmasambhava to restore his health. Upon his arrival, Padmasambhava requested Sindharaja's virtuous daughter, Tashi Kheundron, to be his consort for spiritual practices. Together, they embarked on a seven-day retreat in a sacred cave, now known as Kurjey. After a series of mystical events, including a dance performance that tamed the wrathful deity Shalging Karpo, Padmasambhava retrieved Sindharaja's life-soul, leading to the King's miraculous recovery.

Revitalized, Sindharaja received Buddhist teachings from Padmasambhava, fostering an understanding of virtue and peace. Padmasambhava also mediated a historic truce between Sindharaja and a rival king, establishing a principle of mediation that influences Bhutan's legal system to this day. The legacy of Padmasambhava's teachings and acts of reconciliation continue to shape Bhutan's spiritual and legal practices, making his story a significant part of the country's cultural heritage.

In today's context, Padmasambhava's teachings and the values he embodied—compassion, wisdom, and selflessness—continue to guide the Bhutanese people. The stories of his life serve as moral compasses, inspiring us to strive for enlightenment and to live in harmony with others and the environment.

* * *

Taktsang and the Guru's Legacy

On his inaugural visit to Bhutan, Guru Padmasambhava prophesied his return, this time journeying from Tibet. His second expedition led him to a renowned location that has since become Bhutan's most iconic site—the breathtaking Taktsang. Also known as Tiger's Nest Monastery, this architectural marvel is Bhutan's most photographed landmark.

Defying gravity, Taktsang nestles precariously on a sheer cliff face, 3,120 metres high, in the serene Paro valley. Constructed in 1692, this temple complex is a testament to Bhutan's architectural prowess and spiritual devotion. But to fully appreciate its grandeur, one needs to embark on a demanding trek winding up the rocky mountain trail. The path, snaking around the cliff, is well-trodden by pilgrims, tourists, locals, and mules carrying weary travellers.

The journey, often shrouded in mist, can be challenging, but it offers an unparalleled experience. Hiking among fluttering prayer flags, blue pine trees adorned with drooping lichen, yellow-billed magpies flitting through the leaves, and breathtaking vantage points, this route provides a unique blend of natural beauty and spiritual essence.

For centuries, Taktsang has been a revered pilgrimage site in the Himalayas, attracting eminent figures and Tibetan saints who sought solitude and spiritual enlightenment within its hallowed halls. The eleventh-century yogi Milarepa is among the many hermit-saints who have meditated here. Visitors often speak of a calming energy that envelops the area, despite the physically demanding climb.

The temple complex we see today, clinging to the mountain like an arachnid on a wall, was built 800 years after Padmasambhava's arrival in Bhutan. Despite the area being renowned as a sacred retreat, no architectural structure existed until the seventeenth century. Unfortunately, a devastating fire in 1998 ravaged the monastery, but the Fourth King commanded its restoration following traditional methods and style. Today, Taktsang stands as resplendent as ever, indistinguishable from its original form.

Taktsang's fame extends beyond its precarious perch and extraordinary architecture. The sacredness of this spot stems from popular accounts of Padmasambhava's journey here on a tigress, a manifestation of Yeshe Tsogyal. He meditated in a series of caves for three years, three months, and three days, subduing evil forces and spreading Buddhism among the natives. His meditation cave at Taktsang is now a revered shrine, opened once a year for public viewing.

Bhutan abounds with sacred sites touched by Padmasambhava, including Kurjey Lhakhang and the elusive Singye dzong in eastern Bhutan. Unlike other sites, reaching Singye dzong requires a strenuous three-day trek and special permissions. Although named a dzong or fortified monastery, Singye dzong is actually a lion-shaped cliff believed to house a concealed dzong that will only reveal itself at an opportune time. Despite its secrecy, this dzong is a significant pilgrimage destination, housing a temple founded by Yeshe Tsogyal, Padmasambhava's Tibetan consort. Legend says that visiting it can liberate one from rebirth in the lower realms.

Among the plethora of prophecies Guru Padmasambhava bestowed upon Bhutan, one foretold the emergence of a destined ruler, a unifying force for the fragmented land. This prophecy materialized in 1616 with the arrival of Zhabdrung Ngawang Namgyal (1594–1651), a Tibetan lama of prominent stature. This influential figure, depicted on the large thangka displayed in Parliament Hall, is revered across Bhutan. His bearded visage also graces home shrines and temples, symbolizing his profound impact as a central political and religious figure.

* * *

A Unified Land

Any discussion of great, sweeping change in a society must be seen in the context of its history because these events rarely happen in a vacuum. Bhutan is no different, despite being such a small country. While its kings have abdicated much of their power, our peaceful transition owes much to all of them, and the traditions they have built over the century they have ruled this nation.

Geographically located between the two most populous countries in the world, Bhutan is in a state of perpetual vulnerability. Potential rulers started to sow discord among one another, but Zhabdrung Ngawang Namgyal, a name that resonates profoundly in the annals of Bhutanese history, was a visionary leader who played an instrumental role in the early formation of Bhutan.

Born in 1594 at the Ralung Monastery in Tibet, the Zhabdrung was considered the fulfilment of prayers and aspirations of Drukpa Kagyu followers, marking his life one of spiritual significance from the outset. (Note that while 'Zhabdrung' is a title awarded to great lamas in Tibet, here in Bhutan it nearly always refers to our founding father Ngawang Namgyal or one of his reincarnations.)

At the tender age of twelve, he was recognized as the reincarnation of Pema Karpo, a scholar of unparalleled wisdom within the Drukpa lineage. This dual recognition elevated the Zhabdrung's status, not just as the son of the sixteenth prince abbot, but also as the living embodiment of a renowned Drukpa scholar.

However, this accolade sparked a rivalry. Pagsam Wangpo, from a lineage of spiritual reincarnations or *trulkus*, contested the Zhabdrung's claim, asserting he was the true reincarnation of Pema Karpo. This dispute split the Drukpa followers, sowing seeds of discord that ultimately led to the Zhabdrung's departure from Tibet.

The situation was further complicated by the endorsement of Pagsam Wangpo as the legitimate heir by Phuntsho Namgyal, ruler of the Tsangpa dynasty. This decision not only intensified the strife between the factions of the Zhabdrung and Pagsam Wangpo but also entrenched the schism within the Drukpa school. The fallout divided the Drukpa school into northern and southern branches, with Bhutan's state religion, Drukpa Kagyu, aligning with the southern faction.

It was against this tumultuous backdrop that the Zhabdrung embarked on his historic 1616 journey to Bhutan, following the trail laid out for him by a raven in a dream—an intervention by the raven-headed deity Mahakala. It is a momentous event that Bhutan commemorates even today, over 400 years later. His arrival marked a period of transformation for the country as he worked tirelessly to unify the many warring factions under a single banner. This is the reason the raven watches over Bhutan to this day, as our official national bird.

Shortly after the Zhabdrung arrived in Bhutan, he established the southern Drukpa order at Cheri Monastery in Thimphu. His popularity among the people and monastics was increasing too. When the Tibetans invaded Bhutan to get to him, the Bhutanese must have thought that they were being attacked and mobilized support around him, allowing him to gain appeal among the people. This helped him fend off the first Tibetan invasion by his enemy, the Tsangpa ruler and establish his power base in his new territory.

The Zhabdrung's political acumen shone through in his establishment of a unique dual system of governance in the seventeenth century. He appointed the *je khenpo* (chief abbot) as the head of the religious order and the deb raja (regent) as the administrative head, effectively balancing spiritual and administrative responsibilities. This system also ensured that the governance of Bhutan would not lean too heavily on either secular or religious interests, providing a balanced approach that has persisted over centuries.

His reign, spanning over thirty-five years, was marked by the introduction of a code of law, which helped solidify his unification efforts and establish a sense of national identity. Indeed, it can be said that the Zhabdrung's wise, enlightened leadership was ahead of its time and allowed the system he established to flourish beyond his own lifetime. His political actions laid a strong foundation for the development of Bhutan as a distinct nation, separate from its larger neighbours, and remain a viable nation state to this day.

After unifying the local chieftains into his single Drukyul polity (which roughly matches the geographical borders of Bhutan today), the Zhabdrung realized that this new religious state needed to have its own identity, separate from Tibet. This realization led to the establishment of many customs, traditions, and ceremonies that have lasted till today. The national dress that we wear today, including the variously coloured scarves (known as *kabney*) worn by men to indicate rank, were all instituted by him.

A code of conduct (*driglam namzha*) was also devised during his reign. It sets basic guidelines on what to wear, mannerisms to adopt, and moral etiquette. The driglam namzha protocol even teaches discipline, filial piety, and determines how to conduct oneself while eating, and how one should bow when greeting senior officials.

Besides a cultural identity, the Zhabdrung transformed the landscape with the dzongs (fortified monasteries that also serve as administrative centres) that he built. As he consolidated the regions, he constructed such edifices at strategic points to not only for defence, administration, and accommodation but also as expressions of his military might and dominance. They dot the landscape across the entire country, making them distinct reminders of his rule across the land. Their establishment cemented his rule indefinitely, a move that was no different from European medieval rulers' castle-building in their conquered realms.

* * *

The Dzongs of Bhutan

After a three-year retreat in 1623, Zhabdrung Ngawang Namgyal received visions directing him to unite the Drukpa state under both spiritual and political leadership. He declared himself the ruler of Drukyul ('Land of the Thunder Dragon', now known as Bhutan), and built the first dzong, Semtokha, in 1629. This structure, which served as a fortress, monastery, and administrative centre, became the model for all future dzongs.

Despite an uprising by a faction of five lamas during its construction, he successfully defended his territory. The completed Semtokha dzong was consecrated in 1630. However, a Tibetan invasion in 1634 resulted in the dzong's capture and destruction. It was only restored thirty-seven years later.

Following this incident, the Zhabdrung decided to construct a grander dzong in Punakha, at the confluence of two rivers, fulfilling another prophecy by Guru Padmasambhava. Built in 1637–38, Punakha dzong, also known as 'The Palace of Great Bliss', is considered one of Bhutan's most magnificent, fortified monasteries.

Punakha, a masterpiece of Bhutanese architecture and the resting place of the Zhabdrung's earthly remains, is perhaps the country's most beautiful, fortified monastery. In spring, the dzong's whitewashed walls contrast with lilac jacaranda blossoms, while a traditional wooden cantilever bridge adds charm to the riverside setting. The fortified monastery hosts the Punakha Drubchen, an annual festival commemorating the Zhabdrung's historic victory against the Tibetans in 1639. The sacred relic involved in that battle— Ranjung Kharsapani, a vertebra of Tsangpa Gyarey, the founder of the Drukpa Kagyu school of thought—remains within the dzong, symbolizing its religious and political significance.

Bhutanese elders recount that otherworldly beings assisted in building Bhutan's dzongs, contributing materials for Punakha dzong's construction. However, considering the scale of the architectural work involved, it's also likely that a sizable workforce was employed.

The next dzong to be completed after Punakha was Wangdue Phodrang, about 20 kilometres due south of Punakha. The Zhabdrung accomplished this just one year after being guided to its site in a vision. It sits on a ridge resembling a sleeping elephant and represents the unity he fought so hard to build.

The original building was destroyed by a fire in 2012; His Majesty the Fifth King personally supervised the safe rescue of many priceless relics and artifacts from the flames. An exact replica of the original dzong has since been consecrated and inaugurated to great fanfare, much to the relief of we who believe the Zhabdrung's legacy lives on.

The new dzong is based on painstaking reconstruction of how it looked in its heyday—complete with rammed earth walls, stone masonry and massive timber columns and beams. Its modern reconstruction took over a decade, and one wonders at the miraculous speed with which the original was built!

The dzongs of Bhutan still stand today as a majestic reminder of the nation's past and continue to serve as the monastic and administrative centres of their respective dzongkhags (districts). There are twenty in operation as of this writing, with at least one in every major valley. They are supplemented by over 2,000 lhakhangs (monasteries), each decorated with altars, statues, scriptures, paintings, and silver and gold ornaments. These structures are centuries old and speak of a wealthy past for the nation.

King Jigme is perhaps one of the greatest dzong builders after the Zhabdrung himself. As I write, four have been constructed, including a rebuilt Wangdue Phodrang dzong, along with Drukgyal dzong (reconstructed after a fire in the early 1950s), and the entirely new Denchi dzong. A fourth, the recently completed Pamisa, located above the Paro Valley, is the biggest dzong in Bhutan. Finally, a fifth dzong at Sarpang will soon be completed as of this writing. Over the construction process, I have been privileged to visit these sacred sites on multiple occasions.

My own closest connection is to Drukgyal dzong. Built in 1649 by the Zhabdrung to commemorate Bhutan's victory over combined forces of Tibet, Mongolia, and China, when reconstruction began in earnest to celebrate the birth of His Royal Highness the Gyalsey, Crown Prince Jigme Namgyal Wangchuck in 2016. I had the honour of taking part in the sacred ceremonies to lay its foundation stone on the occasion of his birth.

* * *

By the end of the 1640s, the Zhabdrung's position of power had been fully asserted across Bhutan after his triumphant victories over numerous Tibetan invasions. His success in repelling them consolidated his position as the uncontested ruler of Bhutan. With the help of the *penlop* (governor) of Trongsa, whom he had personally appointed, the Zhabdrung managed to take control of the central and eastern parts.

However, the Zhabdrung and his close aides knew that any news of his impending death would cause mayhem in the country. Hence, it was kept as a closely guarded secret for over fifty years. In 1651, the Zhabdrung went into retreat at Punakha dzong and never emerged again. However, meals continued to be served on time, orders were 'issued' supposedly by him, and someone even pretended to give blessings while hiding behind a curtain.

This ruse temporarily preserved the unification of the country, avoided any dynastic struggle, and kept the Tibetans at bay. His retreat remains an important symbol of Bhutanese nationhood, and we believe him to still be in it. As such, we continue to offer meals and seek his counsel and support; I myself have gone to Punakha to seek his permission before every one of my political campaigns and visited many more times as a politician and prime minister to offer prayers and seek his guidance on important matters.

Despite the difficult time of succession after the Zhabdrung died, his dual system of government continues to be pivotal to this day. This diarchal political system, which he instituted, is one in which the country is headed by a spiritual leader (the chief abbot or je khenpo) and an administrative leader of the secular world (a prime minister). Both leaders hold equal power, and in the Zhabdrung's day, both reported to him as the supreme power—a role held by the king today. The position of the spiritual and secular leaders would rotate, but the Zhabdrung had intended for his position to be hereditary. However, this failed to happen, as he did not have any children.

Despite having been successfully driven from Punakha dzong, the Tibetans were unabated and continued to make subsequent but futile invasions until 1732. The third *desi* (secular ruler) appointed by the Zhabdrung, Mingyur Tenpa, extended the boundaries westwards to Kalimpong, which is now part of India. By 1772, Bhutan had also successfully taken over Cooch Behar, now part of West Bengal,

India. The capturing of Cooch Behar and its king would have significant consequences for the Bhutanese.

However, elected desis continued to rule amid rivalries between various factions, eventually leading to civil war, political infighting, and internal conflicts. The situation gradually worsened and the Tibetans, Gushi Khan, and the Mongols, as well as the Chinese emperor in Beijing, were momentarily involved in the disputes, until a truce was initiated by Tibet and formal diplomatic relations established.

After seventeen Tibetan invasions and finally securing peace with them, Bhutan had to fight off the British East India Company in 1772 and the wider British Empire in 1865. These two battles resulted in Bhutan losing its claim over Cooch Behar and the *duars*, the floodplains that lie at the foothills of the Himalayas.

Meanwhile, within the heartlands of Bhutan, incessant conflicts, political instability, and rivalry for regional supremacy continued. This lasted until a famed warrior, Ugyen Wangchuck, was elected to be the first hereditary Dragon King (or Druk Gyalpo) in 1907.

Just as how Guru Padmasambhava had once predicted that someone named Namgyal would come to rule the land, a similar prophecy proffered by him tells of the emergence of the monarchy in Bhutan: 'On a cliff, in the land of Mon, lies my body in print. There, in Bumthang, where the Wheel has turned, shall arrive a Dharma King, my incarnation!'

The Zhabdrung's Legacy

Zhabdrung Ngawang Namgyal's influence on Bhutan continues to be felt, and his enlightened leadership, innovative political structures and commitment to unity laid the groundwork for the Bhutan we know today. This dual system of rule is not unique to Tibet or Bhutan, and history has seen some countries being ruled by two entities that share equal power. In medieval Europe, treaties were signed to recognize two rulers of equal footing who jointly ruled over a sovereign nation. This would usually consist of a secular ruler and an ecclesiastical ruler.

For a period of time in Hungary, a religiously vested king and a war chief would both rule side by side as two kings. In Japanese history, the powerful shōguns held equal authority to the monarch. Today, the sovereign state of Andorra has a unique diarchy in that it is jointly ruled by two princes or coprínceps: the president of France and the bishop of Spain. Besides the two co-princes, Andorra also has a democratically elected government with a head of government as the chief executive. Andorra's unique system has lasted since 1278 right up to the present day, and the joint rule of the two heads of state are institutionalized in its Constitution.

In a sense, Andorra's diarchical system is perhaps a close reflection of Bhutan's traditional dual system of government. Although it has been substantially adapted since the time of the Zhabdrung, Bhutan today has a prime minister—who is head of government—and a je khenpo, who is a religious head. Together, the two are accountable to the Druk Gyalpo. So, in a way, the Zhabdrung's vision has come full circle.

This dual system is represented in Bhutan's national flag. The yellow portion represents the secular leader and the orange part symbolizes the spiritual leader. The white dragon in the middle is the Druk or thunder dragon. Like Andorra, Bhutan also has a democratically elected parliament.

Today, within the sacred walls of Punakha dzong, the legacy of the Zhabdrung continues to resonate. It is here that his mortal remains are believed to rest in eternal meditation. This fortified monastery also witnessed the dawn of Bhutan's monarchy, with the crowning of the First King Sir Ugyen Wangchuck in 1907. Following this tradition, each subsequent king of the Wangchuck Dynasty has been privately consecrated with the Raven Crown within the hallowed chambers of Punakha dzong.

The dzong's historical significance extends beyond royal coronations. In 1952, it was the stage for the country's first National

Assembly convened by the Third King of Bhutan Jigme Dorji Wangchuck. This event marked a turning point in Bhutan's political landscape, signalling a shift away from absolute monarchy.

In recent times, Punakha dzong captured global attention when King Jigme Khesar Namgyal Wangchuck was crowned there in 2008, and again when he married Queen Jetsun Pema there in 2011. The royal couple received blessings from the holy relic housed within the fortified monastery before embarking on their matrimonial journey.

Punakha dzong's religious and symbolic importance is immense. Holding political events within its precincts is akin to securing spiritual endorsement from the Zhabdrung himself. This ritual lends an air of divine approval to the kings' authority, reinforcing their dominion over the land and its people.

Besides its association with the Zhabdrung and the monarchy, Punakha dzong serves as the winter abode for the Central Monastic Body, known as the *draktshang*. The Je Khenpo, along with his monks, reside here during winter and migrate to Tashichho dzong in Thimphu for summer. This annual custom, initiated by the Zhabdrung in 1641, has been upheld for centuries, further cementing Punakha dzong's central role in Bhutan's cultural and religious tapestry.

Chapter Four

From Monarchy to Democracy

During 2006–2007, the Election Commission will educate our people in the process of parliamentary democracy and electoral practice sessions will be conducted in all the twenty dzongkhags.

After twenty-six years of the process of decentralization and devolution of powers to the people, I have every confidence that our people will be able to choose the best political party that can provide good governance and serve the interests of the nation ...

—King Jigme Singye Wangchuck in his
Nation Address of 2005

Born in Bumthang, the broad-shouldered, sturdily-built Ugyen Wangchuck was trained in combat strategy and warfare since a young age. By seventeen, the future First King had already led troops to battle and was appointed as the penlop of Paro. When he was twenty-one, his father Jigme Namgyal—who was the Trongsa penlop and had once led campaigns against the British—died in an accident, leaving Ugyen Wangchuck with the foundations for a unitary power, as well as his own position of power as the penlop of Trongsa. This further cemented Ugyen Wangchuck's position as the de facto ruler of Bhutan. In the 1880s, Ugyen Wangchuck defeated his opponents who were vying to rule and consolidated his power after seizing control of Semtokha dzong.

But what ultimately helped solidify his rule, leading to that unanimous vote that made him king, was his role as a mediator between the British and Tibetans in 1906. Following the battles in 1865 and the signing of a treaty with the British, Bhutan's relationship with British India had remained firm. When it came to matters related to Bhutan, the British would defer to the sagacious Ugyen Wangchuck.

This proved to be invaluable when the British were attempting to form formal diplomatic relations with Tibet. Ugyen Wangchuck eventually became the key influencing figure in convincing both parties to come to an amicable solution. For his role in negotiating ties with Tibet, the British honoured him with the insignia of the Knight Commander of the Order of the Indian Empire. His statesmanship and masterful mediation tactics resulted in him being regarded as the unquestioned leader of Bhutan, and it greatly helped that he was popular with the British too. Sir Ugyen Wangchuck was even invited to meet the Prince of Wales in Calcutta, where he was received with the same formalities due to an Indian prince.

Going beyond the country's borders to sow seeds of diplomatic relations was a refreshingly new type of leadership that Bhutan had not seen in centuries. Sir Ugyen Wangchuck's discernment, prudent judgement, and cordial relations with Bhutan's neighbours instilled the period of peace, security, and stability the country had longed for. This was the right moment to make an important political transition.

On 17 December 1907, a coronation was held and Sir Ugyen Wangchuck was handed a crown fashioned from his father's helmet. Known as the Raven Crown for its distinctly protruding raven head on top with red tassels flowing from its base, this crown—and its variations—has been handed to all hereditary monarchs since that day. (The raven, undoubtedly, alludes to Mahakala, the deity who first led the Zhabdrung to Bhutan in his prophetic dream.)

On the upturned circular rim of the crown are fearsome skeletal heads embroidered on the sides with motifs of burning flames, a visual reminder of the traditions of Vajrayana Buddhism. Blessed in the presence of the Zhabdrung's remains to imbue it with his powers, the Raven Crown represents the spiritual and secular values of the Bhutanese, and the monarchy as their custodians.[8]

The coronation of the First Druk Gyalpo was a significant turning point in Bhutan's history, leading to consistent foreign relations and policy, guaranteeing our independence and sovereignty. That day has been celebrated as Bhutan's National Day ever since.

Almost a year before the Raven Crown was placed on Sir Ugyen Wangchuck's head, around fifty officials representing every part of Bhutan and segment of Bhutanese society had gathered to elect him king. They placed their seal on a document stating that he was to be 'enthroned as the hereditary monarch, through common agreement'. The abbot, monastic masters, the congregation, state council, regional governors, and all officials and subjects 'unanimously and sincerely' endorsed the First King. The establishment of the monarchy not only ended two centuries of conflict but also spelled an evolved version of the original dual system prescribed by the Zhabdrung, and the beginning of a monarchy that remains one of the youngest in the world.

Sir Ugyen Wangchuck's twenty-year reign heralded the beginning of peacetime in Bhutan. He was known for ruling the country by combining the Buddhist qualities of wisdom and compassion, benevolent traits that would henceforth come to define successive monarchs till this day. The First King continued to maintain close relations with Britain and India, in an attempt to steer away from growing Chinese influence on Tibet.

To avoid any foreign influence or play in national matters, the Treaty of Punakha was signed in 1910 to ensure Bhutan's sovereignty. This was an era of colonization, when the majority of Asian territories were seized by the Dutch, French, or British. Adamant about preserving Bhutan's sovereignty, the kingdom continued a policy of

---

[8] Karma Phuntsho, 'Bhutan's Raven Crown,' Bhutan Cultural Library, at https://texts.shanti.virginia.edu/content/bhutan%E2%80%99s-raven-crown.

isolation and refused to allow an appointed British resident in the land. The Treaty of Punakha stated that the British Government would 'exercise no interference in the internal administration of Bhutan'. But it also allowed the nation to be 'guided by the advice of the British Government' when it came to external relations.

After Sir Ugyen Wangchuck died in 1926, his eldest son, Jigme Wangchuck, succeeded him to the throne. The second Druk Gyalpo reigned for twenty-six years and continued to solidify the political power that his father had established decades ago by making extensive changes to the Zhabdrung's dual system of government. In an effort to ensure political stability and to prevent Bhutan from lapsing into internal disputes and power struggles again, King Jigme Wangchuck simplified the hierarchical system by appointing himself to have absolute power over all religious and secular matters. He also instructed the je khenpo to establish a central monk body.

Bhutan continued to isolate itself from the outside world while also strengthening its relationship with British India. But this proved to be worrisome as India's independence drew closer. Since the First King's reign, Bhutan had depended somewhat on British support. However, as the empire was exiting India, King Jigme Wangchuck was concerned about the ramifications of this in Bhutan. Would it be subsumed into India as a princely state? What would happen to the sovereignty of his country? Concerned with such matters, a Bhutanese delegation was sent to New Delhi to reiterate Bhutan's independent status.

India became independent on 15 August 1947, and two years later, Bhutan and India signed a new treaty in Sikkim. The treaty was a reconfirmation of the earlier one signed between Bhutan and the British. However, this time, Bhutan agreed to be guided by India in its foreign affairs while managing its own internal matters. This 1949 treaty not only forged Bhutan's long-standing friendship with India that lasts till this day but also influenced Bhutan's development, culture, and economy.

Although India no longer guides Bhutan's foreign affairs due to a revised 2007 treaty, the two countries still thrive as close allies and partners, since the friendship was struck up by King Jigme Wangchuck many decades ago. Ever since Bhutan closed its borders with Tibet after the Chinese incursion in 1959, Bhutan has looked southward for political and trade relations. India has since provided most of the development funding and resources for Bhutan, including military training. The Second King's foresight in securing Bhutan's independence also helped secure the monarchy.

The reign of the Wangchuck dynasty seemed promising, even more so when the next king took the throne. Known affectionately as the 'Father of Modern Bhutan', the third Druk Gyalpo, Jigme Dorji Wangchuck, thrust Bhutan into a new era. His father had helped open doors to its neighbour in the south and it was now up to the Third King to fully utilize the opportunity that lay in his hands.

Bhutan's days of isolation ended during the reign of the Third King, from 1952 to 1972. As the world started to see a post-World War II market expansion, Bhutan flourished blissfully in its medieval way of life. But this was about to change. Self-imposed isolation was not feasible in the modern world and if Bhutan wanted to remain independent, the new King knew that it had to be part of a larger global community. Bhutan had to modernize but do so without destabilizing its culture and traditions.

The World Comes to Bhutan

Bhutan was arguably one of the last nations on earth to participate in modernization. For centuries, no roads linked Bhutan to the outside world. This was until 1961, when the first road was built to connect it to India from the southern border, the same road project that my mother played a part in constructing. Today, that first stretch of road in Phuentsholing is marked by a Bhutanese-styled gate. Known simply as the Bhutan Gate, this landmark looms over the black-topped road, demarcating the border that separates Bhutan and India.

The construction of a road that connects Bhutan to its neighbour was just the beginning of many more modern developments that were about to happen in the kingdom.

With funds from India, King Jigme Dorji Wangchuck launched a development phase, albeit a cautious and controlled one. During this period, a dozen hospitals and over 100 schools were built. More roads and highways were constructed to interconnect the Bhutanese people. Bhutan also received technical assistance and training from Southeast Asian countries, and the Royal Bhutan Army and police force were established during the Third King's reign. This was the time when my father first joined the Army.

King Jigme Dorji Wangchuck's overhaul of Bhutan's education system marked a significant turning point in the country's history, paving the way for intellectual diversity and broader worldviews, while also preserving and promoting Bhutanese traditions. Prior to this reform, education in Bhutan had largely been confined to monastic institutions and accessible only to a privileged few. This limited access to education created a narrow spectrum of ideas and perspectives, stifling innovation and progress. By establishing a modern education system, the Third King effectively democratized knowledge, granting more Bhutanese people the opportunity to learn, develop their own ideas, and contribute to the nation's development.

The introduction of new content and a secular worldview in the curriculum fostered thought diversity among the Bhutanese. Exposure to different ideas, perspectives, and cultures encouraged critical thinking and creativity, equipping future generations with the skills needed to navigate an increasingly globalized world.

At the same time, the Third King's decision to change the medium of instruction to English was a strategic move that not only aligned Bhutan with international academic standards but also opened up a world of opportunities for its citizens. English proficiency would allow Bhutanese students to access a wealth of knowledge and resources, further broadening their horizons. This move ended the nation's self-imposed isolation and threw open the doors to globalization, and today, almost every Bhutanese, especially the young, can communicate in English.

Alongside these developments through the 1960s, Dzongkha was formalized as a written language. Dzongkha has its roots in the southern dialects of the Tibetan language. Before the 1960s, written Dzongkha had primarily been used in religious texts and official government correspondence, often influenced by Chhokey, a classical Tibetan language with complex scripts and a vocabulary influenced by Sanskrit and Pali. While Chhokey was in use as a liturgical language in Buddhist ceremonies (similar to the way Latin is used in the Catholic Church), it was not widely spoken or understood by the general population, most of whom lacked literacy in their own language.

By the 1970s, a fully developed written form of Dzongkha emerged, aimed at developing it as Bhutan's national language in the name of cultural and national unity. Furthermore, by building more schools and inviting teachers from India, King Jigme Dorji Wangchuck expanded the accessibility of education throughout Bhutan, allowing even those in remote areas to receive quality education. This move not only promoted literacy and learning but also contributed to reducing social inequality.[9]

While embracing modernity and global perspectives, the Third King also understood the importance of maintaining a strong connection with Bhutan's cultural heritage. His introduction of Dzongkha as the national language in schools ensured that Bhutanese traditions and values would continue to be passed down to future generations, striking a balance between progress and preservation. The transition has not been without its challenges; as we learn primarily in English and gain an international language that

---

[9] Lhundup Dukpa, 'Language Policy in Bhutan,' in Andy Kirkpatrick and Anthony J Liddicoat (eds.), *Routledge International Handbook of Language Education Policy in Asia* (New York, NY: Routledge, 2019).

allows communication all over the world, we correspondingly face challenges in learning Dzongkha and keeping it relevant.

In conclusion, the Third King's educational reforms in Bhutan served as a catalyst for thought diversity and progress while simultaneously safeguarding the country's rich traditions. His balanced approach to modernization and tradition serves as an inspiring example for nations navigating the path between preserving cultural heritage and embracing the demands of a rapidly changing world. Because of his introduction of modern education in Bhutan, 2 May is commemorated as Teacher's Day every year, coinciding with his birthday.

Perhaps the two most significant transformations brought about by the 'Father of Modern Bhutan' have been the abolishment of feudalism and the establishment of a National Assembly. Prior to the shift to democracy in the twentieth century, Bhutan was a feudal society, with power centralized in the hands of regional leaders, religious figures, and the monarchy.

In the feudal system, society was organized into a hierarchy with the king at the top. Below him were penlops (governors) and *dzongpons* (district administrators), both positions involving civil and military leadership. The clergy also held significant power, particularly the je khenpo who was the religious counterpart to the King.

Land ownership played a critical role in Bhutan's feudal system. The majority of the population were serfs working on plots owned by the state, the clergy, and the aristocracy. Serfs provided manual labour and a portion of their harvest in return for protection and the right to work the land.

Within a year of his reign, King Jigme Dorji Wangchuck had established the *Tshogdu* (National Assembly) in Punakha dzong in 1953. He knew early on that a centralized authority, such as the monarchy, was not an efficient system. Earning the trust of the people was crucial to ensuring a secure status for the monarchy and the country. Perhaps the exposure he gained from a Western education in Kalimpong and his study tours to Britain and Switzerland inspired him to transform Bhutan.

While his predecessors were conservative in their approach to governance, the farsighted Third King embraced a more democratic approach. The Tshogdu that he established contained some 138 elected members who represented the people, the monastic community, and government officials. They would discuss various issues and for the first time, elders from different hamlets and districts were invited to voice their concerns and recommendations on ideas and solutions for the country.

In 1965, the Third King went a step further, setting up a Royal Advisory Council of eight members. These members would advise the king and the government, as well as deliberate on appeals made to the king. The Royal Advisory Council, together with the National Assembly, became the formal legislative body that enacted laws and acts. In 1959, the Supreme Law was drafted and passed by the National Assembly. But the laws needed to be interpreted by a body. So, King Jigme Dorji Wangchuck decided to open up the judiciary. He appointed *thrimpons* (judges) in every district, setting in motion an independent judicial system, leading to the establishment of the High Court in 1967.

But for democratic governance to fully take shape, the king would have to reduce his own powers. He did just that in 1969, when he gave up his royal power to veto bills passed in the National Assembly. To send a stronger message that Bhutan should embrace a democratic governing system, the Third King again delegated his power further to the people by subjecting himself to a vote of confidence every three years. The National Assembly now had the power to remove the king, provided there was support from a two-thirds majority, in favour of the next in line of succession. (The vote of confidence can still be enacted today, in which the reigning king can be subjected to a motion for abdication in parliament. This provision was included in our Constitution at the insistence of the Fourth and Fifth Kings. This means that, barring a massive change in our political culture, the people of Bhutan will always have the power to force their king to step down.)

At the same time, King Jigme Dorji Wangchuck also officially abolished serfdom in 1958. By liberating the bonded labourers—who, for many generations, served feudal lords and were landless—the Third King significantly changed the social structure in Bhutan. The freed slaves were now awarded citizenship (some slaves had been kidnapped or brought in from neighbouring regions) and land, including equal rights and opportunities as their former masters. The abolishment of feudalism, including the sharing of political power, thus paved the way for a gradual transition to democracy.

This process, however, was not realized by the Third King in his lifetime. In 1972—a year after Bhutan joined the United Nations—King Jigme Dorji Wangchuck died in Nairobi, Kenya, while receiving medical treatment. The initiative for a democratic Bhutan fell into the hands of his son, the 'Great Fourth' King Jigme Singye Wangchuck.

At only sixteen, the Fourth Druk Gyalpo was the youngest monarch at the time. If his father had held the door ajar for foreign funding to modernize Bhutan, the Fourth King thrust it wide open, though only to a select group. For the first time in history, overseas guests were invited to Bhutan to witness his coronation in 1974. Hotels had to be built to accommodate them, and this first batch of visitors was allowed to visit certain lhakhangs and dzongs, marking the humble beginnings of tourism. Improvements in connectivity and the launch of Druk Air in 1983 saw an increase in the number of tourists over the next few decades.

However, tourism in Bhutan has always been tempered with a 'high value, low volume' tourism policy, which has been able to successfully prevent the over-tourism woes that plague famous landmarks and destinations today. Opening our doors to tourists proved to be a vital move for Bhutan, as tourism today is our second largest revenue generator after hydropower. The revenue generated from tourism provides for free education, healthcare, and infrastructure development in Bhutan. This self-sustainable model was one of the examples King Jigme Singye Wangchuck put forth in his coronation address in 1974. He said that Bhutan must 'ensure economic self-reliance to ensure the continued progress of our country in the future'. For many years, his forefathers had relied mostly on funding from India and other countries. Now, the Fourth King expressed hopes for a self-sustainable Bhutan that would bring more prosperity and stability in the future while pledging to continue his father's work of modernizing Bhutan.

But this did not mean rampant economic development. No story about the Fourth King of Bhutan—or of Bhutan, for that matter—goes without mentioning GNH. When the world is measuring success through economic indicators such as gross domestic product (GDP), GNH is an outlier. What the Fourth King envisioned was a self-reliant Bhutan, built in a way that not only brought economic prosperity but also happiness and contentment. This included political stability and social harmony. He believed that happiness—not economic wealth—is an indicator for progressive development. Much of today's development efforts and decisions stem from GNH guidelines. A framework was subsequently created and methods of measuring the state of happiness in the society are still works-in-progress. We will look at GNH further in the following chapter.

During the Fourth King's reign, material prosperity rose rapidly. Water was safer to drink, healthcare services improved dramatically and more roads were built to connect the people closer to one another. A radio station was set up and television and Internet services were finally introduced to the country in 1999, making Bhutan one of the last countries in the world to have access to them.

Mobile phones arrived in 2003 and by 2011, the country had a 100 per cent mobile coverage. Bhutan's first hydropower project at Chukha was built and after its inauguration in 1988, the project improved the financial capacity of the country drastically. (These are not considered 'dams', as our hydroelectric facilities are 'run-off-the-river' systems that do not require large dams or reservoirs.)

One of my priorities in politics has been building and expanding the hydropower ecosystem in Bhutan, including prospecting for viable projects; designing and manufacturing hydromechanical and electromechanical components; setting up transmission and control systems; and building tunnels, dams, and powerhouses. I am confident that we can become an international player in the region. Today, hydropower remains the top revenue earner for Bhutan, followed by tourism. By 2013, all county offices were connected by fibreoptic broadband networks.[10]

Under the Fourth King, socio-economic development thrived, promotion of Bhutanese culture was enhanced, and efforts to preserve the environment flourished—alongside the modernization of fundamental sectors like education, agriculture, and raw materials.

Continuing his father's reforms in administration and justice, King Jigme Singye Wangchuck took a step further by decentralizing the government even more. *Yargay tshogdu* (development committees) were formed in 1981 at the dzongkhag level to decentralize power from the capital to the districts, so that development programmes could be deliberated at that level. This allowed for grassroots participation in the decision-making process. In 1991, yargay tshogdu were established at gewog level, giving individual gewogs decision-making power.

In 1998, as a means of further decentralizing his executive power, the first five minister-candidates were nominated by the Fourth King, to be elected by the National Assembly (themselves elected and holding legislative power) as ministers. The position of prime minister rotated among them. Five years later, in 2003, His Majesty appointed ten more minister-candidates, of whom six were elected by the National Assembly as ministers. This introduced democratic choice gradually into the system and paved the way for the Constitution to be drafted.

---

[10] Karma Phuntsho, *The History of Bhutan* (Noida: Random House India, 2013), 585.

The *gup*, or head of the county, was initially a hereditary position or selected by elders. But this changed in 2002 with the election of a gup using a secret ballot. This served as the first instance of a nationwide election, a practice that the Bhutanese would soon put to good use when the country became a democracy. Today, gups are elected at the local government level. Elected members of the National Assembly were called *chimmis*, though this would be changed to *thuemis*.

To sum up, secret balloting had already been used in parliament in the late 1990s to elect ministers and members, but Bhutan's kings had been guiding the process along, overcoming popular resistance slowly and instituting limits on their own power bit by bit.

The process of democratization finally materialized when the Fourth King initiated the drafting of the first written Constitution for the country in 2001. It took a few years more of consultation and research before the Constitution was finalized.

A Worthy Example

In December 2005, the Fourth King announced that he would abdicate in two years to make way for a new, democratic Bhutan. His actual abdication, to the surprise of the nation, came just one year later in December 2006—a sign of his resolve and seriousness in leading change and imposing democracy on Bhutan.

The fifth Druk Gyalpo, King Jigme Khesar Namgyal Wangchuck, took the throne at the age of twenty-six and began the task of overseeing Bhutan's full transition to democracy in the following two years. He took charge in his father's shadow, and the Fourth King, known for his wisdom and revered leadership, had left behind big shoes to fill and a nation that deeply respected him. With his father watching closely, the young monarch was under immense scrutiny.

One of the critical tasks he inherited was overseeing Bhutan's transition from an absolute monarchy to a democratic system—a

shift his father had initiated to great resistance from a citizenry
that preferred the stability and security provided of the monarchy.
Complicating matters further, the first elected government was
composed of seasoned leaders who had held high positions
during his father's reign. They were accustomed to the old ways of
governance, and to secure their cooperation, he needed to establish
his own authority and demonstrate his vision and capability for
leading the country.

The Fifth King approached these challenges with a blend
of youthful vigour and deep respect for his heritage. He worked
tirelessly to unify the nation, earning the respect of both the older
generation and the emerging democratic electorate. His leadership
has been marked by a commitment to sustainable development
and GNH, ensuring that Bhutan's progress is measured not just by
economic growth but also by the well-being of its people.

The Fifth King also immediately set about overseeing the
finalization of Bhutan's constitution. Taking personal charge
of the consultation process, he ensured that the transition to a
constitutional monarchy was smooth and inclusive. Under his reign,
key institutions essential for a well-functioning democracy were
established, including an independent Anti-Corruption Commission
and Election Commission, as well as a robust judiciary. These
institutions have been fundamental in promoting transparency,
accountability, and the rule of law in Bhutan.

In preparation for Bhutan's first parliamentary elections,
King Jigme designed and implemented comprehensive training
programmes on electoral processes. This included conducting
mock elections to familiarize citizens with the voting system and
procedures. His meticulous planning and dedication culminated
in Bhutan's historic first parliamentary elections being successfully
conducted, marking a significant milestone in the country's
democratic journey.

This approach not only educated the populace about their
democratic rights and responsibilities but also ensured that the

elections were conducted smoothly and fairly. In December 2007, the first National Council election was held for the twenty-five-member upper house. This was followed by the first National Assembly election in March 2008, which elected the forty-seven-member lower house. Bhutan had fulfilled its transition to democracy successfully and peacefully, with months to spare before the Fifth King's official coronation in November 2008. That year also marked 100 years of peaceful reign of the monarchy, making the occasion immensely significant.

During his coronation speech, the Fifth King laid out the basis of his reign:

> Throughout my reign I will never rule you as a King. I will protect you as a parent, care for you as a brother and serve you as a son. I shall give you everything and keep nothing; I shall live such a life as a good human being that you may find it worthy to serve as an example for your children; I have no personal goals other than to fulfil your hopes and aspirations. I shall always serve you, day and night, in the spirit of kindness, justice and equality.

What the King said on that day resonates with me till this day. Serving the people in the spirit of kindness, justice, and equality is not only the duty of the king but also is the duty of any parliamentarian who is voted into government.

King Jigme's commitment to social welfare is evident in his extensive efforts to address land distribution and poverty. Touring the entire country, he has personally met with farmers and distributed land among those in need. Recognizing the plight of the poor, he established new villages on fertile state land, relocating impoverished families to ensure they have better living conditions and opportunities for sustainable livelihoods. This hands-on approach demonstrates his deep empathy and commitment to improving the lives of his people. His leadership extends to economic development through Druk Holding and Investments (DHI), which manages the country's key economic assets.

Furthermore, King Jigme has been a proactive leader in times of natural disasters. Be it fires, floods, or earthquakes, he is consistently the first to arrive at disaster sites, mobilizing relief efforts and overseeing reconstruction activities. To coordinate and carry out the work of handling emergencies, he founded De-Suung (Guardians of Peace), an organization of volunteers dedicated to tackling various challenges, which I am proud to be part of.

The continuity of Bhutan's revered monarchy is secured by the presence of the crown prince, His Royal Highness Jigme Namgyal Wangchuck. At a mere eight years old, he has already accompanied his parents, Their Majesties the King and Queen, at public events, and even represented the King on his own, instilling a sense of reassurance among the people.

This early exposure to royal duties is a testament to the exceptional parenting of Her Majesty the Queen Jetsun Pema Wangchuck. Beyond her role as a mother and wife, the Queen also guides and provides royal patronage to numerous programmes, including the Bhutan Red Cross Society, the One Gewog One Product (OGOP) initiative to support farmers, Selwa for children with special needs, and the PEMA Center for those requiring mental and psychological support. Her Majesty's unwavering commitment extends to sustainability, environmental conservation, and wildlife protection, ensuring a prosperous future for the nation.

Every nation is built on the foundations laid by its founders, and the Fifth King's example of enlightened leadership is no exception. Their vision, their values, and their sacrifices shape the identity of the country and guide its progress. Our spiritual heritage coming from Guru Padmasambhava, the political groundwork set by our founding father Zhabdrung Ngawang Namgyal, and the wisdom of our kings have all played a crucial role in shaping Bhutanese society.

Yet, we must remember that our founders were products of their time. Their actions and decisions, while they may seem out of step with contemporary norms, should be understood in the context of the era they lived in. It does not mean we should uncritically accept or reject all they did but rather honour their contributions and learn from their experiences.

The duty of present and future generations is not merely to idolize these figures but to build upon their legacy. This involves critically examining our history, acknowledging the flaws, and striving to improve upon them. Recognizing those weaknesses is not an act of disrespect but a sign of maturity and growth as a nation.

In this way, honouring our founders is not about blind adherence to tradition but about drawing inspiration from their vision and courage. It's about perpetuating their commitment to serve the people with kindness, justice, and equality, as our King said. As we move forward, we must carry this legacy with us, adapting it to meet the challenges of our time, and ensuring that Bhutan continues to thrive as a compassionate and just society.

What has made these changes over generations so effective, yet peaceful? Perhaps no cause is so important as trust in our monarchs. The trust that people have in their leaders is the cornerstone of any effective governance system, regardless of its ideological foundation or form. Whether it's democracy, autocracy, socialism, or any other political structure, the efficacy and legitimacy of the government are largely determined by the level of trust bestowed in it by the citizenry.

In democracies, for example, trust enables citizens to believe in the fairness of elections, the impartiality of institutions, and the adherence to the rule of law. It encourages civic participation, fosters social cohesion, and promotes stability. When people trust their government, they are more likely to comply with laws and regulations, pay taxes, and cooperate with public initiatives.

Conversely, a lack of trust can lead to scepticism towards government policies, resistance against legal obligations, and even civil unrest. It can undermine the democratic process, as people may question the credibility of election results or the integrity of elected officials.

In non-democratic systems, trust plays an equally crucial role. Even in autocratic regimes, where power isn't derived from popular vote, the absence of trust can lead to internal dissent, resistance, and potentially, the fall of the regime.

Trust in our leaders (our kings, in Bhutan's case) serves as the social glue that holds a society together. Without it, no system of governance, despite its name or structure, can function effectively or sustainably. Trust, therefore, is not just a desirable attribute, but a fundamental prerequisite for any successful and stable political system.

Democracy: A Tool for Service

While democracy is often viewed as an ideal form of governance, it is not without its challenges. One of these is the risk of conflict, protest, and instability being manipulated by the rich, privileged, and powerful to further their own interests. In a healthy democracy, conflicts and protests should ideally serve as mechanisms for citizens to voice their concerns and effect change. However, when these conflicts persist without resolution or are exploited for private gains, they can exacerbate societal divisions and inequalities.

Sadly, the wealthy and powerful often have resources at their disposal that allow them to navigate these periods of instability more effectively than the average citizen. They may use these resources to influence political outcomes, consolidate power, or even exploit the situation for personal or financial gain. This can erode democratic values and increase the gap between the haves and the have-nots.

This also opens up the possibility of corruption, and in many democracies, politicians require substantial funds from donors to win elections. This is particularly true in countries like the United States, and winners may feel obligated to repay their benefactors—potentially leading to policy decisions that favour a select few rather than the broader public.

This practice is particularly detrimental in poorer nations, where it can perpetuate poverty and hinder socio-economic development.

Therefore, it is critical for emerging democracies to establish an honest precedent in political financing to ensure a fair and equitable system.

Furthermore, enduring conflict and instability can distract us from addressing root issues within society. Instead of focusing on systemic problems like poverty, education, or healthcare, the public discourse becomes consumed by the conflict itself. This distraction allows those in power to avoid making necessary changes that could potentially challenge their position.

The essence of democracy is not about the system itself, it is about serving the needs of the people. In Bhutan, our kings have tailored a unique form of democracy that aligns with our country's distinct needs. This approach is designed to safeguard our sovereignty, nurture our rich cultural heritage, and bolster the welfare of our people.

When we view democracy as the ultimate goal, we run the risk of turning it into a tool that primarily serves those in power. Instead, democracy should be seen as a means to an end, not the end itself. It should be used as a mechanism to empower the people, to uplift their lives, and to address their needs and aspirations—not as a vehicle that only benefits the affluent and influential. At the same time, we must avoid the potential pitfalls of pure majority rule, where the interests of the minority can be completely disregarded. Democracy must respect and protect the rights of each individual, regardless of whether they belong to the majority or minority.

Democracy should be a conduit for societal improvement. It should foster an environment where every citizen's voice matters, where their hopes and dreams are considered and where their well-being is prioritized. It should strengthen our nation's sovereignty and contribute to the happiness and prosperity of its citizens. Our kings have so far ensured that it serves the ordinary people, meeting their needs and making their lives better.

It is cynically said that democracy is two wolves and a sheep voting on what to have for dinner. It is a stark reminder of the dangers of uncontrolled majority rule. It also underlines the importance of checks and balances, safeguarding individual rights, and ensuring that we serve the needs of all citizens, not just those in the majority.

Rather than dividing society into 'sheep' and 'wolves', we ought to ensure that the dinner table is a place of mutual respect and shared prosperity.

Bhutan's democracy is one of the youngest in the world, and it seems to have served our country and people well so far—whether it will continue to excel and thrive remains to be seen. Although Bhutan has managed to retain its sovereignty till this day, we are aware how much of a miracle it has been. Not only are we a landlocked nation surrounded by large countries, such as India and China, but densely populated countries like Bangladesh and Nepal are also in close proximity.

History has shown that small nations like Bhutan can easily be swallowed by larger countries, but clever negotiation and diplomacy by our kings has so far prevented this from happening. To date, Bhutan remains one of the few countries in Asia that can claim to have never been colonized.

But, of course, what is the point of a sovereign nation if its people are not happy?

Part Two

Gross National Happiness and Governance

Chapter Five

Building a Happy Nation

If a government cannot create happiness for its people, that government should not exist.

—Zhabdrung Ngawang Namgyal

As I write this book, I am acutely aware that very few people know about Bhutan. Many would have heard of Nepal, of the Himalayas, of Tibet. But Bhutan, as an independent country, barely registers in people's minds. Granted, we are a small nation with few inhabitants. Imagine a country that is smaller than Switzerland and occupying a slightly larger area than the American state of Maryland, but with a far smaller population. While Maryland has over 6 million residents spread across approximately 12,407 square miles, Bhutan has a mere 735,000 spread across the entire land of 14,824 square miles. Much of this land that is barely habitable—the steep cliffs of the Himalayas and the narrow valleys and dense jungles of the south leads to only 8 per cent of our land area being habitable and farmable.

Self-imposed isolation right up to the 1960s is another cause for such a small population. Although there were close dealings with Tibet in the past, there were also serious differences that led to multiple invasions, as we have seen. When China occupied Tibet in the 1950s, Bhutan immediately sought to close its borders to the north. Towards the south, India was under British colonial rule and, while our forefathers had a healthy respect for Britain's might and conquest of the entire Indian subcontinent, they prevented the British from making inroads into Bhutan through nifty, practical diplomacy.

All this history and geology has culminated in the establishment of a kingdom that is not widely known to the outside world, even today. Even our neighbours in the region barely knew or heard about Bhutan. When I was studying in Pittsburgh and Cambridge, Massachusetts, many Americans I met could not figure out where Bhutan was, despite my best attempts to describe my country to them. Some even thought I was from Bataan in the Philippines or confused it with Nepal!

That has changed. In recent years, Bhutan has slowly gained some level of fame. What was previously touted as the 'last Shangri-La'—a mythical land of remote monasteries and wizened monks—is today known to the world as a carbon-negative country with biodiversity hotspots. Bhutan is also a leading example of sustainable tourism with its tight and unique policy on short-term visitors. Our tourism model has helped stem the tide of over-tourism in Bhutan, although it is proving immensely difficult for other countries to implement. Perhaps this is a case of prevention being better than cure, as it is much easier to control visitor numbers while they are still low than it is after tourism has swelled.

Bhutan is also famous for something else, though. GNH is a unique development philosophy that shifts focus away from unrestrained economic growth to a more holistic approach that aims for a sustainable and equitable society. It is an alternate, home-grown measure of national progress, where we move away from GDP to a more holistic measure of people's happiness and well-being. Note that GNH does recognize the importance of material prosperity, but also gives importance to the non-economic aspects, like balanced socio-economic development, environmental conservation, preservation of culture and good governance.

GNH has excited many on the international front. Economists, scholars, and policymakers have shown increasing interest in GNH at a time when it has been recognized that unchecked economic growth causes complex problems that remain challenging to resolve, such as environmental degradation, disappearance of certain cultures, and worsened health among the population. Other problems that have arisen include growing wealth inequality and outright poverty.

GNH has also struck a chord with private citizens, business people, and civil societies as a method to approach work and life. As more come to learn about Bhutan and GNH, it is easy to see why we are known as one of the happiest countries in the world. How true is this, and moreover, how do you quantify happiness anyway?

I do not want to push any political philosophy in the following pages, only offer up the core principles of GNH as an important part of Bhutan's narrative. I love how compelling and simple, yet beautifully constructed and powerful it is. We often hear about GDP or gross national product (GNP) in the mainstream news, but GNH turns the concept of GNP on its head by changing just one word, while beautifully conveying a meaningful message behind development and growth.

Most Bhutanese grow up today with a keen sense of GNH. It is all pervasive, permeating every aspect of our lives; this was especially the case during the developing years of our country. The Bhutanese view GNH as something organic, an essential part of our national DNA. I do not even remember how it was introduced and it has never been formally questioned or debated, but it has endured, nonetheless.

It is generally accepted that our Fourth King was the architect of GNH in the 1970s. After the death of his father the Third King in 1972, King Jigme Singye Wangchuck suddenly found himself in charge of the country. He was just a teenager then, barely sixteen years old, but wise beyond his years. His coronation in 1974 was when he first spoke about *ga kyid*, a Dzongkha term that sums up prosperity, peace, and happiness into one phrase. 'If everyone of us considering ourselves Bhutanese can think and act as one, and if we have the faith in the Triple Gem, our glorious Kingdom of Bhutan will grow from strength to strength and certainly achieve prosperity, peace, and happiness,' he once said.

The term GNH would not be coined for some time after this incident, but the Fourth King continued to make repeated public pronouncements about happiness and contentment, using the Dzongkha phrases *gatogtog* and *kitogtog* for these ideals. It was in 1979, while returning from the Non-Aligned Movement's Havana Summit in 1979, that the 'Great Fourth' formally articulated the development philosophy of GNH. While His Majesty was speaking to journalists at the Chhatrapati Shivaji Maharaj International Airport in Mumbai on his return from Cuba, an Indian journalist asked him: 'Your Majesty, how big is your country's GDP?'

'For Bhutan, gross national happiness is more important than gross national product,' the Fourth King replied. This proclamation has since been one of the most quoted statements to encapsulate the meaning of GNH, a philosophy that has come to define the nation.

When Bhutanese travel outside to give talks about our country and GNH, and when I make presentations about GNH to a largely foreign audience, this particular quote always attracts the most attention and applause from the audience. People sit up and listen to what and how GNH has helped our country, since we do not follow the conventional GDP measure of progress. They are struck by how profound and relevant his quote is in today's context, even though it was first uttered over forty years ago.

It is almost as though they do not need to hear anything more. Just that single line is enough to inspire them to think about their lives, their economies, and their roles in society a little differently. It has worked better than something a company spending millions of dollars on branding consultants would have come up with. For better or worse, GNH is part of Bhutan's national brand, and many mistakenly still think of us as the world's happiest country and people!

More importantly, it is an idea many nations want for themselves. While happiness as a brand has worked for the kingdom, being so closely associated with it does bring about a unique set of problems which must be faced.

A Government Responsibility

While GNH may seem like a unique approach to a country's development, Bhutan is not the only place in the world that adopts such a method. The late monarch of Thailand, King Bhumibol Adulyadej, implemented a similar development approach known as sufficiency economy philosophy (SEP) in the 1970s. This philosophy was designed to help the kingdom advance economically while exercising moderation, reasonableness, and prudence.

In-line with King Bhumibol's reputation as a wise, respected philosopher king, SEP serves as a tool to enhance GDP through a middle path of economic growth modelled on Buddhism. It does so by emphasizing appropriateness, competitive advantage, and low risk while avoiding over-investment. While both Thailand's SEP and Bhutan's concept of GNH aim to foster sustainable development and enhance well-being, they differ in their specific philosophical underpinnings, frameworks, and methods of implementation. SEP is built on moderation, reasonableness, and resilience, as understood in a Thai context, emphasizing prudence and self-reliance. In contrast, GNH offers a broader framework for holistic development, integrating multiple dimensions of well-being and happiness, unique to Bhutanese culture, into government policy.

As far as I know, only Bhutan *explicitly* assigns the responsibility of making people happy to the government, through Article 9 of its Constitution. As point 2 summarizes it: 'The State shall strive to promote those conditions that will enable the pursuit of Gross National Happiness.'[11]

Elsewhere, it is the responsibility of an individual to seek their own happiness—a right that the government serves to protect,

---

[11] 'The Constitution of the Kingdom of Bhutan,' at https://www.nab.gov.bt/assets/templates/images/constitution-of-bhutan-2008.pdf

whatever one does to attain it. For instance, the US Declaration of Independence affirms that 'All men are created equal, that they are endowed by their Creator with certain unalienable Rights, that among these are Life, Liberty and the pursuit of Happiness.' Notice here that the pursuit of happiness is seen as an individual right, not a government responsibility.

This is also the case in Japan, where Article 13 of the constitution respects the pursuit of happiness:

> All of the people shall be respected as individuals. Their right
> to life, liberty, and the pursuit of happiness shall, to the extent
> that it does not interfere with the public welfare, be the supreme
> consideration in legislation and in other governmental affairs.[12]

Again, 'the pursuit of happiness' is mentioned—part of American values being imprinted on the Japanese Constitution's revision in the wake of the World War II.

Similarly, Singapore's national pledge has citizens promise to:

> [. . .] Pledge ourselves as one united people,
> regardless of race, language or religion,
> to build a democratic society
> based on justice and equality
> so as to achieve happiness, prosperity
> and progress for our nation.

In this instance, it is the responsibility of individuals to create happiness (as well as prosperity and progress) for the nation. This is to be done collectively as a people for the greater good of society and the country; it is not a direct responsibility of the government. At

---

[12] 'The Constitution of Japan,' at https://japan.kantei.go.jp/constitution_and_government_of_japan/constitution_e.html.

its core, the aim of Singapore's pledge is to 'gel people together' and inculcate patriotism at a time of communal tension and racial riots.[13] Yet, at the same time, it is a demonstration of Asian values, such as collectivism and balancing societal needs. GNH does have some similarities to this approach, in that it places the good of a society and country above individual interests.

Many other countries have also included happiness in their constitutions as a pursuit or individual right, including Antigua and Barbuda, Belize, Egypt, France, Ghana, Haiti, Mongolia, Pakistan, South Korea, Turkey, and more.

Doubtlessly, happiness is one of the many important and most desired attributes we want in life. But the link between the government and happiness in Bhutan dates as far back as its founding four centuries ago, when Zhabdrung Ngawang Namgyal pointed out: 'If the government cannot create happiness for its people, then there is no purpose for the government to exist.'

His vision placed the responsibility of making people happy squarely on the government, an approach that continues to form the unique basis of GNH to this day. This philosophy implies that governments should not merely focus on economic growth or material wealth, but rather on the holistic well-being of its citizens. It suggests that the success of a nation should be measured not just in terms of GDP but also in terms of mental wellness, environmental conservation, cultural resilience, and social progress and harmony.

Happiness: The Foremost Purpose

At its heart, GNH means that the happiness and well-being of the people is the foremost purpose of the Government of Bhutan. It requires the government to understand that economic growth alone

---

[13] 'National Pledge: The Origin,' *National Heritage Board of Singapore*, at https://www. nhb.gov.sg/what-we-do/our-work/community-engagement/education/resources/ national-symbols/national-pledge.

is not enough for a country and its people. Single-minded pursuit of economic growth and GDP can actually be detrimental because conventional economic growth is based on consumption. The more people consume, the more an economy grows—whether these are essential or non-essential products. Economic growth requires increasing consumption.

But if there is no limit to economic growth (and if stagnant economies are considered a failure) then there should be no limit to consumption, since the two are correlated. This continued growth at the expense of the environment, society, and even the lives and health of individuals can and does lead to discontentment and unhappiness, especially when people are led towards mindless consumption beyond their means.

One need not look far to see the results. Whether it is the latest car, a trendy smartphone, fashionable clothes, a meal at a swanky restaurant, or an exotic holiday, many people tend to go beyond their means to be able to attain these, with some even going into debt. Too much rich or sugary food, exposure to social media, alcohol and intoxicants, and overworking are all factors that contribute to stress both physically and mentally.

Advertisements, the media, and the Internet have become factors in driving such consumption to the point where people's desire for goods, services, and self-pleasure is simply not satiated. We yearn for something and once we get our hands on it, we are again psychologically driven to yearn for something else almost instantaneously. How many times have you resorted to online shopping to get the latest or trendiest product, only to find yourself either mired in debt or heading back online the next month to buy yet more items? This fuels the economy well enough, but can the same be said for *you*, personally?

In 1968, Robert F Kennedy famously said:

Gross national product measures neither our wit nor our courage, neither our wisdom nor our learning, neither our compassion nor our devotion to our country, it measures everything in short, except that which makes life worthwhile.[14]

Wise as his remarks were, they did nothing to change the system. GDP has predominantly been used all over the world to measure 'everything, except what makes life worthwhile'. I wonder if anyone will ever successfully follow through.

In conventional economies, the purpose seems to be increasing productivity to reach an overall goal of economic growth. You need to work harder, smarter, and quicker to increase economic productivity. The purpose for education and vocational training seems to point to only one thing—enhancing your productivity. Even the establishment of healthcare is carried out with the aim of people falling sick less and contributing more. Vacation time is also tailored to boost productivity, since people feel energized after a holiday and can return to the workplace rejuvenated and ready to give it their all. People are expected to work and save enough for retirement, but during their productive years, they contribute greatly to growing the country's economy.

None of these things are inherently bad, and they have been great blessings to human flourishing. But GNH places them in a different, more important context by turning conventional economic development on its head. Instead of looking at increased productivity to drive economic expansion, productivity is seen only as a tool (not a goal) in achieving the goal of people's happiness and well-being.

Since 1968, the world's GDP has exploded thirty-five-fold from $2.45 trillion to $85.91 trillion, yet we are nowhere near the level of happiness and satisfaction we thought we'd be at.[15] The anticipated

[14] 'Robert F Kennedy's remarks at the University of Kansas on 18 March 1968,' *The John F Kennedy Library*, at https://www.jfklibrary.org/learn/about-jfk/the-kennedy-family/robert-f-kennedy/robert-f-kennedy-speeches/remarks-at-the-university-of-kansas-march-18-1968

[15] 'GDP (current US$),' *The World Bank*, at https://data.worldbank.org/indicator/NY.GDP.MKTP.CD.

utopia of contentment and satisfaction remains elusive, our fingers still grasping at the edges of joy. The march of science and technology has propelled us towards higher living standards, battling diseases, and stretching the human lifespan, carving out lives of comfort and ease. Wages have surged, lifting many from the clutches of poverty, yet a spectre seems to continue haunting our societies.

On the one hand, at least 700 million people are condemned to a life of poverty[16], in which hunger, malnourishment, and deprivation are everyday realities, killing thousands every year. Estimates made by research fellows at the UN suggest, 'To end extreme poverty and absolute monetary poverty worldwide by 2030, it would cost about $70 and $325 billion per year. This may sound like a lot but is only 0.1 per cent and 0.6 per cent of the gross national income (GNI) of the OECD's high-income countries (HICs).'[17] If we wished to eliminate poverty, we could. But do we?

On the other hand, those who escape poverty are faced with the need to feed an insatiable consumer lifestyle. When personal needs remain unmet, the sweet taste of happiness turns bitter.

Our adherence to the GDP model fuels an unquenchable thirst for consumption. The moment the gears of consumption grind to a halt, the economic engine sputters, and lives teeter on the brink of disarray. For many governments, a slowdown in consumption is akin to staring into the abyss.

Following the GDP model creates an insatiable appetite for consumption because the moment you stop consuming, the economy starts floundering and everyone's lives are affected. Therefore, any slowdown in consumption seems to be the biggest

---

[16] 'Poverty ,' *The World Bank*, at https://www.worldbank.org/en/topic/poverty/overview.

[17] 'New estimates of the cost of ending poverty: What does it mean and how much would it cost?,' *UNU-WIDER*, at https://www.wider.unu.edu/publication/new-estimates-cost-ending-poverty#:~:text=To%20end%20extreme%20poverty%20and,%2Dincome%20countries%20(HICs).

fear of most governments these days. Critics have decried this model of capitalism, questioning whether it needs to be reformed.

The deepening climate crisis, slow income growth, the growing gap between the rich and poor and rising job uncertainty challenge the consumption-based capitalist model that so many countries are now bound to. Once people cease to consume, demand drops, jobs are lost, and lives are disrupted. This was evident in the events that transpired during the Covid-19 pandemic in 2020. The global economy crashed as consumption came to a grinding halt.

While millions were in lockdown, so were major economies around the world. Those who survived the pandemic either lost their jobs or barely made it through, with many industries either laying off workers or docking wages. Odd-job labourers who were paid by the hour were unable to earn a living at all. In the US, at least 6 million citizens applied for welfare in a single week.[18] The fragility of the global supply chain was thrust open for all to witness as the supply of goods was severely interrupted, especially essential healthcare equipment that was necessary to prevent many deaths.

The Covid-19 pandemic led to immediate economic recession, where the suffering of so many was something unprecedented and unimaginable. However, in the face of struggle, markets seem to have soared, specifically in the United States. The stock market has continued to climb, despite the Covid-19 outbreak in many parts of the country.

During the same period, in the United States, protests erupted in the wake of George Floyd's death, and a serious dispute arose over the outcome of the presidential election of 2020. Small businesses shuttered across the country but stock prices continued to climb, demonstrating a disconnect between the corporates and the man

---

[18] 'More than 6 million Americans apply for welfare in a single week as coronavirus accelerates unemployment,' *Australian Broadcasting Corporation*, 2 April 2020, at https://www.abc.net.au/news/2020-04-03/covid-19-sees-record-us-unemployment-claims-to-6.6-million/12116594.

on the street. While markets continued their bull run, millions were either dying or had lost their jobs.[19]

Inequality has never been this stark. The rich got richer in the face of a pandemic while others struggled to access healthcare and get food on the table. Is this acceptable? It shouldn't when there are people still suffering, but the fact that we are celebrating our emergence from the pandemic in economic terms hides the heavy price we have paid.

Much like the warnings about climate change, experts had forewarned of an imminent global pandemic for years. But ruling elites chose to ignore the forecasts and focused, instead, on money and power for themselves.

I have even become sceptical of the stock markets. There is absolutely no doubt that they play a vital role in liberal economies, but markets are vulnerable to panic, causing a cascading effect in many areas of commerce and affecting livelihoods. They are also driven by the motive to make immediate (and vast amounts of) profit. In my view, this places a premium not on adding true value to production but on generating that profit through speculation.

The conventional model has, indeed, helped accumulate decades of tremendous wealth. But can it be considered successful if it is prone to fail so easily in the face of an invisible enemy or a financial bubble? With such immense financial growth, how is it that there is no social equality and the wealth gap continues to increase, with a few becoming phenomenally rich while many others struggle to put food on the table?

The implication is disturbing—it would seem we are only to be valued by how we spend and consume. Are we just pawns to make the rich richer? Can something else be done?

Despite living in Bhutan and being fully aware of the downsides of consumerism, I do not claim to be immune to it. Here, we are

---

[19] Emily Stewart, 'Why stocks soared while America struggled,' *Vox*, 10 May 2021, at https://www.vox.com/business-and-finance/22421417/stock-market-pandemic-economy.

generally spared the pull of consumerism—as a small population with a small market, there are no large, glitzy shopping malls and no shiny billboards advertising a celebrity's favourite shampoo, jewellery or streetwear. We do not have TV commercials on our local channels, although we do have access to cable TV from India, where commercials are plenty. The only form of advertising that we may encounter are on the Internet or in magazines, the latter of which we do not have much access to. Hence, we are not hounded by a constant temptation to obtain the latest and fanciest items.

However, Bhutanese do turn to online shopping from overseas merchants, or even ask their friends living abroad to purchase items that are not sold in Bhutan, such as Uniqlo jackets and clothes or Salomon trekking shoes. Online shopping, or shopping via overseas friends, has given us choices from a vast array of goods that we never had access to in the past.

As a grad student in America, I got my first taste of mobile freedom with a Motorola clamshell. But in 2007, the iPhone emerged, sleek and irresistible. I yearned for it, not out of need, but pure desire. However, financial constraints meant waiting until the iPhone 5 to join the club.

Once in, I was hooked. Each new model was a siren's call, promising better photos, quicker emails, and a fresh aesthetic. From the iPhone 5 to the iPhone 14 now, I have upgraded religiously, drawn in by Apple's crafty marketing and rumoured battery draining tactics. If I kept an older iPhone model, I feared being seen as tech-illiterate, and I craved relevance in this digital age. And it hasn't been just the iPhone—the sleek AirPod Pro earbuds soon caught my eye, promising a cool image at the gym or during virtual meetings. What Apple has achieved is the pinnacle of consumerism. It has turned consumerism into a cult, its products a badge of belonging. Each upgrade feels like a necessity to stay relevant, trapping me in their iOS ecosystem. I confess, I'm yet another slave of consumerism!

Even living in the Himalayas does not shield me from the grips of consumption. At an individual level, if your consumption is hard to fulfil, how can you ever be satisfied with life? To achieve more to be 'happy', you end up working more, or worse, taking a loan. Is this really a good recipe for happiness?

The need for consumption must never be met. This relationship between economic growth and consumerism means that once this need is met, the machine grinds to halt and economies splutter. Decreased economic growth is generally considered a failure. Nothing except the bottom line matters.

Even environmental degradation and exploitation are allowed in service of the consumption machine. I have my daughter Galek to thank for making me aware of the plastic microbeads in cosmetics, skincare, and shampoos that are harming the environment. These small, solid, manufactured plastic particles are less than a millimetre in size, do not dissolve in water, and are not captured by most wastewater treatment systems. Instead, the microbeads get washed into the oceans, rivers, or lakes, where marine animals absorb or eat these microplastics.

But what are these microbeads doing in our consumer products in the first place? In skincare, they act as an exfoliant, making our skin 'glow', making us feel that the product is indeed working as it should. Some countries have since banned the use of microbeads in products, but many have yet to do so.

This awareness that my daughter raised in me has renewed my faith in the next generation. Even though Bhutan is a landlocked country with no immediate sea or ocean, Galek is sensibly concerned about the effects of microbeads in the skincare she uses. She has even set certain rules in the house, such as separating waste from recyclables and minimizing the use of plastics, for instance.

Overlooking environmental impacts and vulnerable communities in the quest for GDP growth reveals deep flaws in this model. This narrow focus results in rising inequality, escalating poverty, and increased vulnerability to crises like pandemics or financial downturns. Many economists agree that GDP is imperfect for gauging growth, let alone well-being.[20]

GNH offers a more comprehensive approach. It acknowledges the importance of a strong economy for a comfortable life but insists on balancing modern conveniences with sustainable, inclusive growth. GNH champions social progress and insists that growth benefit people directly. Moreover, it mandates that a nation's development must also respect and preserve the environment.

Social cohesion and a community is vital too for a country to progress. Keeping traditions and culture alive is every bit as important as economic growth because doing so links our present with our past. Bhutan being the last Vajrayana Buddhist kingdom in the world means that our role as stewards of this tradition is even more crucial now than ever. For a thousand years, Tibet, Ladakh, and Sikkim had all once been Vajrayana Buddhist kingdoms that thrived in the Himalayan belt. But geopolitical events in the last century led to the fall of all these kingdoms, except for Bhutan. Today, it is the last custodian of the Vajrayana Buddhist tradition, and the faith is even seeing a renaissance of sorts.

But it is not just about preserving this proud heritage. Bhutan, although largely a Buddhist kingdom, also includes other ethnicities and religions. It is important to celebrate diversity and good values that we should keep for posterity and pass on to the next generation. Culture and traditions keep communities together and give them an identity. They link us to our past and present and allow us to have something to look forward to in the future. Most importantly, a vibrant culture lets us understand and learn more about ourselves.

What is needed to establish all these factors—sustainable and equitable socio-economic development, environmental conservation, and preservation of culture—is ultimately good, trustworthy, and capable governance. It is the foundation that holds

---

[20] Amit Kapoor and Bibek Debroy, 'GDP Is Not a Measure of Human Well-Being,' *Harvard Business Review*, 4 October 2019, at https://hbr.org/2019/10/gdp-is-not-a-measure-of-human-well-being.

everything together and enables these aspirations to be achieved. Without good practices, like participatory governance, stringent anti-corruption measures, comprehensive planning, and effective delivery of services, achieving any of the concepts of GNH would be a dream at best.

What Makes Us Happy?

When I give talks about Bhutan's GNH philosophy, its origins and how it is been used as an alternative development indicator in the kingdom, I am frequently asked two questions. The first is: 'What makes people happy?' The second is: 'What is the government's job in ensuring that people are happy?' In other words, we need to draw concrete principles that define happiness and the role that political leaders play in bringing it about.

Let's get into the details. It is obvious that happiness is subjective, so what makes me happy may not work for you. For example, some people would be happy to have a Kit Kat as a treat. The cocoa in chocolate helps the brain release 'feel good' chemicals or endorphins. But, for me, I prefer the hot chillies in our national dish *ema datsi* (chilli cheese). Fair warning: It is a staple here, and we devour chillies as though they are vegetables! Some people may enjoy the adrenaline rush that they get from doing something adventurous like bungee jumping. Personally, I prefer a stroll in a forest or a week's trek up the mountains. Some people are happy with a few glasses of wine, others are happy to be able to take a holiday to a destination that they have been saving up to go to, and still others are happy as long as they have a roof over their head and a stable income. The point here is that happiness is different for everyone, for me, for you, for your neighbour and for your friend.

For us, in Bhutan, happiness is different. Even the term 'happiness' holds a different meaning in our local language. The Dzongkha word for it is *gakyid*, which holds a more profound and deeper meaning than merely the emotion of happiness. *Ga* refers to *ga tok tok*, a state of satisfaction and contentment, while *kyid* or *kyid tok tok*, which means a state of peace and equanimity. Happiness, therefore, is more than just that fleeting, euphoric feeling of pleasure. It is much more than that dopamine hit each time we do something that feels good. It is definitely much more than that chilli fix, bungee jumping, or a relaxing stroll in the woods!

When we talk about happiness in Bhutan, we are referring to more sustained happiness and contentment. Yes, immediate gratification (like you might get from a glass of wine or a holiday) is also important in our daily lives. We fully acknowledge the purpose it fulfils in the present moment. But contentment relates to what we already have in our lives, and what we make of it. It is perhaps best seen as 'sustained happiness' or 'life satisfaction'.

In 2011, I had the privilege of speaking at a TEDx talk in Thimphu, in which I first shared my personal philosophy on happiness. It is a belief that has guided me throughout my life and one that I am keen to delve deeper into now. I have always held steadfastly to the conviction that the cornerstones of happiness and contentment in life are security, identity, and purpose. Each of these elements plays a crucial role in our overall well-being, shaping our experiences, thoughts and emotions.

Security, both physical and emotional, is paramount. In its absence, we often find ourselves in a state of constant unease, unable to fully enjoy life's moments or reach our potential. It is not just about financial stability or safety from harm, though these are undoubtedly important. It is also about feeling secure in our relationships, knowing that we're loved, respected, and understood.

Money is, of course, essential in today's world. Job security gives one a sense of continuity and self-esteem, and financial security provides for basic necessities such as a place to live in, clothes on your back and food on the table. Saving up enough for retirement also gives us the security that comes from having enough to survive.

At a psychological level, relationships with your family, relatives, or friends are also important. Having people to love and support you in times of trouble is vital for a sense of security. Maintaining good health is another crucial part of being happy and feeling secure about oneself. Without good health, money and relationships would lose their meaning.

Besides investing time in maintaining one's body, investing time in one's mental health is also essential. Taking time out to destress, relax, or even meditate does wonders for one's mental well-being. I strongly believe that all these factors are fundamental for a sense of security.

Then, there's identity—the understanding and acceptance of who we are. Our identity is our compass, guiding us through life's labyrinth, helping us make decisions that align with our values and beliefs. Without a clear sense of identity, we risk losing ourselves in the crowd, becoming chameleons changing colours to blend in rather than standing out as individuals.

How can one be satisfied in life if one does not know who one is? This is tied closely with a sense of belonging, either to a country, a community, or even a club. Some identify with the work they do, be it being a doctor, a lawyer, or even a photographer. Some find their sense of identity through spirituality, while others gain a sense of identity through something as simple as being part of a charity, a football fan club or even a poetry society.

Without identifying with something, life can be rather inconsequential and immaterial, even. If someone identifies as a part of a charity then they have someone and something to strive for, such as preventing domestic violence or raising funds for the marginalized. Identifying and belonging to something, therefore, gives us much-needed feelings of self-worth, and purpose and meaning to life itself. Otherwise, we would be living our daily lives aimlessly.

Last but certainly not least is having a sense of purpose. It gives our lives direction and meaning, turning routine tasks into integral steps towards a larger goal. Without it, life can feel aimless, like a ship adrift at sea. A sense of purpose energizes us, fuels our passion, and keeps us motivated even during challenging times.

Thus comes the importance of purpose, which is intrinsically linked to identity and security. Something in you must drive you to wake up every day. There must be fire in your belly. Someone who identifies as being a doctor or teacher wakes up every day with a purpose of saving lives or educating the next generation. At the same time, she is part of a fraternity of doctors or teachers, developing friendships and relationships that are beneficial to her as a person, emotionally and professionally.

This sense of purpose does not always have to be professional. Even a football fan club member benefits greatly from being part of a larger community. Not only does a fan develop a strong sense of identity and purpose but he also forms a sense of camaraderie with others with similar identity and purpose. This helps boost his emotional health greatly.

So, if these factors can boost happiness, it is obvious to me that we should be investing our time and efforts in these areas. But with one caveat—it must be sustainable. Neighbourhood gangs, for instance, provide their members a sense of security, identity, and purpose. Moral judgements aside, many members are indeed happy, in a sense. They belong to an exclusive club that exchanges code words or hand signs, and they learn how to fight and defend themselves and their territory. But there is one problem: Their happiness is not sustainable. Should the law catch up with them, that whole system of security, identity, and purpose can collapse. Happiness is lost, among many other problems that come with that.

Religion, I find, is another area where people find security and identity. You have a group of like-minded people whom you can share your beliefs with, and you also have the security of a higher power on your side, no matter what religion you believe in. Although religion is sustainable in that it is able to make people happy, various faiths save their best rewards for the afterlife. They do give meaning and dignity to life in the present and provide a strong sense of the pillars of happiness. At their root, religions bring happiness and purpose, which is why they have endured as long as people have been around.

As for my own happiness, I have projected how I would like to live after I retire at sixty-five—a milestone that is approaching faster than I anticipated! I have defined some targets for security, identity, and purpose that I hope to achieve and am actively working on them.

In terms of security, I prioritize physical fitness by maintaining a healthy diet, regularly working out, and scheduling periodic medical check-ups. Equally important is mental fitness, which I achieve through meditation, yoga, and continuous reading to expand my knowledge and maintain mental clarity. Financial fitness is another cornerstone of my strategy, encompassing prudent savings and smart investments to secure a stable future. Finally, emotional fitness remains crucial, involving activities and practices that nurture my emotional well-being and resilience.

My identity is strongly tied to my roles as both a public servant and a volunteer. As a committed member of my political party, I dedicate myself to serving the people and advancing our collective goals for progress. Beyond my official duties, I take pride in volunteering with organizations such as De-Suung and the Red Cross. These roles allow me to contribute to community well-being and respond to the needs of my fellow citizens, further grounding my sense of purpose and identity in service.

Ultimately, my overarching purpose centres on public service with the ambition of transforming Bhutan into a developed country. Every initiative I undertake and every policy I support is driven by this vision, and whatever happens during my political career with the People's Democratic Party and as a public servant, I hope to do more to make Bhutan a developed, prosperous country.

I have some savings and hope to build on that a bit more. My kids are grown up, and I have a happy family life. I have some close friends and make international ones, too, when I travel. To me, the journey is as important as the destination, and the beauty of all this is that I am already feeling happy while working towards my goals.

These three pillars—security, identity, and purpose—are, in my view, the foundations of a contented life. Their absence can lead to a perpetual state of anxiety and discontent. But when they are present and balanced, they create an environment within us that fosters genuine happiness and satisfaction. I believe this triad holds the key to living a fulfilling, happy life.

Ordinary Happiness: The Government's Role

If what makes people happy is so subjective then what is the government's role in making people happy? In my view, the government's job is to enable circumstances that make people happy—such as a sense of security, identity, and purpose—by providing for the underlying conditions that make them feel so.

In Bhutan, this takes the form of free education, free healthcare, and social security and welfare for the destitute—without interfering with each individual's rights. This is actually an extension of the ideas of security, identity, and purpose that we have discussed before, only facilitated by the authorities so that each person has the opportunity to build a happy life for themselves and their loved ones, on their own terms.

This is what the Zhabdrung meant in the quote that opens this chapter. Whatever the form its leadership or methodology takes, each government should provide these conditions at the societal level. This way, at least the very basic well-being of citizens is taken care of, thus freeing up such bread-and-butter concerns to allow them to pursue their individual happiness. The ability to peacefully go to a pub, engage in free discussion on various topics and return home safely signifies a society where citizens enjoy personal security, freedom of thought and speech, and the right to peaceful assembly. These are not just abstract concepts, but tangible experiences that directly impact people's quality of life.

If a government cannot guarantee these basic freedoms, its legitimacy and purpose come into question. After all, one of the primary responsibilities of a government is to ensure the safety and well-being of its citizens and to uphold their rights and freedoms. The true measure of effective governance lies not just in economic indicators or policy outcomes but in the everyday experiences of its citizens. It emphasizes that governance should ultimately serve the people, safeguarding their rights, ensuring their safety, and facilitating their freedom to think, speak, and engage with others. The government must reliably ensure that society in general is safe, that money in the bank is safe, and that your job is secure.

If good health is important then government public policy must ensure that people have access, whether paid or free, to the best possible quality of healthcare. Even social security is something a government should look at if it wants its people to be happy. When we are old or in need, the government must provide a social net for us to fall back on.

For the government in Bhutan to provide the conditions for necessary for people's well-being, GNH had to be formulated into government policies. A 'recipe' or 'formula' for happiness had to be concocted. This formula is popularly known as the Four Pillars of GNH. Its ingredients include socio-economic development, environmental conservation, preservation of culture, and good governance.[21]

We have briefly looked at all these factors earlier, and indeed, they have resulted in beneficial outcomes for Bhutan. They were formulated and put into practice by human beings and are certainly not perfect. If we are to secure happiness for everyone, we must also acknowledge that each pillar also comes with problems and unforeseen consequences that must be managed.

Sustainable Development and Conservation

One of the Four Pillars of GNH is controlled socio-economic development, which must be sustainable and equitable. Being

---

[21] GNH was first articulated in 1999 with five central tenets (balanced and equitable socio-economic development, environmentally sustainable development, human development, culture and heritage, and governance). They were reformulated in 1998 as 'four major goals of GNH' (economic self-reliance, environmental preservation, cultural promotion, and good governance). The current Four Pillars of GNH were defined in 2005.

blissfully isolated from the world has meant that, for most of its history, Bhutan's GDP barely existed.

As recently as six decades ago, life in Bhutan was medieval at best. Everyone lived on subsistence farming. There were no cars or roads, and trade was limited to those who came and went on horseback, trading with our neighbours in India and Tibet. While glistening skyscrapers dotted the skyline of many cities, especially in America, Bhutan was a medieval kingdom stuck in time—until 1961, when we opened our doors to modernization.

Our first five-year economic development plan was introduced then. Living standards were low and Bhutan's per capita GDP was estimated at US$51, the lowest in the world then.[22] By contrast, America's per capita GDP then was already a remarkable US$355. Today, Bhutan's economy is still considered small, despite being one of the fastest-growing in South Asia.[23]

In 2019, GDP stood at US$2.84 billion, ranking amidst other small nations such as Lesotho, Timor Leste and the Central African Republic.[24] This is still a very small amount, and many billionaires in America have a higher net worth than the entire GDP of Bhutan. There are a whopping 400 billionaires in America alone and a staggering 2,755 billionaires in the world—an unprecedented number that grew immensely during the pandemic in 2020.[25] Even India's richest man, Mukesh Ambani, owns a $2 billion home worth Bhutan's entire GDP.

---

[22] In today's value, $51 would be around $104.

[23] According to the Asian Development Bank, economic growth averaged at 7.5 percent a year over the past three decades. See: https://www.adb.org/countries/bhutan/overview.

[24] Ranking is based on nominal GDP See: https://www.worldometers.info/gdp/bhutan-gdp.

[25] Rob LaFranco and Chase Peterson-Withorn (Eds.), 'The Forbes 400,' *Forbes*, at https://www.forbes.com/forbes-400; Kerry A Dolan, 'Forbes' 35th Annual World's Billionaires List: Facts And Figures 2021,' *Forbes*, 6 April 2021, at https://www.forbes.com/sites/kerryadolan/2021/04/06/forbes-35th-annual-worlds-billionaires-list-facts-and-figures-2021.

Despite how small our economy is, its growth has been phenomenal. In just one generation, we have gone from relying only on subsistence farming and minimal trade to a country that is set to graduate from being a least developed country by 2023.[26] In thirty years, life expectancy in Bhutan has increased from forty-five to seventy years, and literacy has also increased from 50 per cent to 72 per cent, with youth literacy reaching 93 per cent. In the past fifteen years, poverty has decreased from 31 per cent to 8 per cent. This has been thanks to Bhutan's economic advances, which have greatly improved life for everyone.

But it is not just economic advancement. One of the greatest outcomes of Bhutan's approach to socio-economic development has been these advances remaining environmentally sustainable. We have been able to make progress without causing deforestation, strip mining our mountains, or selling out to large-scale tourism. This must have been a difficult and costly decision for our Fourth King when he ascended the throne in 1972. He could have easily resorted to cutting down the trees in the kingdom to export ample amounts of timber to neighbouring India or mining the vast quantities of untapped natural resources from the mountains. But King Jigme Singye Wangchuck was adamant about preserving his land for the people.

Today, we are reaping the benefits of this wise decision he made decades ago. We now enjoy clean and fresh air in a region with intact biodiversity, known in the rest of the world as the only carbon-negative country. Furthermore, this preservation of biodiversity and nature has allowed us to tap into one of our largest resources—hydropower.

Hydropower has become the biggest economic engine for Bhutan today. Economically, it is the biggest earner for the country. While hydropower does damage the environment, the run-of-the-river hydroelectric system that we enjoy in Bhutan because of our

---

[26] According to the United Nations, the least developed country (LDC) category is assessed using three criteria: human assets, economic vulnerability, and gross national income per capita. (See: https://www.un.org/development/desa/dpad/2018/its-official-and-historical-three-more-countries-will-graduate-from-the-ldc-category.)

fast-flowing rivers causes minimal environmental impact.[27] In turn, this bodes well for us because of the renewable energy it is generating.

Moreover, development of hydropower plants in Bhutan has been slow and deliberate. All hydropower production is owned by the government, with loans and technical assistance provided by the Government of India. This means that India buys all excess power to help feed its appetite for more energy while offsetting its own carbon emissions. To maintain this balance, private enterprises have not yet been allowed to invest or come into this sector. Water is a resource that belongs to the country and its people—it must be tapped in a way that benefits the entire country, not just one corporation or a few individuals.

Preventing hydropower from being privatized safeguards our natural resources from being exploited. However, future governments will certainly come under a lot of pressure to privatize hydropower. As long as government-owned companies, such as the Druk Holdings Investment group, do a good job and manage this precious resource well, there is no reason to involve private firms in the foreseeable future. Bhutan remains the only South Asian country with surplus energy available for export and continues to have large reserves of untapped hydropower resources.[28]

* * *

Policy Brief: A Place for State Ownership

Globally, state-owned enterprises (SOEs) have become prominent players in essential sectors such as energy, technology, and finance,

---

[27] Bhutan's hydropower sector is predicted to more than double over the 2020s, with more than 5,200 MW produced from six plants. After domestic needs are met, most of the power is exported to India. Revenue reached Nu 12 billion (US$146.5 million) in 2021 and continues to fluctuate around this figure. See: Thukten Zangpo, 'Hydropower revenue to drop by 4 percent,' Kuensel, 26 December 2022, at https://kuenselonline.com/hydropower-revenue-to-drop-by-4-percent.

[28] 'Bhutan's Hydropower Sector: 12 Things to Know,' Asian Development Bank, 31 January 2014, at https://www.adb.org/features/bhutan-s-hydropower-sector-12-things-know.

which are foundational for creating next-generation industries. For developing economies like Bhutan, nurturing and growing SOEs is vital to manage national resources strategically and to establish an economic foundation conducive to innovation and private sector growth.

SOEs help enable countries to achieve long-term national aspirations and global sustainability goals, and are well-suited for investments in disruptive innovation, which is essential for creating new jobs and building a new economy. Additionally, SOEs support strategic businesses, foster good corporate governance, and are key vehicles for deep research and development (R&D).

In Bhutan, SOEs are cornerstones of the economy. They provide essential infrastructure, ensure efficient public services, and drive economic diversification beyond agriculture and hydropower. However, these enterprises face the challenge of integrating commercial goals with social objectives while keeping the country's long-term strategic vision in mind.

Druk Holding and Investments (DHI), established in 2007 by His Majesty the King, manages the Royal Government of Bhutan's investments for the long-term benefit of the people. DHI holds shares in twenty-four companies across various sectors, including manufacturing, energy, natural resources, and technology. With assets totalling around $3.33 billion and contributing 25 per cent of the country's GDP, DHI plays a significant role in the economy. Its contributions in taxes, royalties, and dividends account for about 40 per cent of the government's yearly revenue.

Thus, SOEs play a pivotal role in economic growth. Although there was a period when privatization was favoured, state-owned enterprises have seen a strong resurgence in countries like China, United Arab Emirates, Russia, Indonesia, and Malaysia. In Bhutan, I believe that SOEs under the DHI are integral to our economic structure. They allow us to foster a free market-driven economy, while maintaining certain strategic controls.

However, it is crucial that SOEs do not gain an unfair advantage over their competitors in the private sector. It's about creating a balanced ecosystem where both can thrive, and SOEs are likely to play a significant role in shaping Bhutan's economic landscape for many years to come.

* * *

I am not for one moment saying privatization should not happen! The privatization of certain sectors of the economy has benefited Bhutan. In the 1970s, most of the businesses were owned by the government, such as the bus services, hotels, and tour operators. In the 1980s and 1990s, the government gradually delegated its ownership to private owners, and today, private companies own thousands of tour companies, hotels, and bus operators. Even in the telecom and banking sector, government ownership has been divested, enabling these industries to boom in Bhutan and provide valuable services for its people.

While all this sounds good and prospects are bright economically, one big issue remains unfixed—unemployment. Bhutan's unemployment rate was 2.19 per cent in 2019 while youth unemployment has remained high at over 9 per cent since 2013.[29] In 2023, overall unemployment reached 5.1 per cent, with youth unemployment being as high as 29 per cent due to Covid-19! Fortunately, unemployment rates have fallen since then, and as I write this in early 2024, overall unemployment is now 3.5 per cent, with youth unemployment at 16 per cent.

Bhutan, with its small population, naturally has a smaller workforce. To invigorate our economy, we need to bolster our labour force, yet we're grappling with unemployment. This highlights the fragility of our economic structure, a predicament further exacerbated by the Covid-19 pandemic.

Our most persistent challenge lies in diversifying our economy to create more appealing job opportunities for our youth. Presently, the civil service is Bhutan's largest employer, primarily due to limited

---

[29] 'Youth' refers to people aged 15 to 24. See: Aaron O'Neill, 'Bhutan: Youth unemployment rate from 2003 to 2022,' *Statista*, 12 July 2023, at https://www.statista.com/statistics/811680/youth-unemployment-rate-in-bhutan.

prospects in the private sector. The civil service can only absorb a finite number of graduates, leading many to seek opportunities abroad, particularly in Australia, Kuwait, and America. This issue of unemployment remains a lingering concern that past and present governments have strived to address. Unfortunately, it is likely to persist in the near future, unless an innovative solution can be found and implemented—and it must be compatible with our approach to sustainable development.

Bhutan has indeed managed to embrace the world in terms of modern economic development, but at a small price. Our environment has suffered, but minimally, and our culture is evolving. While we still hold on to our traditional values, we have also been opening up to global trends, and pop culture, the Internet, and the usage of English are commonplace in Bhutan now. In other words, we have managed to steer development on our own terms, avoiding the pressures that come with a country integrating into the global trade system. This has helped us ensure that our development is socially equitable and that our people are well looked after.

Despite our small economy, healthcare and education in Bhutan are entirely free. Good health is undoubtedly a determinant of happiness, and free access to public health has been firmly established in the country, to the point it is even enshrined in the Constitution.[30] In the past, healthcare workers would have to trek long distances over many days just to administer vaccinations to children in remote villages or to ensure pregnant women are given prenatal care. Today, together with donors, partners, and aid providers, hospitals and health facilities are located throughout the country, ensuring that medical care is accessible to every Bhutanese person.

Provision of free healthcare even extends beyond primary health services. Should anyone need to undergo a complicated medical procedure for which the skills or equipment are not available in

---

[30] Article 9.21: 'The State shall provide free access to basic public health services in both modern and traditional medicines.'

Bhutan, they are sent abroad for treatment, and the state pays for this in full. This practice continues today, and almost every cancer case or organ transplant is treated overseas.

* * *

Policy Brief: The Bhutan Health Trust Fund

The Bhutan Health Trust Fund (BHTF) is a unique and pioneering initiative aimed at financing the purchase of essential drugs and vaccines to support Bhutan's primary health care system through effective, sustainable investment. It was established in 2003, and in 2013, during my first tenure as prime minister, my team and I had the honour of operationalizing it. Our work saw its endowment doubled, reflecting its critical importance and success.

BHTF's vision is providing an efficient means to ensure the sustainability of primary health care services in Bhutan. Its mission focuses on mobilizing, investing, and managing resources effectively to generate sufficient income for the procurement of essential drugs and vaccines. This enables free healthcare to be sustained through consistent supply, with as much self-reliance and as little financial uncertainty as possible.

BHTF has made significant strides in ensuring the sustainability and uninterrupted supply of critical health care components. Since its inception, it has funded critical healthcare needs, including vaccines and cold chain equipment worth Nu 420.88 million annually. For FY2023–2024, it committed Nu 525 million for essential drugs and vaccines.

Notably, BHTF introduced vital vaccines like Hepatitis B, HPV, and MR between 2003–2006. It also co-financed pentavalent vaccines with the Global Alliance for Vaccines and Immunization (GAVI). This started in 2010, becoming fully self-financed in 2014. This funding has enabled Bhutan to maintain immunization coverage above 90 per cent since 2010, currently standing at 96 per cent. Furthermore, it allows the government to annually provide free flu shots to senior citizens.

Managed by an autonomous board of seven members chaired by the Health Minister, BHTF sources its funds from health contributions, revenue from investments, and donations from individuals and organizations. Each donation is matched by the Royal Government of Bhutan, ensuring robust financial backing. The BHTF continues to be a cornerstone of Bhutan's healthcare system, demonstrating a successful model of sustainable health financing.

* * *

Education plays a principal role in advancing GNH in the nation. Free education for Bhutanese from early childhood all the way through to tenth grade is a provision in the Constitution, ensuring that everyone is educated up to that point.[31] My children and I are beneficiaries of this. Over and above this Constitutional provision, those who qualify receive free college education.

It does not stop at free schooling. School-going students are provided free food, uniforms, shoes, textbooks, stationery, and so on. In colleges, students are also given monthly stipends. Access to education has truly been one of the biggest game changers and social equalizers in Bhutan. In fact, most of Bhutan's bureaucracy and politicians are the first generation of Bhutanese who have gone to school. Like myself, they come from families with simple backgrounds. The new elite today, whether politicians or businesspeople, consists mainly of people from poor families or who had parents who couldn't read or write, just like mine.

And just like me, most of us were sent overseas to pursue an education simply because Bhutan did not have enough schools. Like myself, those who made it to college overseas did so on scholarships. Some even studied in some of the world's best universities, and

---

[31] Article 9.16: 'The State shall provide free education to all children of school going age up to tenth standard and ensure that technical and professional education is made generally available, and that higher education is equally accessible to all on the basis of merit.'

almost all have returned home to advance their careers instead of staying abroad. Free education has changed our lives tremendously.

Beyond these, social support is extended to the poor as well. We have a unique tradition where anyone who is destitute can appeal directly to the king for help, and many people who face financial, legal, land, or citizenship problems do so. As only the king can distribute land, it is common for His Majesty to do so to anyone who is landless or owns land that is not fertile for agriculture. Everyone also has life insurance subsidized by the government, which is typically more than enough to conduct death rites. In Vajrayana Buddhism, a lot of emphasis is placed on rituals for the deceased so as to ensure that loved ones are guided to an auspicious rebirth. Such rituals can last for several weeks.

Both life and house insurance are also available at subsidized rates. So, if your house is damaged in an earthquake, you will be compensated or if your crops are ruined by wildlife, you will get compensation for that too.

All these social welfare instruments have resulted in a spectacular drop in poverty. Our poverty rate halved in 2007 and by 2017, only 8.2 per cent of the population was living below the national poverty line.[32]

Pitfalls to Avoid

A danger in social development—where the government and king provide for almost everything—that I see and am concerned about is complacency. If we're not careful, we may end up developing a sense of entitlement, rather than wanting to give back or to work hard to earn and enjoy our own accomplishments.

When people start taking without giving back or without questioning how the government mobilizes resources and provides services, self-entitlement may creep in, becoming a difficult-to-reverse

---

[32] 'Bhutan and ADB,' *Asian Development Bank*, at https://www.adb.org/countries/bhutan/poverty.

problem. It is imperative that everyone understands how free provision comes about and is prepared for changing circumstances.

One of the emerging threats I identify is the rampant pursuit and eventual hoarding of wealth, which is increasingly apparent in Bhutanese society due to our societal advancements. Not long ago, in the 1950s and 1960s, vast tracts of land were under the control of historically affluent aristocratic families. These families wielded significant power and influence over their respective regions. They were economically superior, employing numerous individuals and often serving as mediators and local government leaders. Everyone else must have lived in abject poverty.

As is common globally, elites' wealth, titles, and authority in Bhutan too were passed down to their descendants. However, the introduction of free education and healthcare drastically altered this dynamic due to the Third King's freeing of serfs and granting them land. Education was also free and a blessing for ordinary people who eagerly made use of it, but many of the aristocracy saw it as a mandatory duty that they could spare their children from.

Consequently, while these children remained at home to assume their inherited status and wealth, a new, modern Bhutan was being shaped by those who received education, either locally or abroad. These educated individuals began entering the civil service and private sector, becoming decision-makers and achieving entrepreneurial success. They, too, ascended to an elite status, surpassing even the aristocrats in terms of wealth and influence.

While the old idea of aristocracy has largely been replaced, its legacy persists in a new form, and the emerging concern is that these recently prosperous families may amalgamate their power through intermarriage between the rich and powerful, potentially misusing their authority to fortify their positions. Instead of prioritizing public service, they might concentrate on personal gains such as purchasing land in Thimphu, constructing homes, or securing loans.

If these actions are conducted within legal parameters, there's no issue. However, if they're carried out at the cost of others or through illicit means, we could face significant problems in the future. Once this new wealthy class begins consolidating power, we risk reverting to a similar societal structure as the 1950s, ironically coming full circle despite the introduction of free education and democracy being intended to level the playing field.

On the one hand, these modern elites might monopolize opportunities, hindering other Bhutanese citizens' progress or fostering a sense of entitlement among themselves. On the other hand, the new elite could drive and become the champions of further socio-economic development. Therefore, their conduct in the future will be crucial for the nation's social harmony. We must be vigilant, ensuring that everyone, especially ordinary people, have opportunities to climb the ladder to prosperity.

This trend is not unique to Bhutan. Across the globe, dynastic wealth is enduring and being consolidated. For instance, in America, out of the twenty wealthiest families in 2020, thirteen were already among the top twenty in 1983.[33] These affluent families often use their wealth to exert political influence and further their interests, and it is crucial that we prevent such a scenario from unfolding in Bhutan.

Environmental Conservation

I'll share more about this in chapter seven, but for now, suffice it to say that the quality of natural environmental surroundings contribute to happiness and contentment among people. Being exposed to green environments promotes better mental well-being, reduces stress, and improves positive emotions.[34] Walking through

---

[33] Chuck Collins, 'Report: Silver Spoon Oligarchs: How America's 50 Largest Inherited-Wealth Dynasties Accelerate Inequality,' *Inequality.org*, 16 June 2021, at https://inequality.org/great-divide/report-inherited-wealth-dynasties.

[34] Christian Krekel and George MacKerron, 'How Environmental Quality Affects Our Happiness,' *World Happiness Report*, 20 March 2020, at https://worldhappiness.report/ed/2020/how-environmental-quality-affects-our-happiness.

the beautiful pristine forests right in our backyards does wonders for our emotional well-being. Our nature reserves are teeming with wildlife. This is important for the Bhutanese psyche, as we have lived in harmony with nature and its surroundings for centuries.

Our strong belief in spirits and deities of the natural world is one of the many reasons why we hold such respect and veneration for nature. We believe that any damage to our environment angers the protective deities, and disasters will befall us if this happens. If someone in the family was gravely ill, we conduct rituals to appease the deities and to 'remove' the obstacles. This fear is doing us good because as a result, we have managed to protect our environment for thousands of years.

Being the world's only carbon-negative country instils great pride in many Bhutanese at a national level. We identify with this reputation and feel a sense of responsibility in protecting our environment from harm. Being carbon-negative means we are not exposed to as much air pollution as our immediate neighbours are. But pollution knows no boundaries and, soon, we will also be affected by the actions (and inaction) of other countries, such as our larger neighbours India, China, and Bangladesh. In addition, once complacency sets in and our natural surroundings start being taken for granted, our own people are not willing to look after the immediate environment that they live in.

The world is also in dire need of more leaders who can fight climate change at a national or even a global level. We need such leadership at all levels, especially internationally in the form of individuals, agencies, or NGOs. While Bhutan as a small country has managed to receive wide acclaim for being a carbon-negative country due to wise leadership, we run the risk of undermining all that once we start getting complacent.

Cultural Preservation

Despite potential issues that we need to be mindful of, this is ultimately what GNH is about—economic development at a pace that is within our control and sustainable while allowing people to tangibly benefit from it. Our King has repeatedly mentioned that our society must be harmonious, and GNH helps ensure that any development is not too rapid and Bhutan remains peaceful, retaining its traditions and culture too. We are fortunate that in Bhutan, our rituals and traditions are practised widely and frequently, which tends to slow down and cease over time in more secular societies.

Religion pervades every person's life in Bhutan. Everyone, from farmers to civil servants and even the king himself, is constantly immersed in a religious heritage spanning centuries, through wall murals, statues, and even customary rituals that we conduct on auspicious days for good luck or well-being. His Majesty is not just considered the head of our Vajrayana Buddhist tradition because, per the Constitution, he is overseer and guardian of all religions in the land.

Religious festivals are held throughout the year across the country, retreats are organized by monasteries and even in our daily lives, most of us have a habit of chanting sutras and prayers twice a day. Some of us, who have the time, meditate daily, and it is not surprising for a family member to suddenly decide to go on a pilgrimage or a three-year meditation retreat out of the blue. (Mother once completed a three-year retreat, spent two weeks catching up with friends and family, then entered a second retreat. As I write, she's completed five years in retreat!) Every Bhutanese home has a small prayer room, replete with relics, statues, paintings, and an altar to offer incense.

Spirituality is the common thread that links us together in the last Vajrayana Buddhist kingdom in the world, and it is thriving like never before.[35] New monasteries are being built all the time, dzongs are constantly being renovated and monk numbers today are at an all-time high.

---

[35] Bhutan's state religion is Drukpa Kagyu, one of the sub-schools of the Kagyu tradition, which originated in Tibet.

Our architecture is another visual cue and reminder of our heritage. Anyone who visits Bhutan will notice that our buildings almost always look the same! Whether it is a five-storey office building (we do not have skyscrapers here), a five-star resort, or a traditional farmhouse, you can tell that it is a Bhutanese building. This is because all building facades in Bhutan must follow certain guidelines that showcase intricate timber windows, doors, and pillars. Some are elaborately painted with Buddhist iconography—designs and colours that are commonly seen in the kingdom. Some carvings even creatively use foliage designs to symbolize harmony and the hierarchy of people, animals, and nature.

These days, more and more creative young architects have returned from their studies overseas and begun to incorporate Western, modern architecture and traditional Bhutanese form in new projects—not just in Bhutan but also in other countries. The first such example is the University of Texas in El Paso (UTEP), where a number of Bhutanese pursue their studies. Its website (www.utep.edu/bhutan) shares how their campus came to resemble a Bhutanese one. In times to come, we may see more evolutions of traditional designs that incorporate modern touches in exciting new ways.

But the most obvious symbolism of our proud heritage is our national dress: the gho and kira. For many visitors to Bhutan, it is almost like a step back in time when they see us walking the streets in our traditional costume. This resurgence is relatively recent, and, in the 1970s, most civil servants wore Western suits to work. Today, that is unheard of, as all offices require workers to be dressed in the national costume. Even when visiting temples or monasteries, all of us wear the gho or kira to this day. Many years ago, I visited Dechenphug Monastery in pants, like many others would then, but it is now considered unimaginably disrespectful to do so.

We have our Fourth King to thank for this revival. He famously wears his gho whenever he is seen in public—whether he is playing basketball, cycling, travelling abroad, or even fighting militants, as he did in 2003. Upon seeing this, people followed suit and now wear ghos and kiras to all official functions, important events, and even during day-to-day activities. After all, as a tiny nation sandwiched between two giants, it is even more imperative that we keep our unique cultural signifiers alive.

I am always in my gho whenever I attend meetings, official or private, at home or abroad. I even gave our traditional dress a specific mention during a TED talk in Vancouver, describing it as having 'the world's biggest pocket'. Every Bhutanese is proud of their national costume, and we never find it a burden or cumbersome to wear. Its beautiful riot of colours and intricate designs are so pleasing to the eye, we are always more than happy to wear it!

* * *

Policy Brief: The Challenges of Diversity

Most foreigners see Bhutan as a homogenous society. In fact, we are made up of diverse peoples and cultures. As Bhutan becomes more modernized and diverse, we need to make space for other ethnicities and cultures due to the unique geography of the region. Although we are known to be a Buddhist kingdom, Bhutan also has a significant population of Hindus. Southern Bhutan is dominated by Hindus who are mostly immigrants from Nepal and their culture, food, and traditions are distinctively different. It is important that we celebrate these cultures too. We run the risk of undermining these cultures if we do not celebrate diversity.

Besides Hindus, a small community of Bhutanese are Christians. Due to Buddhism's dominance, they shy away from involvement or engagement in public life. A significant challenge is bringing them into the mainstream while balancing their faith with its focus on society. Having grown up in Dr Graham's Homes, a Christian missionary school run by Presbyterians, I know they generally do commendable work among disadvantaged communities. However, the methods employed in Bhutan have raised concerns; some offer the poor material incentives such as money, food, and clothes to encourage conversion.

This approach undermines the principles of religious freedom enshrined in Bhutan's Constitution, which ensures every citizen's right to practice their chosen faith without coercion. Furthermore, it risks creating an environment where conversions are driven more by immediate material needs than genuine belief. If Christianity is to spread, let it be because its ideas and philosophy are accepted freely by others. If they resonate with individuals, conversions should occur organically, without external incentives.

Ethnically, Bhutan is also home to the Ngalops, Sharchops, and Kheng—notable Buddhist minorities. Another significant minority is the Lhotshampas, a Nepali-speaking community that predominantly follows Hinduism. Besides these, there are indigenous groups like the Brokpa, Layap, Monpa, and Doya, who are considered original inhabitants of Bhutan. The numerous castes and ethnic communities among the Lhotshampas such as Bahun, Chhetri, Gurung, Limbu, Newar, Rai, and Tamang further enrich Bhutan's cultural landscape.

The integration of these cultures into Bhutanese society is an ongoing process. His Majesty champions promoting unity while respecting diversity. Public discussions about Bhutan's ethnic diversity have become more frequent in recent years, indicating a shift towards a more inclusive society as we work to integrate diverse communities while retaining our heritage.

* * *

Our cultural retention is a historic miracle, given how far the Vajrayana Buddhist tradition has shrunk from the days when it was practised throughout the region, even as far as Mongolia. It could have been easily diluted along the way as Buddhist kingdoms gradually collapsed around us. Our unspoilt environment and reputation as being the only carbon-negative country in the world is even a more unlikely outcome.

Good Governance

This is where good governance is vital in ensuring effective and quality leadership. Good governance as one of the Four Pillars of GNH is the tool to realizing everything else. It balances the importance of economic growth with sustainability, environmental conservation, and cultural preservation. It also ensures that the other pillars are prioritized properly. Studies have shown that good governance produces higher levels of happiness and lowers inequality of happiness among citizens.[36]

The biggest outcome of good governance in Bhutan is obviously our democracy. It is even more precious due to it being a gift from our monarch, not a freedom we have had to fight for. Bhutan's democracy is unique in its peaceful genesis, but this does not make it immune to the threats that have plagued governance since the beginning, such as corruption. Once good governance is lost, we can forget about conserving the environment, preserving culture, and socially equitable economic growth.

For good governance to work, leadership is critical, especially in the early stages of development of a society or a country. These institutions to provide checks and balances, and to ensure good, efficient governance, were put into place by the King before the first elections. These include the Election Commission, the Anti-corruption Commission, the Public Service Commission, an expanded judiciary, an independent media, and civil society organizations. It has worked well so far, as we have had four elections with four changes in government with a smooth transition each time.

GNH fundamentally contrasts GDP. The seemingly idealistic nature of GNH makes it is difficult to implement. However, the Four Pillars of GNH have served as the foundation for governmental planning for many years.

The notion of GNH was first introduced in the eighth five-year plan, and the Four Pillars were incorporated as central values in the tenth five-year plan, spanning 2008 to 2012. To ensure

[36] J.C. Ott, 'Government and Happiness in 130 Nations: Good Governance Fosters Higher Level and More Equality of Happiness,' *National Library of Medicine*, 26 October 2010, at https://www.ncbi.nlm.nih.gov/pmc/articles/PMC3068254.

that government policies align with GNH principles, the former Planning Commission was restructured and rebranded as the GNH Commission in 2008.

Are We Truly Happy?

What precisely do we mean by *happiness*? If we were to refer to our GNH survey, then yes, around 95 per cent of us say we are happy. While we Bhutanese are often called 'the happiest people in the world', I submit that we are really not in a material sense. As long as happiness is measured in different ways by different people, we can strongly declare ourselves happy in some senses, but we cannot do so in others.

When I speak about happiness to an international audience, I always ask people where they think Bhutan ranks in the World Happiness Report (WHR), an annual report released every 20 March on International Day of Happiness. Published by the United Nations, the WHR is believed to be the most comprehensive international report of happiness available.

More often than not, the audience is always eager to say that Bhutan is number one. But when I show them that the WHR ranks us as the *ninety-fifth* happiest country in the world, people are shocked.[37] How can a country that professes to follow a GNH philosophy not be the happiest in the world? Could so many videos, tourism promotions, documentaries, and news articles be wrong?

It all depends on how we measure such a subjective quality. If we use economic success, we definitely are not the 'happiest' by that standard—not by a long shot! We have resource constraints. Our economy is small and we have a long way to go in terms of improving our healthcare, quality of education, and job provision. I think I can say with confidence that we are not the happiest people in an economic sense.

---

[37] 'World Happiness Report 2019', *World Happiness Report*, at https://s3.amazonaws. com/happiness-report/2019/WHR19.pdf

According to the World Happiness Report, Finland has consistently secured the top position as the happiest country worldwide for several years, followed by Denmark and Norway— all of them Scandinavian countries.[38] Meanwhile, our neighbouring countries, China and India, lag significantly behind, ranking ninety-third and one-hundred and fortieth respectively.

However, different indices present contrasting findings. For instance, the 2016 Happy Planet Index crowned Costa Rica as the world's happiest country, with Mexico and Colombia trailing closely in second and third places. In this particular index, Bhutan occupied the seventy-fifth spot.[39] As for the Scandinavian frontrunners in the previous index? Finland ranks thirty-seventh, Denmark thirty-second, and Norway twelfth.

Another ranking, the Global Happiness Report issued by Ipsos, positions Australia and Canada at the forefront as the happiest nations, succeeded by China and Great Britain. In this case, Bhutan was not included in the study.[40]

These striking discrepancies highlight the inherent complexity and controversy in quantifying happiness. Such drastic variations in results are due to the novelty of measuring happiness, as most nations have yet to adopt this practice. Moreover, different agencies employ diverse metrics, which leads to inconsistent outcomes. Unlike measuring economic growth, where countries with the highest GDP are more or less consistent, results of measuring happiness will never be consistent, as all three indices use varying methodologies.[41]

---

[38] 'World Happiness Report 2024', *World Happiness Report*, at https://happiness-report.s3.amazonaws.com/2024/WHR+24.pdf

[39] 'Happy Planet Index,' at https://happyplanetindex.org/countries.

[40] 'Global Happiness Study,' at https://www.ipsos.com/sites/default/files/ct/news/documents/2019-08/Happiness-Study-report-August-2019.pdf.

[41] The World Happiness Report uses six variables: GDP per capita, social support, healthy life expectancy, freedom, generosity, and absence of corruption to calculate happiness. The Happy Planet Index is calculated by combining life expectancy, experienced well-being, inequality of outcomes, and ecological footprint. The Global Happiness Survey was conducted as an online survey with a sample of over 1,000 respondents in twenty-eight countries.

Nonetheless, there is one constant across all indices: Bhutan frequently falls short in these rankings. This discrepancy arises because the prevalent metric used in these happiness indices is economic success measured mainly by per capita GDP, which overlooks many aspects that our own GNH Index considers, such as psychological well-being, time freedom, and cultural resilience. I will discuss these further in the next section.

Sadly, Bhutan has not been included in the recent WHR of 2020. Apparently the Centre for Bhutan Studies and the National Bureau of Statistics could not come to an agreement with Gallup (who did the polls for the report) on how to conduct the polling. Gallup would not reveal its methodology, and there were no details on the data that was to be gathered. As far as the Centre for Bhutan Studies and the National Statistical Bureau were concerned, neither did anyone from Gallup ever visit Bhutan nor did they contract the exercise to anybody or any organization in Bhutan.

Since we were not confident about what data Gallup was collecting or how it was doing so, Bhutan decided to pull out of the exercise. It is more the pity that not only was the WHR first inspired by Bhutan but March 20 is also celebrated as World Happiness Day as a direct result of Bhutan's initiative at the United Nations, but we must acknowledge that it has grown beyond its initial foundation.

The Nine Domains of Happiness

In 2006, the Centre for Bhutan Studies reviewed and expanded the scope of the Four Pillars. By that time, GNH had caught on with many academics and scholars, and two international conferences on GNH had already been held.

Based on the plethora of information that was available on GNH or GNH-like concepts or projects, the Centre for Bhutan Studies expanded on the four main tenets of GNH into what we now know as the nine domains: health, education, living standards, ecological diversity and resilience, good governance, cultural diversity and resilience, community vitality, psychological well-being, and time use.

I like to think of the domains as the foundations of happiness and well-being. Health, education, and high living standards are all regarded by countries as front and centre of their development agenda. Increasingly, countries are also beginning to recognize the importance of and prioritize good governance and protecting the ecology. As for the rest of the domains (cultural diversity and resilience, community vitality, psychological well-being, and time use), which we consider as critical public policy, they rarely register as priorities for other governments. These elements, which I consider to be cutting edge governance thought and policy, are perhaps more abstract and less easily measured. That said, they are equally important to the overall well-being of a society.

However, governments would be remiss *not* to consider them at some level. Cultural diversity and resilience celebrate the richness of different traditions and ways of life, fostering social cohesion and mutual respect. Community vitality speaks to the strength and vibrancy of social networks and communal bonds, which are essential for social support and a sense of belonging. Psychological well-being highlights the importance of mental health and personal fulfilment, while time use refers to the balance between work and leisure, acknowledging that overwork can lead to stress and burnout.

While it is not suggested that these domains should be universally adopted in their exact form by all governments, especially those with differing cultural contexts, they do present valuable considerations. They highlight the need for a comprehensive approach to development that addresses not just economic growth but also social, cultural, and environmental factors. In essence, they underscore the importance of creating conditions that allow people to thrive and achieve a high quality of life in all its multifaceted dimensions.

I was sceptical at first when the nine domains were introduced but was won over when we realized this was a way to truly determine

GNH levels and show us where the government can improve the well-being of our people. The GNH survey would also provide a wealth of data for the government and help us plan policies or prioritize development work. Personally, I feel, besides policymakers, the public should read the survey's findings for themselves and incorporate the takeaways from the results in their own lives.

Measuring Happiness

Despite how unrealistic or idealistic it may seem to measure happiness, it needs to be done. It provides valuable data and insights to countries, particularly those that rank low on the index, to take the information and use it to improve or derive better policies. It is most definitely not a race to the top. Finland does not receive an award and the lowest ranking country does not get penalized either, but the idea behind the rankings is ultimately to help improve the well-being of people.

So why is not Bhutan anywhere near the top? Perhaps we are not meant to be. We are a small developing nation that has little compared to others. To enhance well-being, we need more technology and resources, which we lack. We can't argue with the fact that economic prosperity is critical for happiness, and indeed, we are nowhere near the top few 'happiest' countries by the standards they use.

But this does not mean that GNH is not working for us. Not only have life expectancy and literacy rates increased, poverty has decreased, and infant mortality rates have also plummeted from 140 per 1,000 live births to 15. We have a strong cultural identity as the only surviving Vajrayana Buddhist kingdom. More than 70 per cent of our land is under forest cover. And in terms of governance, democracy has been introduced seamlessly and smoothly in the country. Our institutions are in place and functioning, and we have already seen four different governments through four elections.

But happiness, we believe, still must be measured in some way, so we know how our citizens are doing and whether they are happy with their situation. Measurements of happiness in Bhutan started long before the World Happiness Report, with nationwide GNH Index surveys being conducted in 2010, 2015, and 2022. The indicators and questions are developed by the Centre of Bhutan Studies as a way to measure not happiness itself (which is subjective) but whether the country is achieving optimal GNH levels.

The GNH Index, a remarkable Bhutanese innovation, developed and spearheaded by Dasho Karma Ura, the president of the Center for Bhutan Studies, was born from a series of pilot studies and surveys in 2008. In the inaugural 2010 survey, the centre reached out to a diverse cross-section of 7,142 Bhutanese citizens. Over the span of three weeks, fifty-five enumerators were trained at the Centre of Bhutan Studies to translate English questions into Dzongkha and other dialects. This linguistic army then dispersed across Bhutan's vast terrain, taking nine months to complete the survey.

The questionnaire, extensive and comprehensive, required about three hours for each respondent to answer. We delved into the lives of farmers, civil servants, housewives, and monks—Bhutanese from all walks of life. Beyond standard queries about household data, demographics, and education levels, we sought to understand their psychological well-being, social support, sense of purpose in life, stress levels, emotions, health, personal time usage, food and nutrition, community participation, connection with nature, and perceptions of crime and safety.

Some questions might seem unusual to outsiders, but they are deeply rooted in Bhutanese culture. For instance: 'Do you consider karma in your daily life?', 'Can you recite a couple of *lozey* (creative poetry) lines?', or 'Do you pay homage to the local deity in your village or community?' We even explored physical health, alcohol consumption, familial knowledge, school and community concerns, and personal support systems.

Once the survey results were collated, respondents were categorized into 'happy people' and 'not-yet-happy people'. We found that 89.6 per cent of the people were happy with, interestingly, 40.9 per cent found to be 'deeply happy', having achieved 'sufficiency' in six of the nine domains. The survey revealed intriguing insights, such as men are happier than women, higher education does not necessarily lead to happiness . . . and the happiest group is the one that is unmarried![42]

That final revelation never fails to get a laugh whenever I share it, but the reason is simple—the unmarried include monks and nuns, who rate themselves as highly content.

In 2015, a second nationwide GNH survey found the Bhutanese slightly happier than before. The rate of people considered happy had risen to 91.25 per cent, and people found to be 'deeply happy' had risen to 43.4 per cent from 40.9 per cent.[43] Once again, men were happier than women, but more education led to more happiness, and urban dwellers were happier than rural folks. An interesting observation was that Bhutanese were sleeping more and working less, a positive trend considering the global problem of sleep deprivation.[44]

The 2022 GNH survey revealed that the number of people found to be happy had increased again to 93.61 per cent, with 48 per cent of the people claiming to be 'deeply happy'.

Looking closely at work-related data, it was found that women worked more than men because household chores are considered work, an aspect not factored into conventional GDP calculations. Recognizing unpaid labour can have significant implications for global economics, potentially adding trillions to the world economy if this value could be quantified.

So, what makes Bhutanese happy according to the survey? Money tops the list, followed by good health, and assets like land or homes. Spirituality, community, and environment are other important

---

[42] For the latest details, see: www.grossnationalhappiness.com.

[43] Gyalsten K. Dorji, '91.2 % of Bhutanese are happy: GNH survey,' *Kuensel Online*, 4 November 2015, at http://www.kuenselonline.com/91-2-of-bhutanese-are-happy-gnh-survey.

[44] According to GNH surveys, the average time spent sleeping was 8.8 hours, and time spent working 7.9 hours.

factors, though they rank behind these material concerns. While these findings may seem contradictory to the GNH philosophy and sound like they are being taken for granted, they do underline the importance of basic needs and the value Bhutanese place on their unique cultural and environmental heritage. This is just a snapshot of the nation at a certain point in time and may continue to change as Bhutan develops.

The Oxford Department of International Development contextualizes the results as such:

> The 2022 GNH Index, with a value of 0.781, reflects a growth rate of 3.3% compared to the 2015 GNH Index of 0.756, faster than previous growth. The GNH Index in 2010 was 0.743. The GNH value ranges from 0 to 1 where higher value represents greater well-being and happiness.[45]

Three surveys are not enough to establish a trend, but the numbers do point to certain significant situations in Bhutan. If you unpack the GNH Index, it has 33 indicators with 124 variables. These variables form the building blocks of the GNH Index and by looking at individual parts that make up the whole, the government is able to pinpoint the areas that need improvement.

To ensure fairness, the GNH Index has not used any data from the government and political leaders have been left out of the process entirely, only being shown the findings when the surveys have been completed. In this way, they have remained as true as possible to ordinary people's thoughts and feelings.

GNH in Business

A revelation recently struck me—the potential of Bhutanese GNH surveys to revolutionize the business landscape. Imagine

---

[45] 'Bhutan Gross National Happiness index shows increase since 2015 despite pandemic,' *Oxford Department of International Development*, 24 May 2023, at https://www.qeh.ox.ac.uk/news/bhutan-gross-national-happiness-index-shows-increase-2015-despite-pandemic.

businesses harnessing insights from these surveys to restructure their operations, amplifying the GNH levels across all stakeholders, from owners, management, workers to shareholders. This would not just be an internal transformation; it would ripple outwards, enhancing the environment, community, customers, and even the supply chain.

In 2016, I found myself irresistibly drawn to this concept of GNH for businesses. So much so, that I fervently appealed to Dasho Karma Ura and the Centre for Bhutan Studies to adapt it for the business world. My advocacy bore fruit when they initiated a GNH certification pilot for select corporations in Bhutan.

This innovative idea sparked enthusiasm beyond Bhutan's borders. International colleagues in India, Switzerland, Thailand, Brazil, and Belgium were electrified by the prospect of a GNH certification for businesses. An undercurrent of desire is palpable, a yearning to shift from businesses solely focused on bottom-line profits to adopting a more holistic, inclusive approach.

Many companies engage in corporate social responsibility (CSR) or economic, social, and governance (ESG) projects aimed at combating poverty, climate change, protecting the environment, women's rights, or promoting education. However, integrating a GNH-oriented approach into business operations can allow these values to be ingrained in the company's ethos.

While companies acknowledge the importance of these values and dedicate funds towards projects that align with them, often these values remain external. They are not fully absorbed by the companies or their employees. CSR or ESG initiatives are frequently treated as mere checklists, a way to demonstrate to employees and communities that 'good' is being done.

By internalizing these causes, making them part of the company's DNA, their impact can be magnified. The company can become sustainable and undoubtedly lead to happier, more fulfilled employees. The contribution to CSR programmes cannot just be financial but be woven into the very fabric of the company, creating a more values-driven, impactful entity.

GNH Goes Abroad

In the 1970s, our visionary Fourth King voiced an unconventional aspiration for Bhutan: we would pursue national happiness, not mere economic wealth. The idea was revolutionary and unprecedented, a beacon of hope in a world fixated on relentless economic expansion. Little did we know that GNH would eventually shine brightly on the international stage.

It took several decades before other nations began to question their single-minded pursuit of economic growth. Today, more nations are intrigued by our unique approach, keen to understand how happiness can be used as a measure of prosperity. In 2011, Bhutan, as a proud member of the UN, proposed a paradigm shift towards a more holistic economic model, one that recognizes happiness and well-being as universal aspirations. This proposal was embraced by the UN General Assembly with a resolution acknowledging that GDP falls short of capturing these broader objectives and highlighting the imperative for sustainable development.

Bhutan's government hosted a landmark meeting during the sixty-sixth session of the General Assembly, named 'Happiness and Well-being: Defining a New Economic Paradigm'. This historic gathering convened representatives from governments, religious organizations, academia, and civil society, all united in their quest for a more meaningful economic model. Our King further directed the formation of an International Expert Working Group, comprising eminent scholars from around the globe. Their mission? To translate the principles of GNH into a new economic paradigm and policy objectives that could potentially be adopted worldwide.

The fruits of their labour were presented to the UN General Assembly and led to the establishment of the International Day of Happiness on 20 March 2013. This joyous occasion has been celebrated annually ever since. The WHR, launched on this day every year since 2012, is a testament to the growing global recognition of the importance of happiness.

Remarkably, Bhutan was featured in the inaugural report as a case study, demonstrating the profound philosophical underpinnings of our approach to happiness and its policy implications. Surprisingly, this report was overlooked when the very same UN released its own version of the WHR.

In 2015, the UN turned its focus towards defining a new development paradigm, resulting in the Sustainable Development Goals (SDGs). These ambitious goals aim to have developed and developing countries partner to eradicate poverty and hunger, reduce inequality, promote sustainable cities and communities, and drive urgent action against climate change. It seems that the world is finally catching up with Bhutan's vision of a balanced and sustainable future.[46]

Many elements of the SDGs and GNH are consistent with one another, as both frameworks aim to create a balanced and sustainable development approach that goes beyond economic growth. Bhutan has incorporated the SDGs into its GNH development framework, illustrating the commonalities between the two. For instance, Bhutan has prioritized SDGs one (no poverty), thirteen (climate action), and fifteen (life on land).[47] This decision aligns with the nation's GNH goals, as all sectors of the government are required to plan their sector plans based on the GNH goals. We continue to work alongside the UN to help achieve its global objectives, in a spirit of collaboration and mutual influence.

The first international conference on GNH was held in February 2004 and was attended by scholars, policymakers, and development economists from several countries. Since then, seven more such conferences have been held in Canada, Brazil, Thailand, Malaysia,

---

[46] For more information on the 17 SDGs, see: https://sustainabledevelopment.un.org/sdgs.

[47] Oana Forestier and Rakhyun E. Kim, 'Cherry-picking the Sustainable Development Goals: Goal prioritization by national governments and implications for global governance,' *Sustainable Development*, Volume 28 Issue 5, pp. 1269-1278.

and Bhutan, and have been instrumental in generating interest in GNH and in Bhutan itself.

The most recent GNH international conference was held in Sarawak, Malaysia, in November 2018, and it remains a priority for me to encourage more international discussion on GNH around the world and assist any agency interested in adopting its tenets in their own countries and organizations.

More importantly, at a national level, many countries are considering moving away from unfettered growth and wasteful consumption to development that is more 'human'. In 2010, the UK launched the National Wellbeing Programme that looks at datasets to monitor national well-being. In the Middle East, the United Arab Emirates launched a national programme for happiness and well-being, appointing a Minister of State for Happiness and Wellbeing to oversee plans and policies to achieve a happier society.

Positions such as chief happiness and positivity officers have been created to help drive this programme. Madhya Pradesh was one of the first states in India to appoint a minister of happiness in 2017 who would oversee a 'happiness ministry' that was modelled after Bhutan's GNH Index. Unfortunately, after a scandal-laden term, the minister of happiness was booted out in the 2018 state elections.

Canada, in a dedicated pursuit of happiness, embarked on an eleven-year journey to craft its unique happiness index—The Index of Wellbeing. With a brigade of researchers at the helm, Canada's approach mirrors Bhutan's revolutionary GNH Index, albeit with eight domains instead of nine and sixty-four indicators—half the number in Bhutan's model.

In 2018, the land that bore 'The Father of Capitalism' Adam Smith, Scotland, took a surprising turn. They announced their leadership in establishing the Wellbeing Economy Governments group aiming to challenge GDP's narrow scope as the sole measure of progress. This eclectic group is a global coalition, encompassing

Scotland, Iceland, and the distant New Zealand, each actively involved in crafting their unique well-being strategies.

New Zealand, in particular, made waves in 2019 by announcing its inaugural 'well-being budget'. Billions were allocated to bolster mental health services, combat child poverty and family violence, and transition towards a sustainable, low-emission economy. The then-Prime Minister Jacinda Ardern upheld the environment and the well-being of her people as the 'true measure of success'.[48]

It is heartening to see these nations band together, prioritizing happiness and the welfare of their vulnerable citizens. But one can't help but wonder, why did it take so long? If countries are now gradually embracing GNH, does it validate our long-standing belief in this approach?

Finally, will they succeed on the scale they envision? It is too early to tell, but the burgeoning interest in sustainable development worldwide is a promising sign of a potential paradigm shift in our understanding of progress and prosperity.

Development with Values

The ideals of GNH are a topic that is ripe for scholarship, and the amount of literature on it is quite bewildering. GNH is so well-studied and debated by both local and international scholars that there is a danger of over-complicating the concept. Perhaps this prompted our Fifth King to encapsulate and simplify the whole intent of GNH into a statement that could be understood easily. In the bustling Madhavrao Scindia Memorial Lecture hall in New Delhi, during his inaugural state visit to India in 2009, His Majesty distilled the essence of GNH into a simple but profound phrase: 'development with values'.

---

[48] Emma Charlton, 'New Zealand has unveiled its first "well-being" budget,' *World Economic Forum*, 30 May 2019, at https://www.weforum.org/agenda/2019/05/new-zealand-is-publishing-its-first-well-being-budget.

To him, GNH represented development steered by deep-seated human values. This vision of growth, imbued with moral integrity, has become the cornerstone of Bhutan's evolution. The GNH Commission—the guardian of our five-year development plans—ensures that this blend of progress and principles permeates every facet of our national fabric. Each policy is meticulously scrutinized by this commission, using a unique metric that determines its alignment with GNH. Policies that fall short are sent back for refinement until they resonate with our cherished values.

During my tenure in government, I witnessed this rigorous screening process firsthand. Over its lifetime, the GNH Commission, chaired by the prime minister and comprising eleven government secretaries and other ex-officio members, has employed a comprehensive tool featuring twenty-six criteria. Draft policies have to pass this exacting test before landing on the commission's table. While most have succeeded, some falter due to budgetary restrictions, resource limitations, or political considerations. (The GNH Commission was disbanded in October 2022, as part of the Royal Civil Service Commission's reorganization of civil service agencies, and its functions distributed to other divisions.)

During my first term as prime minister, I recall the Mineral Development Policy failing to clear the screening tool twice, largely due to it not meeting certain criteria. After four painstaking years of amendments, including clauses for environmental protection, anti-corruption measures, and community involvement, it finally made the cut.

The GNH Commission may have disbanded, but that does not mean our attitude towards it has changed. At the national level, GNH is a solemn commitment of the state and the incumbent government. At a business level, it provides a framework for organizations to infuse their operations with its principles and values. It has been deeply woven into the fabric of Bhutanese life and is more than just a development philosophy—it is a way of living.

We expect our government to uphold GNH in all its endeavours. It is become part of our national DNA, guiding our professional and personal actions. Our unique philosophy has projected Bhutan's voice on the international stage, offering a positive influence at a global scale, and its constitutional inclusion ensures that GNH will continue to shape and honour Bhutan's trajectory for generations to come.

But the bottom line is that for GNH to work, good governance is crucial. It is the central pillar on which GNH stands. Meritocracy, justice, and the rule of law are all important for a country and its government to function. It is not enough to claim GNH's ideals, as a nation must actively build care for people, integrity, and trust in the authorities into everything it does.

Adopting GNH Around the World

Adopting GNH as a measure of societal progress necessitates its deep and thoughtful integration into the existing framework and culture of a country. It cannot simply be imposed or added without due consideration for the unique circumstances, values, and political philosophies of the country.

Here are some principles that can guide this process in a culturally and politically agnostic manner:

1. **Holistic understanding:** GNH is a holistic concept that goes beyond economic parameters to include spiritual, physical, social, and environmental dimensions of well-being. Stakeholders need to understand this holistic nature and embrace it as a comprehensive approach to national development rather than just as a way to improve economic success.

2. **Inclusivity:** All sections of society should be involved in defining what happiness means to them. This ensures that the GNH model is reflective of the collective aspirations and values of all citizens, irrespective of their cultural, political,

or socio-economic backgrounds. Public awareness about the importance of GNH and its implications for societal well-being should be promoted through education, public discourse, and media.

3. **Adaptability:** While the GNH model has been successful in Bhutan, other countries must adapt it in ways that suit their unique contexts. This may involve adjusting the various domains and indicators of GNH to reflect the realities and priorities of the country. This could serve to foster national unity and mutual understanding, as different groups bring their concerns and circumstances to the table.

4. **Political will:** The adoption of GNH requires strong political commitment and leadership. Politicians and policymakers must be willing to shift from traditional economic measures of progress to a more holistic and sustainable approach.

5. **Policy integration:** GNH should be integrated into policymaking at all levels of government. This includes incorporating GNH principles into national planning, budgeting, and decision-making processes.

6. **Continuous measurement and evaluation:** Regular assessments should be conducted to measure progress in achieving GNH. These assessments can guide policy adjustments and ensure that the GNH model remains relevant and effective over time.

7. **International cooperation:** Countries should collaborate and learn from each other's experiences in implementing GNH. This can facilitate mutual learning and the exchange of best practices.

These principles offer a starting point for countries considering the adoption of GNH. However, the success of this endeavour ultimately depends on the willingness and ability of each country to redefine progress in ways that prioritize the holistic well-being of its citizens.

Implementing a happiness or well-being index in a freedom-oriented society like the US, which places high value on individual liberties and limited government intervention, can be challenging. However, it's not impossible; the key lies in creating an approach that aligns with the country's core values while promoting sustainable development and well-being.

1. Firstly, such an index must respect personal freedoms and individual rights as enshrined in (for instance) the US constitution. The focus should be on creating an environment that allows people to pursue their own definition of happiness and well-being rather than enforcing a one-size-fits-all model.

2. Secondly, the process should be transparent and involve public participation. Citizens could be involved in determining which domains and indicators are included in the index. This would ensure that the index reflects the values and priorities of the American people, increasing its acceptance and legitimacy.

3. Thirdly, instead of giving more power to the government, the role of the government could be reframed as a facilitator in creating conditions that promote well-being. This could include policies that encourage economic stability, social equality, environmental sustainability, and access to healthcare and education.

4. Fourthly, checks and balances should be put in place to prevent the abuse of power. This could involve oversight from independent bodies, and regular reviews of the index and its impact.

5. Finally, a happiness or well-being index is not a panacea for all societal issues but a tool to guide policymaking and foster a broader conversation about what constitutes progress and success in society.

In a society like the US, where trust in government varies, it's essential that any attempt to implement such an index is done in a way that fosters trust, promotes transparency, and respects individual freedoms. Each step of the process should be communicated clearly to the public to ensure understanding and buy-in.

In conclusion, while it may present challenges, the adoption of a happiness or well-being index in countries around the world could offer a fresh perspective on societal progress and success, encouraging a shift towards policies that promote holistic well-being and sustainable development. Themay be required to apply GNH by governments at the national level. But the same holds true for application of GNH at community level (local governments) and in businesses—an encouraging move that has also generated interest from businesses in measuring their performance within the framework of GNH for business.

I'm excited about the possibilities that our very own GNH could help businesses worldwide shift their focus from solely maximizing shareholder profits to enhancing the well-being of all their stakeholders—employees and their families, management, the community, customers, the environment, and shareholders alike.

Chapter Six

Signing Power Away

Each word has earned its sacred place with the blessings of every citizen in our nation. This is the People's Constitution.

—His Majesty the Fifth Druk Gyalpo,
Jigme Khesar Namgyal Wangchuck

My hands were shaking. I opened them to see sweat glistening in the grooves of my palms. As if to check if I was dreaming, I reached up to touch my forehead and felt beads of cold sweat. Suddenly, the atmosphere seemed heavy, except for a slight buzz in my ears.

I focused my attention on the ritual going on. Monks were chanting prayers accompanied by the rhythmic pounding of drums, ringing of bells, and sounding of horns, but all I could hear was the reverberating beat of my heart. I reached into my gho to look for a hanky to wipe my face with but gave up after riffling around for a few seconds.

'I shouldn't move too much,' I told myself, 'or else I might draw unnecessary attention to myself.'

Without warning, silence fell. The monks had finished their prayers, marking the beginning of the actual event I was there for: the signing of the Constitution. I looked around to see what the others were up to, trying to get a hint of what they might be thinking. Seated next to me and on the rows of benches behind were all the members of parliament from both the ruling and opposition parties, and members of the National Council. This may have been something of an overstatement, as the opposition consisted of just me and one other member!

We had been voted in during the first National Assembly Election in 2008. There were seventy-two of us, and we were all here to sign the Constitution—twenty-five members of the National Council; five appointees of His Majesty; twenty representatives, one from each dzongkhag; and forty-seven from the National Assembly. We were the first fully-elected bicameral parliament, and no one before us had experienced what we were going through now.

I examined the faces of the forty-seven National Assembly members and saw anxiety written all over them. I was relieved to know I was not the only one feeling nervous. But I had the most to fear—I was in the very first opposition party of Bhutan and there were only two members: myself and fellow party member Damcho Dorji. Both of us made up one of the world's smallest opposition parties, facing a whopping forty-five-member ruling party!

I was petrified. As if to hide how scared I was, I placed my hands inside the folds of my kabney (worn as part of protocol, since we were in Tashichho *dzong*) and quickly averted my gaze to the ground in front of me. No one said a word as we sat with our bowed heads in the grand assembly hall. Perhaps it was the grandeur of the place. Its square pillars were embellished with auspicious signs, clouds, and various Buddhist symbols painted in gold, red, blue, green, and white filled every inch of the columns.

Similar patterns adorned the thrones, ceilings, walls, and tables in the hall, adding to the magnificence of the place. We were all seated facing an altar that had two statues: a tall one of Buddha and the Zhabdrung, almost as though he was there to witness this momentous event. In front of the two statues were a bowl of fruit and a row of *tormas* (ritual cakes made from dough and butter) dyed in white, yellow, red, blue, and green. These items were for the deities of Bhutan, offerings to them to ensure a successful outcome for the ceremonies happening that day.

But much more significant were the prayers we all offered that day that the Constitution would service present and future generations. This moment, this place, and the significance of it all was not lost on us. We were in the presence of the most revered personalities in the kingdom: the reigning Fifth King, his father the Fourth King, and the Je Khenpo. Our country's most eminent figures had gathered on this auspicious day to bear witness to the signing of the Constitution, a document that heralded the beginning of democracy in our country.

One by one, our names were called to proceed to a grand ceremonial table, where a large book the height of a man's torso was placed amidst several symbolic *khadars* or silk ceremonial scarves. The table itself was hugely significant too. Carved and adorned with two dragons, the eight auspicious symbols, and other floral motifs, this was the very wooden table where Gongsar Ugyen Wangchuck had been ratified as Bhutan's First King over a hundred years ago. At the same table where people had hoped he would put an end to centuries of civil warfare and mayhem, a new democratic Bhutan was beginning, in which the powers of governance were being handed back by the King to the people after an unprecedented hundred years of peace, prosperity and happiness.

Paradoxically, I was growing increasingly anxious, as if I were betraying my conscience. That Constitution amounted to taking power away from our beloved monarch, which some part of me still thought of as betraying our ancestors—the ones who had placed his forefathers on the throne in the first place.

It is important to note that even if this was our kings' wish, it was still not easy breaking from a tradition of monarchy that had brought peace, prosperity, and stability to Bhutan. The people of Bhutan adore our kings, yet that day, we were there to sign their powers away by forming a democratically elected government.

I wondered what the people of Bhutan would think. We had been voted in by them, yet they had said time and again that they did not want democracy. From the drafting of the Constitution to the mock elections that were held as a dry run before the first election, the citizens of Bhutan had expressed that they much preferred the rule of an absolute monarchy to a democratically elected parliament.

Before I had time to sort out my thoughts, I heard my name being called: 'Leader of the opposition party, Tshering Tobgay.'

I could feel my whole body shaking as I stood up. I took a few quivering steps towards the grand table. Carefully holding my kabney and spreading it out to cover my lower body, I stopped and took one step forward with my right foot, bowed deeply to the King who was standing at the other side of the table, and took a step back before I moved forward again towards him.

As I approached, I beheld a rectangular book before him with Dzongkha written horizontally across it in gold ink. The pages were bound in the form of the traditional Buddhist scriptures commonly seen throughout monasteries and temples in Bhutan. The King had already signed this copy of the Constitution in gold ink, using a bamboo quill with a nib crafted by local artisans.

His Majesty handed me the pen I would use to sign away much of his power. I bent down and did so.

'*Tashi delek*,' he congratulated me. I made a slight bow, averting my gaze to avoid eye contact with the King, and shuffled backwards before turning around toward my seat.

It is done, I thought to myself, as I glanced up and saw the King's father, the Fourth King, looking quite content. He looked so much like a proud father, as he observed what was happening in the Grand Assembly Hall. His presence and approval were a reassuring sign that we were indeed doing the right thing.

The Making of a Constitution

Across sovereign nations, the constitution is regarded as a sacred document that upholds the rights and liberties of its people. It is a fundamental set of laws that determine the governance of the country and reflects the unique philosophies and objectives of the people in the land.

Constitutions also prepare a people for the future by promoting progress, stability, and values, and make up a key pillar of democracy. They defend political processes of a country for generations to come by harnessing the power of the people and define the relationships between different entities within the state, their powers, and their responsibilities.

Thus, a constitution profoundly affects how well a country functions and the quality of life in it, including how people are protected, recognized, and respected as individuals. Most importantly, a constitution binds political players and the government by a set of laws that determine how they are to function, within limits, to prevent instances of corruption, dictatorship, and oppression. Ultimately, a constitution embodies the identity of a people, declaring to the world what they stand for as a nation and their vision for the future.

Codes of law have been known to exist since prehistoric times— the earliest known is said to have been composed by the Sumerian king Urukagina of Lagash in 2300 BC. There has been some debate surrounding the first written constitution in pre-modern times. Is it the one written by Athens' ruler Solon in 594 BC or the Constitution of Medina, drafted by the Islamic prophet Muhammad in 622 AD? Most such constitutions were partially written, but the first completely written national constitution is that of the United States, ratified on 21 June 1788. Since then, the idea of a single national constitution has become popular all over the world.

Poland and France adopted their first constitutions in the 1790s, and the European Revolutions of 1848 resulted in the creation of dozens of new ones that year alone. It became clear that changes of government were marked by adopting a new constitution. Today, almost every country in the world has a codified constitution, with a few exceptions such as Saudi Arabia, the United Kingdom, Israel, and New Zealand.

Bhutan's Constitution was ratified on 18 July 2008. Prior to democracy, Bhutan, like every other civilization, had its own set of laws and codes of justice. The Zhabdrung promulgated the first set of laws for the country, which achieved unity for the land by the time of his passing in 1651. Known as Kathrim, the laws were based closely on Buddhist principles, with specific references to ten pious acts and sixteen virtuous acts of social piety. These laws included refraining from taking life, refraining from being malicious, and banning dishonesty, greed, selfishness, and being short-tempered.

After the Third King established the National Assembly in 1953, he also abolished serfdom and slavery and enacted the Thrimzhung Chhenmo ('Supreme Law') in 1959. The document was similar to other constitutions, guaranteeing fundamental rights, equality of persons before a court of law, the right to own and inherit properties without discrimination, and the right to marriage and family.

In November 2001, the Fourth King set into motion an important step towards democracy—by inaugurating the drafting ceremony of a new Bhutanese Constitution. Thereafter, the drafting committee started getting busy with creating one of the most important documents in Bhutanese history.

The Constitution of Bhutan ranks among the fifteen shortest in the world. Comprising thirty-five articles in total, the Constitution is comprehensive yet brief. It consists of only twelve chapters, which are further divided into thirty-five articles and 352 clauses, and is only 3,814 words long. (This is still longer than, say, the Constitution of Monaco.)

On the contrary, the longest constitution in the world happens to be that of the largest democracy in the world—the Constitution of India. Containing 444 articles and 106 amendments, it is 146,385 words long in its English language version. This makes it thirty times longer than the US Constitution, and it is still growing. The Indian Constitution, composed between 1947 and 1950 after its independence from the British Empire, is also one of the most-amended constitutions in the world, with 127 formal changes to date. It is a mammoth task to read through the whole document!

Every constitution in the world is unique to its country. It is mostly derived from the nation's own historical, climatic, economic, cultural, and geographical conditions. It reflects the history, culture, aspirations, and vision of the people in the nation. Besides embodying these features, a constitution defines the various arms of government, their roles and responsibilities, and includes in these details, certain checks and balances to prevent power from being concentrated in the hands of one person or a group of people. These are some of the universal features of most constitutions around the world and Bhutan is no exception.

Our Constitution guarantees free speech, the right to assembly and private property ownership, and allocates power to government institutions. However, there are many aspects of Bhutan's Constitution that are unique and almost unheard of elsewhere. These features determine the length of a monarch's rule, provisions for the abdication of the king, along with sections covering the environment, parliament, and welfare. These unique aspects, which you might find fascinating, are what I want to focus on.

During my tenure in active politics, I have referred to the Constitution umpteen times, mainly because I wanted to familiarize myself with the workings of the state and institutions but also because I found certain provisions rather fascinating, intriguing, and courageous. It compels me to think about how my nation would respond to certain situations that I see in other countries.

Most constitutions around the world were introduced either by popular demand from the people or because it was the need of the hour. This is especially so when a country is trying to establish a fairer, democratic society, typically after a time of crisis. This happens often when a country becomes independent, such as India, or when a dictator falls or during events of massive upheaval, such as the Arab Spring, the fall of the Berlin Wall, and the end of apartheid in South Africa. In certain countries, pressure from foreign powers has led to a constitution being made, such as in post-war Japan where the US guided the drafting of a new Japanese Constitution after World War II. On some occasions, constitutions have been promulgated by authoritarian regimes after a coup.

In other words, constitutions are mainly written in times of strife with the purpose of moving forward as a society. Rarely has one been written during peacetime, since there is no need for one when there is peace and stability, and citizens are happy and prosperous. This is the first thing that makes the Bhutan Constitution stand apart from others in the world. Our Constitution was introduced at a time of extended peace, stability, and tranquillity. We had progressed into a modern economy, living standards had improved, and people were largely satisfied. Bhutanese felt fortunate to be led by a king who had their best interests at heart.

On 4 September 2001, at the height of his popularity, His Majesty the Fourth King Jigme Singye Wangchuck decreed that a written constitution be promulgated for the kingdom. '[The] destiny of the nation lies in the hands of the people, we cannot leave the future of the Country in the hands of one person,' he said, declaring that democracy would henceforth be the bulwark of the people of Bhutan.

His insistence on a transition from an absolute monarchy to a democracy did not go down well with the people. They were surprised and in disbelief. But the Fourth King was adamant that it was the best time to initiate the drafting of a constitution. As His Majesty explained:

Bhutan, through good fortune and fate, could not hope for a better moment than now for this historical development and would never find another opportunity like this to introduce a Constitution that would provide a democratic system of government best suited for the future well-being of the nation.

Today the King, government, clergy and the people in all sections of society, enjoyed unprecedented levels of trust and fidelity. The security of the country was ensured and the people enjoyed peace and stability. Bhutan's relations with its close friend and neighbour had reached a new height and the country also enjoyed growing relations with its developmental partners as well as other countries that appreciated the Kingdom's wholesome policies for development and change.

In many countries, constitutions were drafted during difficult times, under pressure from political influences and interests, but Bhutan was fortunate that the change came without any pressure or compulsion.

Indeed, our Constitution is a product of *evolution*, not *revolution*. It is also a product of peace and of our King's wisdom and purest motives. We were extremely careful about what would and would not be constitutional, and despite its brevity, it took us seven long years to formulate. India's took three years to be written; the United States' was created, approved, and ratified in two.

The seven-year journey of the Bhutanese Constitution from conception to ratification is one of the longest in world history, but it would finally be adopted by the first elected parliament on 18 July 2008. While the process was a lengthy one, it would not have been possible had the country not been peaceful. Any strife or conflict would have put a stop to the drafting. Thankfully, it was written at a time of peace and stability, without any breaks in between. Also, it was guided not only by one king but two, who oversaw the process from beginning to end.

The entire undertaking was as seamless as it could be, so much so that it did not feel like an abrupt change of leadership when the Fourth King handed over his duties to the Crown Prince.

True Representation

Most constitutions around the world begin with a declaration: 'We, the People', which raises the question: 'Is the constitution truly representative of the people?'

The American Constitution is probably one of the most recognizable constitutions in the world that many know begin with 'We, the people of the United States', a statement many people take great pride in. However, does the constitution truly reflect the will of the people? And were the people consulted or involved in the drafting? How do millions of people, who might adopt the constitution in a national vote, collectively write a document that everyone agrees on?

There are many ways to write constitutions, whether it is by an elected group of people who represent the public or by an appointed group. The latter happened in the US, where delegates from various states convened to write the constitution—fifty-five delegates representing all thirteen states (except Rhode Island) attended the Constitutional Convention.[49] It was a well-educated group comprising merchants, farmers, bankers, and lawyers, with notable representatives such as Benjamin Franklin, Thomas Jefferson, and James Madison. To ratify the US Constitution, all states had to sign and approve the document before it became law. The Constituent Assembly of India had 389 members of different castes, religions, regions and genders. Benin's constitutional body was a national conference of 500 members while Kenya used a committee of just nine experts. Spain's constitution was written by seven parliamentary members. In Tunisia, over 200 people were elected to a constitutional committee.

There is no right or wrong while forming constitutional committees. The most important guiding principle is legitimacy, whether the committee is made up of a group of politicians, political scientists, lawmakers, scholars, businesspeople, or elected members of the public.

Likewise, in Bhutan's Constitution, the preamble begins with 'We, the people of Bhutan . . .' which, to me, is a true representation of a constitution written by the people and for the people. Almost every person and most definitely every household had a say in drafting it. Here's how it came about.

When the Fourth King decreed for a constitution to be written for Bhutan, a thirty-nine-member Constitution Drafting Committee was formed. Under the chairmanship of former Chief Justice Sonam Tobgye, the committee consisted of elected representatives from the twenty dzongkhags, members of the Royal Advisory Council (elected by the people), civil servants, the judiciary, monks from the Central Monastic Body, and the speaker of the former National Assembly.

One of the advantages of Bhutan beginning modern development relatively late is that we have been able to learn from

---

[49] 'Constitution,' *History*, 28 March 2023, at https://www.history.com/topics/united-states-constitution/constitution.

the rest of the world, especially our neighbours. We are always reminded to learn from successes and to not repeat mistakes. Thus, the committee took reference from other constitutions around the world. Bhutan's Constitution needed to be progressive, and so the drafting committee reviewed over 100 constitutions. Vajrayana Buddhist and other Bhutanese texts comprising 7,455 pages were also consulted.

We also studied the very basis of the Bhutanese nation, including its religious, cultural, philosophical, and political founding. The committee also looked at previous royal decrees and keynote addresses on policies and rights, both in terms of political and Buddhist discourse. This included the types of rights, liberties and freedoms, human rights conventions, protocols, and other international and regional instruments. Many experts were sought but to avoid diminishing the public's receptivity to the constitution, Bhutan engaged a senior advocate of the Supreme Court of India, Mr K.K. Venugopal, to assist the process with the eye of an impartial international expert.

The committee also considered formal and informal comments from the UNDP, UNICEF, the Centre for Human Rights in Germany, Swiss independent development organization Helvetas, the Danish International Development Agency, as well as Bhutanese scholars, civil servants, judges, lawyers, jurists, and academics. Editorials from Bhutan's flagship newspaper *Kuensel* were also collected and analysed.

After three and a half years of studying and working on the Draft Constitution, in close consultation with the Fourth King, the first draft was finally distributed to the people of Bhutan in March 2005. An auspicious day was chosen and the box of the Draft Constitution to be sent to the High Court, wrapped in yellow silk cover. A conch shell was blown to mark the momentous occasion. (The conch shell is one of the Eight Auspicious Symbols in Buddhism and represents the supremacy of Buddha's teachings; it is associated with truthful speech and strength.)

The Draft Constitution was then distributed to the 'four corners' of the land, as representatives from a district in the north, south, east, and west were issued a copy. (This was a symbolic tradition established by the Zhabdrung to demarcate the boundaries of the Bhutanese state.) Then, copies were sent to households, government officials, students, institutions, and foreign agencies. In order to reach out to Bhutanese residing overseas, the Draft Constitution was also uploaded on the Internet.

Four months later, His Majesty the Fourth King held consultation sessions in seven districts across the country to seek the opinions and comments of the people on the Draft Constitution. The first consultation kicked off in Thimphu at a place called Lungtenphu (a fitting name meaning 'place of destiny'). The consultation process went on for seven whole months, eventually spanning all twenty districts across the country and involving both the Fourth King and his son, the Fifth King. Both kings participated in discussions with local communities, where at least one participant from each household attended. This effectively meant that almost every Bhutanese in the country took part in the public consultation.

I clearly remember one incident arising from the very first public consultation in Lungtenphu. One of the first concerns to be raised was from an old man who stood up and asked why the Constitution was silent on the number of queens that the serving king could take. Perhaps it should be clear that the king could take only one wife?

The Fourth King, who was chairing the discussion in person, answered the old man: 'Perhaps future kings will not be foolish to have more than one wife.' His Majesty's answer was probably a reflection on his personal life. The Fourth King is married to four queens—all of whom are sisters—and has sired ten children in total. (The reigning King Jigme Khesar Namgyal Wangchuck is the eldest son of the Fourth King and the Queen Mother Gyalyum Tshering Yangdon Wangchuck. Polygamy and polyandry are not explicitly outlawed in Bhutan, and there is no specific prohibition on taking more than one spouse. However, such practices—which were borne out of economic necessity—are very much a thing of the past as Bhutan opens up to more economic opportunities. These days Bhutanese, whether in rural or urban areas, prefer to have a single partner over multiple.)

Like the rest of Bhutan, I was shocked to hear that question asked to the Fourth King's face, given how disrespectful it was to such a sacred figure (the reincarnation of the Zhabdrung no less). Nevertheless, I think the more salient point is the precedent this question set. Such an act would be well-remembered as a message that the discussion forums were to be taken seriously and that any question by any citizen would be honoured—even about the personal life of the King. We could not afford to have any sacred cows.

Our kings were foresighted enough to realize that the reverence they commanded from the people could actually have been a barrier to the new Constitution, viewed as it would be as a 'gift from the throne' that was not to be criticized or questioned. We would have ended up heaping praises on it with no substantive criticism, something the Fourth King wanted to prevent, so I am convinced that this question was planted by the king himself.

Was Democracy Even Needed?

Was there ever a pressing need for parliamentary democracy in the serene kingdom of Bhutan? This question surfaced during numerous consultations leading up to the shift towards democracy, sparking intense debates about its necessity.

We had learned lessons from the tumultuous experiences of our neighbours, India and Nepal, which had embraced democracy long before us. We watched the loud, often chaotic rallies in India, which starkly contrasted with our tranquil Bhutanese way of life.

The violent upheaval of Nepal's monarchy, marred by a series of brutal murders and bloody insurrections, was something we found difficult to comprehend. The instability of Nepal's government—marked by several changes in leadership in the past five decades, each marred by its own wave of unrest—further reinforced our belief that democracy might bring turbulence and chaos to our peaceful nation, which had flourished under the careful rule of our monarchs.

Our people were vocal about their apprehensions regarding parliamentary democracy. There was a widespread sentiment that democracy was being ushered into Bhutan prematurely, raising concerns that the welfare of the people might be overshadowed by political manoeuvres. In response to such scepticism, our Fourth King firmly stated: 'We should not be deterred by the fact that democratic political systems have not been working in some countries.' His words were a clear rebuttal to those of us disheartened by the disorder we had witnessed in foreign democracies. Emphasizing the inherent goodness of democratic principles, the King added:

> The principles and ideals of democracy are inherently good and a democratic system is desirable for Bhutan. If the lessons of some democracies are not encouraging, it is not because the concept of democracy is flawed. It is because of mismanagement and corruption by those who practice it.

Despite his wise words and gentle persuasion, many Bhutanese still clung to the comfort of the familiar, preferring an absolute monarchy over the uncertainties of a democratic system. This preference contradicted the popular notion that monarchies are outdated and should be abolished. People resisted change, but as history has shown us, change is inevitable.

There was one last step. The final draft for the Constitution had to be discussed in parliament, signed and adopted before it came into effect. But there were two hurdles to cross: not only did the new parliament have to be elected first, but the Constitution also had to be debated by the newly-elected parliament. After the public consultations were completed, the first National Assembly election was held on 24 March 2008. Two months later, the draft Constitution was put before the newly-elected parliament for debate. This became one of their first responsibilities and a gravely important one too.

The new government took to the task immediately. They debated and discussed the provisions one by one over ten days of parliamentary debate, which was broadcast on television. Some of the major discussions surrounded the local governments, which were non-partisan independents.

It was speculated that the discussions were seemingly an attempt to establish control over the local governments by making them accountable to the central government or even the speaker of parliament. Thankfully, this did not happen. Other members of the then government even criticized the Royal Civil Service Commission, which is a constitutional body responsible for civil servants, for having too much power without accountability.

Another issue I remember being discussed was the draft Constitution's silence on capital punishment. The last executions in Bhutan took place in 1964. They were of a group of three officers behind the assassination of the late Jigme Palden Dorji—the Third King's brother-in-law and the first person in Bhutan to hold the title of *lyonchen* (prime minister)—during pre-democratic days. The execution by firing squad took place at Changlimithang in Thimphu, and the public was allowed to view the execution. The death penalty would not be imposed again, but it was only in 2004 that the Fourth King abolished it outright. This was enshrined in the final Constitution after parliamentary debate; as Article 7, Section 18 says, 'A person shall not be subjected to capital punishment.'

As I sat through the parliamentary sessions, watching the government painstakingly dissect each clause of the Draft Constitution, my frustration mounted. My objections to many of the points raised were not merely born out of my role as the opposition leader but rather from a place of principle. I firmly believed that the Draft Constitution should be accepted without dispute. After all, the Drafting Committee, under the watchful eyes of two successive kings, had devoted seven years to its creation. They had conducted extensive research, sought expert consultations, and carefully considered feedback and comments before refining the language into simple Dzongkha. This was done so that our people could easily understand it. Furthermore, they had translated the draft into two additional languages (Tshangla and Lhotshampa), thereby extending its accessibility. It had also been made widely available online, and many valuable comments and suggestions came from viewers (including foreigners!) who had studied it.

Moreover, while our kings might have discouraged this perspective, our people saw the Constitution as a gift from the throne. In their eyes, we should have approved it on that basis alone. We had also been elected to parliament based on the Draft Constitution, and since it had been carefully drafted and thoroughly vetted enough to be the legal basis for any election, it should ideally have passed without further question.

In other words we, the elected representatives, owed our positions in parliament to this very Draft Constitution. It was the foundation of our mandate, and without it, we wouldn't be sitting in parliament to begin with. To question everything at this stage, as I saw it then, was arrogant and irresponsible.

The chairman of the Drafting Committee, Sonam Tobgye, explained the Draft Constitution clause by clause, line by line and word by word. I could imagine his frustration at having almost a decade's worth of his work being questioned, almost interrogated, by us young members of parliament. Once, during a recess, I walked up to him to apologize. 'You must be rather frustrated with all the debate going on,' I said.

He replied with his signature generosity and understanding: 'This is my job. And you're just doing your job too.'

On 18 July 2008, the Constitution was finally endorsed in a momentous occasion at Tashichho dzong. An auspicious day was chosen and the final Constitution, which today is kept locked with

our guardian deity Mahakala, was brought out in a religious parade
to the Grand Hall in Tashichho dzong, where King Jigme Khesar
Namgyal Wangchuck signed it with a quill dipped in golden ink.

This is a sacred document that we cannot tinker around with
easily. We can't just change it to meet our immediate political
conveniences. That day's signing also put an end to all discussions
on it. Having 'We, the People' in the preamble of our Constitution
is truly deserving. We the People have studied, deliberated, and
exchanged our views on it for years. We the People have examined
it thoroughly in languages we could comprehend and have
understood its provisions. We the People have truly 'written' the
Constitution of Bhutan, and now we the People will protect and
safeguard it—remaining true to its precepts and principles—while
working together towards the vision and ideals it set out for us.

Why Is Bhutan's Constitution Unique?

Constitutions are often written at a time when a country is undergoing
a historical and momentous change, such as a transition in the type
of governance or to a democracy. Sometimes, it happens when
coups occur, such as when armed forces take over a government
by force. Or, in some countries, a constitution is written when an
elected person decides to change the rules.

Likewise, in Bhutan, the Constitution was devised to impose
and formalize democracy, and the institutions required for that
democracy to function well. The Constitution also (for the first
time) formalized the institution of the monarchy, clearly defining
its powers and responsibilities and including provisions to dilute the
king's powers—something that is unique and unheard of in most
countries with a monarchy.

According to our Constitution, Bhutan is a democratic
constitutional monarchy, something that cannot be changed simply
by parliamentary processes. This can only be done through a
national referendum. Like any constitutional monarchy, there will

undoubtedly be an article to do with the monarchy, its prerogatives, succession, power, and immunity. The Constitution solidifies the position of Bhutan's monarch, which has been a symbol of national unity since 1907.

Our king is the head of state, a universal principle of other constitutional monarchies among the world, and a figure who must be apolitical and neutral. In Bhutan, he is the head of both spiritual and temporal matters. He is also the protector of all religions in Bhutan—not just the state religion of Drukpa Kagyu but also of other faiths that Bhutanese practise, such as Nyingma and Hinduism, as well as other religions and any other spiritual traditions. Consistent with most constitutional monarchies around the world such as in Monaco, Jordan, and Belgium, succession of Bhutan's monarchy is a hereditary one based on primogeniture, where the eldest son is normally the heir apparent. Currently, the Fifth King's eldest child is a son, Crown Prince Jigme Namgyal Wangchuck, who is slated to succeed the Golden Throne in the future.

Hereditary succession of the eldest son is almost universal wherever monarchies exist. But, in Bhutan, there are conditions, even exceptions to this. The eldest prince may not automatically be given the crown by the reigning king. In fact, if the reigning king deems his eldest son to be too incompetent or mentally incapacitated to rule, it is his sacred duty and prerogative to deviate from primogeniture succession by bypassing the senior prince and handing his crown to another legitimate child, even if the child is a princess. In the event there are no descendants, the crown will pass to the nearest collateral line of descendants with the principle of lineal descent, with preference being given for the elder over the younger as per Article 2, Section 3(d).

Indeed, in Bhutan, it is perfectly constitutional for the throne to pass to a queen should a departing king not have any sons at all. Our Constitution is a visionary one, as it ensures that the country and people will not end up in the hands of an incapable monarch. By providing clear lines of succession, Bhutan's Constitution safeguards the future of the monarchy should any unforeseen circumstances occur in the future. There is even a clause to prevent the throne from being passed to a person who has physical or mental infirmities: '[The title to the Golden Throne of Bhutan shall] Not pass to children incapable of exercising the Royal Prerogatives by reason of physical or mental infirmity' [Article 2, Section 3(e)]. Also, the crown will not be handed to a presumptive monarch who is married to a non-natural born citizen of Bhutan.

In a royal address delivered at the closing of the seventh session of the second parliament on 8 July 2016, the Fifth King has explicitly stated he 'has the responsibility to raise the prince in a manner that he was brought up by [his] great father,' and that he would 'ensure the Royal Prince is able to serve his people and country exceptionally well when his rule comes'.

In other words, Bhutanese monarchs must ensure their heirs are capable of ruling, otherwise, provisions of the Constitution will take over and determine the next steps should this fail to happen.

Retiring a King

I first heard of India's Taj Mahal in one of my history classes at Dr Graham's Homes, and its story has always stuck with me. Dubbed as one of the seven modern wonders of the world, this UNESCO World Heritage site is a lasting monument of romance. Mughal emperor Shah Jahan had it built to house a mausoleum for his wife Mumtaz Mahal, who had died after giving birth to their fourteenth child in 1631.

The Shah immediately commissioned the Taj Mahal to be built and for the next twelve years, the country's resources and people were focused on this massive project. Soon after its completion, Shah Jahan was usurped from this throne by one of his sons, Aurangzeb.

In what may have been an act of mercy, the Shah was placed under house arrest at the nearby Agra Fort, and was looked after by his favourite daughter, Jahanara. The Agra Fort is about

2.5 kilometres northwest of the Taj Mahal, so Shah Jahan would still be able to see the monument that he had built through a tiny window. I can imagine him by his window every day, looking out at the ivory-white marble mausoleum and longing for his dead wife.

It is also said that when Shah Jahan grew old, his eyesight started to fail him. Jahanara brought a mirror to be placed near the window, so that her father would still be able to see the Taj Mahal. To me, this is a powerful story of romance, devotion, and dedication . . . but it is also one of misguided priorities and misuse of resources.

Shah Jahan himself was also extremely lucky to live out his natural life—overthrown kings have usually been imprisoned for life, mutilated or killed outright. After he died, he too was put to rest in the Taj Mahal, beside his beloved wife.

History has seen sons, brothers, wives, uncles and even cousins deposing their father-king, often by force. Think Cleopatra[50], Egyptian pharaoh Rameses III, and the sons of William the Conqueror[51], among many others. Such events are always ugly and create huge rifts, fear, and instability among the people. To prevent this from happening in Bhutan, one more provision was added that was seen as a truly groundbreaking and revolutionary move—decided on and fiercely defended by none other than the Fourth King himself. During the drafting, His Majesty incorporated a clause in the Constitution that *requires* the reigning King to step down at the age of sixty-five: 'Upon reaching the age of sixty-five years, the Druk Gyalpo shall step down and hand over the Throne to the Crown Prince or Crown Princess, provided the Royal Heir has come of age.'

---

[50] Cleopatra ordered the killing of her younger brother Ptolemy XIV and installed her infant son as co-regent in 44 BC. She also ordered the killing of her rival younger sister Arsinoe. Rameses III was murdered in a conspiracy led by one of his wives, her son and a group of officials.

[51] Upon William the Conqueror's death in 1100, war broke out between his two sons Robert and William over control of England and Normandy.

This means the King must retire at sixty-five, and his heir must also be at least twenty-one years old before he can ascend the throne. If the heir is not of age when the King retires, a Council of Regency will exercise royal prerogatives until the heir presumptive turns twenty-one.

This unique provision was lauded by international observers, including the Danish International Development Agency, which hailed it as 'a positive and remarkably innovative move'. J.S. Verma, former Chief Justice of India, has said of it:

> Now I am not aware of any other place where anyone in power is prepared to step down voluntarily unless there is a divine mandate [. . .] It is the people's representative, who can sit in judgement over the King's conduct also to decide whether he has committed violation of the provisions of the Constitution. I think that's something extraordinary.[52]

This did not go down well with the people, and it became an emotional and hotly debated issue. The public in every district opposed this clause. Nobody wanted to see their beloved king be forced to retire! However, the Fourth King was adamant about having this provision in the Constitution and spoke about it on many occasions. His Majesty gave several reasons as to why this clause was necessary.

First, if the king occupies the throne till his death, he may not be able to carry out his duties to the nation to the best of his ability. In no way will this benefit the country, His Majesty explained. As the king grows old, he will definitely have health problems that will impede his performance, thereby causing problems for the people and country, he added. He also stressed that the king will only be a burden if he is not physically fit to carry out his duties.

---

[52] From a talk given by Justice Verma in Bhutan, 13 October 2010. See: Lyonpo Sonam Tobgye, 'Making of the Constitution of the Kingdom of Bhutan,' *Academia*, 27 January 2014, at https://www.academia.edu/34887081/Constitution1_of_bhutan.

His Majesty even used himself as an example in his speeches:

> If we do not include this provision in the Constitution, future
> kings may not be willing to step down to hand over the throne.
> For example, 30 years from now I will be 80 years old. At that age,
> I could neither be useful to the country nor to the people. I may
> not even be useful to myself.

He also reiterated that Bhutanese should not think only about the
present but of the future as well. His Majesty's opinion was that
when the entire country is in mourning, it is certainly not a good
time for an heir to ascend to the throne. 'If a king is enthroned at the
time of mourning, the security and the sovereignty of the country
would be at greater risk,' explained the Fourth King.

As he gave these explanations to the public during one of the
consultation sessions in Thimphu in October 2005, nobody had a
clue that the Fourth King was going to announce his abdication
a year later, way before the constitutional retirement age of
sixty-five. The entire nation was bewildered; many did not see this
coming and even though we knew his reign would end someday, we
thought he would rule till his retirement age at least.

But, in 2005, he announced his abdication in favour of the
Crown Prince. 'The Crown Prince has much to learn about the
responsibilities that go with ruling the country,' the Fourth King
said. 'I have decided to step down so that the new king will be able
to gather experience before the parliamentary elections in 2008.'

These days, the Fourth King is thoroughly enjoying his
retirement and is occasionally spotted cycling around Thimphu in
his gho (with no security detail following him). As a result of his
abdication, today we have a king in retirement, a reigning King, and
a future King in the current Crown Prince. I do not think Bhutan
has ever seen such an auspicious moment, with three monarchs in
our midst!

Throughout his thirty-four-year reign, the Fourth King had
been steering the country towards democracy through various

means. His final and greatest service to his people was to step down in preparation for a 'new' Bhutan. Perhaps His Majesty was right: Change normally comes during times of crisis, but it is better to make it when things are stable and peaceful. Also, a new democracy with a new king heralds new beginnings. Maybe that was what the Fourth King had hoped for—to begin things with a clean slate.

A Mandate of the People

Bhutan's constitutional early retirement for reigning kings is indeed a good idea. Usually, the new monarch's accession happens instantly upon the death of a reigning king, hence the proclamation: 'The King has died. Long live the King!'

With a retirement clause for Bhutan's monarch, this situation is unlikely to occur unless the king passes suddenly. More importantly, it pre-empts a situation of forced abdication through a coup or some other situation leading to the king being overthrown.

It helps that we Bhutanese, despite revering our kings, do not regard them as having a 'divine right' to rule. Many monarchs, including the British monarchy, justify their rule as such—they believe they are God's representatives on earth, so they cannot resign. Until her death in September 2022, Queen Elizabeth II was the world's longest-reigning monarch. During her twenty-first birthday speech in 1947, she declared her intention never to retire, vowing to dedicate her life to the Commonwealth.[53]

It is not an easy task for a monarch to resign either, if their office is regarded as a mandate from heaven. This is the reason why most monarchs rule until their deaths and, until recently, maintained a stronghold over absolute power. For instance, Japan faced a

---

[53] Queen Elizabeth II declared this at her twenty-first birthday speech in 1947, before ascending the throne in 1952. See: 'Not performed for 200 years in Japan, abdication seen recently in monarchies in Europe — and Bhutan,' *The Japan Times*, 30 April 2019, at https://www.japantimes.co.jp/news/2019/04/30/national/not-performed-200-years-japan-abdication-seen-recently-monarchies-europe-bhutan.

constitutional crisis when former emperor Akihito expressed his desire to relinquish the Chrysanthemum Throne after a thirty-year reign. In Japan, the emperor is traditionally known as the 'heavenly sovereign', with no provision in the constitution to allow a reigning emperor to step down. Japan's Imperial Household Law also stipulates that a new heir can ascend the throne only upon the death of the emperor. For 200 years, no monarch in Japan had abdicated and every emperor had since ruled till his death. As early as 2009, Emperor Akihito had been subtly hinting at handing his position to the crown prince.

In 2016, he addressed the nation by saying that with his declining fitness level, '[it] may become difficult for me to carry out my duties'. It took nearly two years before the eighty-five-year-old emperor was granted a one-time exception to abdicate after the Japanese parliament enacted a special law allowing him to do so. The government initially feared that permitting abdication might be unconstitutional, as the emperor's actions are restricted by Japan's post-World War II constitution. Since the end of World War II, the emperor has held a symbolic role without governing powers, ensuring that the will of the emperor does not supersede existing laws.

Monarchs around the world, such as those of the Netherlands and Belgium and even Pope Benedict XVI, have abdicated due to old age or sickness, preferring not to rule till their deaths. So, why is it that, in Bhutan, it is possible for a king to retire or resign? This boils down to how our monarchy began in the first place. Instead of claiming a mandate from heaven, our First King became a hereditary monarch because of a mandate from the people, not God or heaven. He was elected king in 1907 to end two centuries of civil war.

This means that despite our reverence of them, to the point of them almost being god-like to us, it is crucial to remember that Bhutan's kings never claimed to have a divine right to rule. Our love for them is born out of their compassion, their work, and the sacrifices they have made for the country. It comes from what they have done not who they are. The king rules because we the people let him—this is still the case, even if we believe, as we do of our Fourth King, that he is an incarnation of Cherenzig or Avalokiteshwara, the Buddha of Compassion, as well as the Zhabdrung.

Because people mandated his rule, they can strip it away, as instituted and enshrined in the Constitution by our kings. In other words, our kings made sure that while the Constitution reinforces the institution of the monarchy, it also provides clauses for a king's power to be legally taken away.

Constitutionally, the monarch is regarded as sacrosanct and not answerable in a court of law.[54] He is the only person in the kingdom who is allowed to award titles and grant citizenship, *kidu* (welfare handouts), and amnesty. However, there are clauses in place for the king to be made to step down should he wilfully violate the Constitution or suffer from permanent mental disability.

A motion can be tabled against a king at a joint sitting of parliament if no less than two-thirds of the total number of members of parliament submit such a motion. The chief justice will preside over this joint sitting. Should no less than three-fourths of the total number of members of parliament pass the motion for abdication, the final decision on the king's abdication will be made through a national referendum. This means the decision on whether a king is to abdicate from the throne will lie in the hands of the people through a simple majority of the total number of votes cast. If the resolution is approved, the king will then have to relinquish his throne in favour of the heir apparent.

This unique provision in the Constitution ensures the sovereignty of the people while keeping abdication serious enough to only be considered in extreme cases, such as the stability of the nation. As the Fourth King has said, the country is more important than the king, therefore it is imperative that clauses for the removal

---

[54] The Druk Gyalpo shall not be answerable in a court of law for His actions and His person shall be sacrosanct [Article 2, Section 15].

of a king are put in place. 'The King can do no wrong' is not a consideration here!

By implementing this provision, together with the clause about retirement at sixty-five, the monarch himself had allowed the powers of the monarchy to be diluted for the sake of the country and people. This benevolent move is an unprecedented one and is perhaps one of the most unique aspects of Bhutan's Constitution. It also demonstrates that our monarchy is not authoritative or dictatorial. It reigns by the principles of democracy with the power vested in the people, instead of one's birthright.

As mandated by the Constitution, one of the king's crucial duties is to grace every inaugural and final ceremony of each parliament session. Since the inauguration of the first democratically elected parliament, His Majesty the Fifth King has maintained an unbroken record of attendance at these parliament sessions, a testament to his unwavering dedication.

These sessions serve as a platform for His Majesty to address not just the parliament but also the nation at large, given that these proceedings are broadcast live on television. These addresses often include announcements of significant national importance. A notable example was the royal wedding announcement, where His Majesty unveiled his plans to marry and expressed his unwavering faith in Her Majesty Jetsun Pema as the future queen of Bhutan.

Moreover, these sessions provide His Majesty with the opportunity to underline the responsibilities of the government, advocate for ethical practices, and stress the importance of preserving our distinctive political system. The Fifth King consistently reminds the government that their success is contingent on their diligence and the support of the people. However, should they falter, it is both his duty and the responsibility of the citizens to hold them accountable.

The Constitution also affirms the king's role as the supreme commander in chief of the armed forces and militia. This is also the case in other constitutional monarchies: Thailand, the United

Kingdom, Malaysia, Brunei, Denmark, Norway, Saudi Arabia, and Spain all have their monarchs as the leader of their country's armed forces.

It is an imperative move that keeps the military outside the influence of politics. Defence and security of the nation is solely the responsibility of our king, which is why in Bhutan, we do not have a defence minister within our cabinet, unlike other constitutional monarchies such as Spain, the United Kingdom, Thailand and others.

Not having a defence minister in an elected parliament is not standard practice and probably flies in the face of democratic principles, but in Bhutan's context, it is important for the king to be the one commanding our military. First, for a small country with limited resources, a disciplined and motivated army is critical. If the army was answerable to the government of the day, they would not be as motivated as they would be if they were fighting for the king. Second, if the government is involved, it runs the risk of politicizing the army, or the army pandering to the government for malicious motives. Either way, it is not an ideal situation—governments have been overthrown by their own armed forces before.

The army must be kept in check by a neutral party. It is stated in our Constitution that Bhutan will never declare war against a foreign state, as Article 28, Section 6 declares: 'Bhutan shall not use military force against a foreign State except in self-defence or for the purpose of maintaining its security, territorial integrity and sovereignty.' The Royal Bhutan Army may be a small force of just over 10,000, but it has a storied history of defending the country against much bigger powers, and as we have noted, it has participated in armed conflict as recently as 2003 to defend its country from foreign militants.

This declaration may sound silly on the surface—how can tiny Bhutan wage war against larger powers? However, it has indeed happened before and could happen again, as Bhutanese troops have invaded territories such as Tibet, Sikkim, and parts of India. This clause is set in place to prevent future unnecessary warfare and is a laudable declaration that stems from Buddhist principles and a positive diplomatic policy. This clause was inserted of our own accord—no foreign power imposed it on us, unlike Japan's post-war Constitution, which, under the supervision of the United States, renounced its right to wage war.

Besides the army, the civil service and clergy must also be neutral and apolitical. In Bhutan, civil servants are not permitted to join or form political parties unless they resign, but they are allowed to vote. However, monks, nuns, or other religious figures are not allowed to join politics or participate in the electoral process. They may not campaign, join a political party, or even vote. Members of the royal family are also not allowed to do so, unless they renounce their status, a rule in place under the Election Act of 2008. These groups of people must remain above the conflict that comes with politicking.

One final note about our royal family—that is, the king, his siblings, their spouses, and their children. The Constitution does allow them to receive annuities from the state, and while I am not at liberty to give the exact amount, it would be fantastic if I could. It is actually *less* than the earnings of many private citizens and public servants, and this amount has never been increased. During my first tenure in office, a raise in their annuities was considered . . . only for the Fifth King to refuse to even let us discuss it!

Some of our royal family own some real estate, but they are not the most prosperous businesspeople. They are nowhere near the richest people in Bhutan and are perfectly fine with this. As for the King himself, he has no personal wealth whatsoever, in comparison to the world's wealthiest royal families. For instance, the King of Thailand's net worth is estimated to be $43 billion while the Sultan of Brunei's is $28 billion.

His Majesty himself resides in a small, single-storied palace below the magnificent Tashicho dzong. Most visitors mistake the large, grand Tashicho dzong as the palace itself! He also drives a small, electric car, with no security convoy following him around.

In living so modestly, the Fifth King is following the example of his father the Fourth King, who is known for his humble lifestyle—he lives in a cluster of log cabins in a pine forest. (We call it Samtenling Palace, despite its unassuming nature.) The Fourth King also prefers to drive around in his old and trusty vehicles to newer, more fancy ones.

The powers and scope of the monarchy in Bhutan are outlined and defined very clearly in our Constitution. It also prevents the King from gaining too much power, as parliament is prohibited from amending any sections within Article 2 on the institution of the monarchy to give the king more powers. Future kings will have to comply with all the provisions listed in Article 2, and if anyone wants to change anything, it will have to be through a national referendum, where the people will decide directly.

So, while the institution of the monarchy is immutable, its mandate is and will always come from the people of Bhutan.

Chapter Seven

Carbon Negativity and National Leadership

We have an economy that needs to grow, whether or not it makes us thrive; we need an economy that makes us thrive, whether or not it grows.

—Kate Raworth, *Doughnut Economics*

In the annals of our history, the transition from an absolute monarchy to a constitutional monarchy represents a significant milestone. This was a move inspired by enlightened leadership, where personal power was willingly surrendered for the greater good of the nation.

As we have seen, our kings have made one bold decision after another to 'sign away' power from themselves to the people, by entrusting it to a democratically elected parliament. This was not a demand voiced by the people; it was an initiative taken by the monarchy, reflecting their deep commitment to the welfare and progress of Bhutan.

This transition to democracy parallels another remarkable achievement of Bhutan—carbon negativity. Our country has always placed enormous emphasis on environmental protection. We understood early on that economic development should not come at the expense of our environment. This philosophy, deeply rooted in our culture and spirituality, has been championed by our enlightened leaders. Despite the allure of rapid industrialization and its immediate economic benefits, they chose to prioritize the environment, understanding that such an approach might impose hardships on our people. Simultaneously, they ensured that social welfare needs were met, despite the sacrifices required for environmental preservation. Both transitions have a common thread—a focus on long-term stability and sustainability over short-term gains. Both decisions required immense courage and foresight, reflecting the wisdom of our leaders.

What augurs well for the future, and what I have shared over the course of this book, is our social change engineered by stable, trustworthy national leadership that ensures a peaceful environment for future generations. These leaders embody the principles of GNH and are a testament to the enduring wisdom, courage, and compassion of Bhutan's enlightened leadership.

Caring for Nature

I first used the term 'carbon negative' in 2016 during my TED talk in Vancouver, Canada, where I spoke about the kingdom and our pledge to remain carbon neutral for all time. Since that talk, 'carbon negative' is now—to my great satisfaction—a term that is widely used to describe Bhutan.

At that time, our tiny kingdom was the only carbon neutral country out of the nearly 200 countries in the world. But instead of using the term 'carbon neutral', I chose to use 'carbon negative' instead. Neutrality implies that we sequester what we emit. But, in Bhutan, we sequester several times more than what we emit. To drive home this point, it made more sense to me to use 'carbon negative'. Bhutan generates around 2.2 million tonnes of carbon dioxide, but our forests sequester 6.3 million tonnes of it, nearly three times the amount we produce. We are a carbon sink for nearly 4 million tonnes of carbon dioxide each year.[55]

---

[55] 'Bhutan: the world's first carbon-negative country,' Climate Action, 18 January 2017, at https://www.climateaction.org/news/bhutan_the_worlds_only_carbon_negative_country.

Of course, Bhutan is a tiny country and, in the grand scale of things, 4 million tonnes of carbon dioxide is really no reason for us to be blowing our own trumpet, but 4 million tonnes is equivalent to having flown from Paris to New York 4 million times! So, it is a relatively large amount of carbon emissions that our forests are sequestering. According to estimates from 2020, China absorbs just 18.4 per cent of the whopping 12,295.62 million tonnes of carbon dioxide it emits.[56] There is also a concern that India's forest cover is losing its absorption capability, and it has pledged to grow sufficient forest cover to absorb 2,500 to 3,000 million tonnes of carbon dioxide.[57] This would be sufficient to absorb most of the 3,166.95 million tonnes of carbon dioxide that it emitted in 2021, but without further action, it may be too late.[58]

Unlike people, greenhouse gases do not need passports, and we in Bhutan can testify to the borderless nature of air pollution. Every winter, haze from neighbouring countries enters Bhutan; it is a global issue that requires a global solution. The fact that Bhutan is carbon negative is not good enough. Many countries must aspire to do so, and big countries and companies that are heavily polluting must become carbon neutral.

Bhutan was a carbon neutral oasis by 2009, long before the term 'carbon neutrality' became a global buzzword. Despite its early pledge to maintain this status forever, the world barely batted an eyelid. Even powerful environmental bodies like the United Nations Framework Convention on Climate Change (UNFCCC) and UN

---

[56] Yongjie Hu, Ying Li, Hong Zhang, Xiaolin Liu, Yixian Zheng, and He Gong, 'The trajectory of carbon emissions and terrestrial carbon sinks at the provincial level in China,' *Nature*, 9 March 2024, at https://www.nature.com/articles/s41598-024-55868-y; 'China,' *Climate Watch Data*, at https://www.climatewatchdata.org/countries/CHN?end_year=2021&start_year=1990.

[57] 'Here's why forest restoration is key to India's ambitious climate goals,' *World Economic Forum*, 23 March 2022, at https://www.weforum.org/agenda/2022/03/forest-restoration-india-ambitious-climate-goals.

[58] 'India,' *Climate Watch*, at https://www.climatewatchdata.org/countries/IND?end_year=2021&start_year=1990.

Environment Programme (UNEP) failed to spotlight Bhutan's audacious promise.

Today, Suriname and Panama have joined Bhutan in being recognized as carbon negative countries by the Energy and Climate Intelligence Unit. These countries have made significant strides in maintaining a balance between emissions and absorption rates.

While Suriname's dense forests absorb one million more tonnes of carbon than it emits annually, Bhutan too continues its commitment towards carbon neutrality. Around 735,000 people live in Bhutan, while in Suriname, the population stands at 563,000. More than 90 per cent of Suriname's territory is covered with forests, which absorb more than 8 million tonnes of carbon emissions annually, while emitting 7 million tonnes, qualifying it as a carbon negative country.[59]

The question then arises—how do these relatively unknown, small countries manage to achieve what larger nations can't? The harsh reality is that we have irreversibly altered our atmosphere over the last 300 years through industrialization. Pre-industrial era, every nation was likely carbon-neutral.

* * *

Carbon Negativity and Neutrality

Recent strides in environmental sustainability have seen several countries, including the Comoros Islands, Gabon, Guyana, Madagascar, and Niue, achieve carbon neutrality, with Panama even reaching carbon negativity alongside Bhutan and Suriname. Each of these nations has made significant efforts to balance their carbon emissions with activities that offset an equivalent amount of carbon dioxide, or more than they emit.

The Comoros Islands, an archipelago in the Indian Ocean, have committed to achieving carbon neutrality through various initiatives.

---

[59] 'Suriname is a Carbon Negative Country,' Discover Suriname, at https://www.discover-suriname.com/news/suriname-carbon-negative-economy-country.

These include reforestation programmes, investments in renewable energy sources such as solar power, and enhancing agricultural practices to reduce methane emissions. The country also focuses on preserving its rich biodiversity and marine ecosystems, which play crucial roles in carbon sequestration.

Similarly, Gabon, located on the west coast of Central Africa, has established itself as a leader in sustainable forestry management. The country has vast tropical rainforests that act as significant carbon sinks, absorbing more carbon dioxide than the nation emits. Gabon's commitment to strict conservation policies, sustainable logging practices and expanding protected areas has been instrumental in maintaining its carbon neutral status. Additionally, Gabon invests in renewable energy projects to further reduce its carbon footprint.

The small South American country of Guyana also has a substantial portion of forested land, which helps it sequester large amounts of carbon dioxide. The government has partnered with international organizations to implement reducing emissions from deforestation and forest degradation (REDD+) programmes. These initiatives focus on conserving forest cover, promoting sustainable land use, and supporting eco-friendly economic development. Guyana's Low Carbon Development Strategy (LCDS) further underscores its commitment to maintaining carbon neutrality while fostering growth.

Madagascar, an island nation off the south-eastern coast of Africa, is known for its unique biodiversity and extensive forests. The country has taken significant steps towards carbon neutrality by implementing reforestation projects, protecting existing forests and promoting sustainable agricultural practices. Madagascar's efforts are also supported by international funding and partnerships aimed at conserving its natural habitats and reducing deforestation rates.

Finally, Niue, a small island nation in the South Pacific, has achieved carbon neutrality through innovative approaches to energy and environmental management. The country has invested heavily in renewable energy sources, particularly solar power, to reduce reliance on fossil fuels. Niue also emphasizes community-based conservation projects, and sustainable development practices to maintain its carbon-neutral status.

Like Bhutan and Suriname, Panama has achieved carbon negativity, meaning it absorbs more carbon dioxide than it emits. This accomplishment can primarily be attributed to Panama's extensive forest cover, which acts as a significant carbon sink. The country has implemented robust conservation policies, reforestation initiatives, and sustainable land-use practices to enhance its carbon sequestration capacity. Additionally, Panama's commitment to renewable energy and low-impact agriculture further supports its carbon negative status.

These countries have demonstrated remarkable progress in their environmental efforts, each leveraging their unique natural resources and implementing forward-thinking policies to achieve and maintain carbon neutrality or negativity, setting examples for other nations seeking to develop economically in an environmentally sustainable way. Perhaps the time is ripe for an alliance of carbon negative countries that showcases the work done to reach carbon negativity and call for more action from the industrialized world.

* * *

Despite the impact of the Covid-19 pandemic, even a drastic reduction in human activity did little to curb carbon emissions. However, not all hope is lost. Instruments like the Paris Agreement bring together nations in a unified effort to limit global warming. Countries like Denmark, France, Norway, Sweden, New Zealand, Hungary, and the United Kingdom are leading the race to net-zero emissions.

Critics may argue Bhutan's carbon-negative status is due to its lack of industrialization and underdevelopment. While it is true that Bhutan hasn't contributed significantly to industrialization, it is a fallacy to link underdevelopment with carbon neutrality. Many underdeveloped countries are also not industrialized, yet they are net carbon positive—some heavily so.

The fact remains that industrialization is the primary reason for our current environmental predicament. Almost every country in the world is generating more carbon than absorbing it. This did not even stop with the Covid-19 pandemic and the largest decline of global greenhouse gases on record (roughly 2.4 billion tonnes) triggered by forced lockdowns and travel restrictions.

To make things more precarious, 2023 was the hottest year on record.[60] This is on the heels of the past eight years all being the warmest on record, as estimated by the World Meteorological Organization.[61] Are we heading towards a point of no return?

Bhutan's achievement does not diminish due to its lacking industrialization. Instead, it highlights a possible path forward for other nations. The question remains—how did Bhutan, a country smaller than Switzerland, not just meet but surpass global carbon emission goals? This is a question worth exploring as we tackle the monumental task of reversing climate change.

Bhutan's geographical location undeniably plays an essential role in its carbon negative status. Although nestled within the majestic Himalayas, a significant portion of Bhutan's southern districts bask in tropical, humid, and balmy conditions. The country's landscape stretches from a mere 100 metres above sea level to a staggering 7,500 metres at its pinnacle. This vast altitude range, combined with our location just outside the tropics (around 27 degrees north in latitude) and our proximity to the Bay of Bengal, creates ideal conditions for a range of biodiversity.[62] From lush sub-tropical forests in the southern hills to cool coniferous forests at higher altitudes, the region supports varied ecosystems. Additionally, our sparse population density alleviates pressure on these rich forests, helping preserve their natural state.

---

[60] 'Copernicus: 2023 is the hottest year on record, with global temperatures close to the 1.5°C limit,' *Copernicus*, 9 January 2024, at https://climate.copernicus.eu/copernicus-2023-hottest-year-record.

[61] 'Past eight years confirmed to be the eight warmest on record,' World Meteorological Organization, at https://wmo.int/news/media-centre/past-eight-years-confirmed-be-eight-warmest-record; 'Ten Hottest Years on Record,' *Climate Change Guide*, at https://www.climate-change-guide.com/hottest-years-on-record.html.

[62] 'Bhutan,' *CIA World Factbook*, 3 June 2024, at https://www.cia.gov/the-world-factbook/countries/bhutan.

However, there's another ingredient in Bhutan's recipe for carbon negativity that often goes unnoticed—spirituality. As the last Vajrayana Buddhist kingdom globally, Bhutan preserves many aspects of the ancient animistic religion, Bonism. A cornerstone of Bonism is nature worship. We revere every mountain, lake, river, spring, forest, and tree as the dwelling place of deities or saints. Desecrating these natural abodes could invoke their wrath. Hence, respecting and worshipping nature is deeply ingrained in Bhutanese life.

A vivid example of our harmonious co-existence with nature is our ground-breaking ceremony or *salang tendrel*. Just as Chinese feng shui offers fruit and incense to the God of the Land before construction begins, or Japan's Shinto rituals involve striking a pile of soil with a ritual hoe and offering a sprig from the sacred sakaki tree, we in Bhutan seek permission from the nagas, the serpent deities believed to own the land. Be it for a humble house, a grand office building, or a project like a road, bridge or hydropower facility, lamas conduct *pujas* (rituals) for the nagas, seeking their approval to 'borrow' their land. A vibrant sand depiction of a naga, usually female, is drawn on the ground, facing a specific orientation. Offerings are made to local protective deities for blessings, and the foundation stone is laid only after receiving the lama's indication that the naga has granted us permission.

This belief that the earth belongs not to us humans but to non-human entities is not only profoundly beautiful but also sacred. While legal documents may suggest we 'own' a piece of land or a house, our ground-breaking ceremonies serve as poignant reminders that we're merely temporary custodians, borrowing the land from its true owners in the spiritual realm. The salang tendrel ceremony epitomizes Bhutanese connection with nature—a belief so deeply rooted that no Bhutanese would dare commence construction without first seeking the deities' approval.

In an Abrahamic context, the sense of environmental reverence can be adapted into the concept of stewardship. In Christianity,

Judaism, and Islam, there's a shared belief that God created the world and entrusted its care to humans. This responsibility, often referred to as stewardship, mandates people to look after the environment, not for their selfish needs but for the benefit of all creation.

The Abrahamic religions hold that God created us in His likeness and placed us on earth, which He also created. God continues to create future generations in His likeness as well. Therefore, it is our sacred duty to protect earth for these future generations, as they are God's creations too. Similarly, Buddhism holds that, through reincarnation, we will be reborn. If this is the case, it would benefit us to protect the natural environment and earth for our own future rebirths.

In the book of Genesis in the Bible, humans are given dominion over the earth, which is a clear call to care for and cultivate the world responsibly. Similarly, in Islam, mankind is considered as *khalifa*, or stewards of Allah on earth. Jews have also developed the biblical commands into a concept called *tikkun olam*, which means repairing or healing the world. All these systems recognize that individuals have a responsibility to make the world a better place, which includes caring for the environment. Even without religious beliefs, one can appreciate the intrinsic value of nature and the services a healthy ecosystem provides, from the air we breathe to the food we eat.

Whatever our beliefs, there is a moral obligation towards future generations to leave them a planet that is healthy and thriving. These different contexts all share a common thread: a profound reverence for the environment and a recognition of our responsibility to protect it.

The Road to Net Zero

The Paris Agreement stands as a beacon of global unity in the fight against climate change. For the first time in history, a legally binding agreement has rallied all nations towards a shared objective: to limit global warming to 1.5 degrees Celsius compared to pre-industrial levels. In addition to setting this ambitious goal, the agreement provides financial, technical, and capacity-building support to those countries in need—a testament to the spirit of international cooperation.

Indeed, the Paris Agreement is a bold stroke in our battle against climate change, but it's precisely what we require in these critical times. Countries like Denmark, France, Norway, Sweden, New Zealand, Hungary, and the United Kingdom have already embraced this challenge, committing to net-zero emissions through legislation aimed at achieving this target by 2050 (2045 for Sweden).[63]

Furthermore, at least twenty other nations have drafted policies or enacted decarbonization plans with the aim of eliminating their contribution to global warming within three decades or less. While many parts of the world are still deliberating over the specifics, these actions demonstrate that change is not just possible but underway.

However, the journey ahead is far from easy. The scale of the task requires an unprecedented level of commitment and action. Encouragingly, Bhutan's two neighbours, both with massive populations and correspondingly large carbon footprints, have pledged to achieve net-zero emissions. China, the world's largest emitter, aims to reach this goal by 2060.[64] India, the third largest emitter, has also greatly reduced its emissions. As of 31 October 2023, non-fossil fuel-based energy sources accounted for 43.81 per cent of India's total electric power installed capacity (186.46 GW). Additionally, India's emission intensity of GDP was reduced by 33 per cent between 2005 and 2019, meeting a target set for 2030.[65]

---

[63] 'Sweden Plans to Be Carbon Neutral by 2045,' *United Nations Climate Change*, 19 June 2017, at https://unfccc.int/news/sweden-plans-to-be-carbon-neutral-by-2045.

[64] 'Carbon neutrality in China,' *China-Europe Carbon Neutral Sustainable Urban Development*, at https://chinaeucn.com/carbon-neutrality-china.

[65] 'India achieves two targets of Nationally Determined Contribution well ahead of the time,' *Ministry of Environment, Forest and Climate Change*, 18 December 2023, at https://pib.gov.in/PressReleaseIframePage.aspx?PRID=1987752.

Both countries have made significant strides in expanding their renewable energy capacities to meet growing energy demands and combat climate change; China is the world's largest producer of renewable energy, particularly in solar and wind power, and continues to invest heavily in renewable energy infrastructure and technology.

India is also rapidly advancing in the renewable energy sector, with significant investments in solar and wind power. It ranks among the top countries globally for total installed renewable energy capacity, driven by favourable government policies, incentives, and international cooperation.[66] This world leadership shows the crucial role that China and India play in the global transition towards more sustainable energy systems and reducing dependence on fossil fuels.

Despite the enormity of the task, the Paris Agreement and the actions of these nations provide a glimmer of hope. They serve as a reminder that, together, we can turn the tide against climate change.

I am aware that the idea of 'fighting climate change' can be somewhat misleading because climate change is a natural phenomenon that has occurred throughout the history of our planet. Changes in the planet's climate have led to significant events, such as the Ice Ages. However, when we talk about the need to fight climate change today, we're referring specifically to anthropogenic or human-induced climate change.

Human activities, particularly the burning of fossil fuels like coal, oil, and gas, have dramatically increased the levels of greenhouse gases in the earth's atmosphere, leading to a rapid rise in global temperatures—a phenomenon known as global warming. It's resulting in long-term shifts in climate systems, including melting polar ice, rising sea levels, and shifting precipitation patterns. These changes pose significant risks to human societies and natural ecosystems around the world. As we saw in the introduction,

---

[66] Uma Gupta, 'India installed 7.1 GW of renewable energy capacity in March,' *PV Magazine*, 24 April 2024, at https://www.pv-magazine-india.com/2024/04/24/india-installed-7-1-gw-of-renewable-energy-capacity-in-march-2024.

Bhutan faces threats to lives and livelihoods in the form of melting Himalayan glaciers, causing severe GLOFs.

Therefore, when we talk about fighting climate change, we mean taking action to reduce human emissions of greenhouse gases and to mitigate the negative impacts of the changes that are already happening. This includes transitioning to renewable forms of energy, improving energy efficiency, protecting and restoring forests, and adapting our cities and agricultural practices to cope with changing climate conditions.

We also need to invest in new technology to sustain civilisation while removing the global threat posed by runaway carbon emissions. If technology has led to global warming, it can provide ways to tackle it as well. It's true that we can't stop climate change entirely, as some level of natural change will always occur. However, by reducing our impact on the climate, we can help slow down the rate of change and give both human societies and natural ecosystems a better chance to adapt and survive.

Spirituality is a critical component in the conservation of sacred spaces globally, but it's only a starting point. Policies, legislation, and strategic planning also play a pivotal role in preserving our forests and environment. This principle has been embraced by Bhutan for decades, prioritizing environmental protection as a national policy long before it became a popular trend.

The commitment to environmental conservation is so profound in Bhutan that it is one of the four pillars of our GNH. This development policy strikes a balance between economic growth, sustainable development, cultural preservation, good governance, and environmental conservation. The Constitution of Bhutan legally enforces the protection of the environment, mandating that a minimum of 60 per cent of the country must forever remain under forest cover.

Bhutan's commitment to this mandate has been impressive, with approximately 70 per cent of the nation currently covered by forests, exceeding the constitutional requirement. This commitment to protect our forests dates back to 1974 when our Fourth King decreed it as a policy. Notably, an entire article out of the thirty-five in Bhutan's Constitution is dedicated to environmental preservation. It entrusts every Bhutanese citizen with the responsibility to protect and conserve the environment and charges the government with safeguarding the biodiversity, preventing pollution, and curbing ecological degradation.

This commitment is unique; Bhutan's Constitution is possibly the only one globally with a substantial legally binding section devoted to protecting the environment. Beyond this top-down approach, other policies prioritize forest preservation in Bhutan. For instance, forests are prioritized over agricultural land, requiring permission before any tree can be felled, even on private property.

This contrasts sharply with situations in biodiverse regions like Borneo and the Amazon, where deforestation is rampant due to agricultural activities like oil palm plantations. In Brazil, despite the Forest Code requiring landowners in the Amazon to conserve 80 per cent of native vegetation on private property, deforestation has surged to its highest level since 2008, accelerated since Brazilian president Jair Bolsonaro took office in 2019.[67] However, efforts have been made to reverse this trend, with a joint declaration in 2007 by the governments of Brunei, Indonesia, and Malaysia to conserve around 220,000 square kilometres of rainforest.[68]

Bhutan has managed to keep forest fires relatively small and controlled, thanks to strict regulations and the concerted effort of advocacy programmes, the armed forces, voluntary groups, citizens, and even monks. Although Bhutan does not face the risk of the

---

[67] 'Brazil's Forest Code,' *Nature*, at https://www.nature.org/en-us/about-us/where-we-work/latin-america/brazil/stories-in-brazil/brazils-forest-code; Diana Roy, 'Deforestation of Brazil's Amazon Has Reached a Record High. What's Being Done?' *Council on Foreign Relations*, 24 August 2022, at https://www.cfr.org/in-brief/deforestation-brazils-amazon-has-reached-record-high-whats-being-done.

[68] Barbara Fraser, 'Is deforestation in Borneo slowing down?' *Forests News*, 15 January 2019, at https://forestsnews.cifor.org/59378/has-borneos-deforestation-slowed-down.

large-scale disasters seen in places like California, Australia, and the Amazon, we take forest fires seriously, recognizing the importance of preserving our precious environment.

My parents were no exception. Growing up in Thimphu, my brother and I spent our winter vacations playing in the fields near our family home. Our house was nestled just below a burgeoning forest, a dangerous playground according to our parents. They feared we might find a box of matches and inadvertently set the woodland ablaze. During winters, our flammable pine forests were (and still are) a tinderbox waiting to ignite, packed with dry twigs, weeds, and shrubs. Yet, our parents' primary concern was the potential devastation of wildlife, the insects, birds, and other creatures that called the forests home.

My mother, a devout Buddhist, worried about the karmic consequences of such an act. The idea of us accumulating negative karma by causing harm to these creatures tormented her. Over time, her repeated warnings about playing with fire became ingrained in us. Today, after witnessing the forest grow over three to four decades, I find myself echoing her concerns to my own children.

Our proximity to the forest brought frequent visitors—pheasants, deer, wild boars, and occasionally, bears. These animals, particularly the boars and bears, would wreak havoc on our land, ploughing through everything indiscriminately. As a child, it was hard for me to understand why we couldn't protect our land and crops by killing these animals. But, in Bhutan, hunting is illegal, and while there are exceptions for landowners when non-endangered animals destroy their crops, people generally choose not to harm them.

One vivid memory from my childhood encapsulates this sentiment. One day, I saw my mom visibly distressed as she watched us running after stray dogs that were chasing after a deer. 'Why are you chasing the deer away?' she asked. 'Animals, especially wild deer, will never approach a human habitat unless they're seeking help. It must be desperate.'

'Why would it come to our house?' I remember asking her.

'Perhaps it was being hunted by a leopard or wild cat,' Mother replied. 'Instead of helping it, you boys are encouraging the dogs to go after the deer.'

She then explained to us that wild animals tend to stay away from human beings and would never venture into a village, especially during daytime. If they do so, they're either foraging and will run away after eating, or they're seeking help from humans.

This wisdom stayed with me, shaping my perspective on animal–human interactions. In 2018, while serving as prime minister, I was reminded of it when a Royal Bengal Tiger was spotted in Thimphu. The tiger had ventured into the city and was found drinking from a stream, as it was ill. It was captured and monitored, and, unfortunately, died a few days later.[69] This event reinforced my belief in the importance of maintaining harmony between humans and wildlife.

Living in a country dominated by forests and jungles, we often encounter wildlife. However, the farmers bear the brunt of these encounters. Wild animals frequently wander onto farmland, destroying crops and livestock. Farmers are even prohibited from cutting down trees encroaching on their land without special permission. Despite these hardships, farmers respect the laws, understanding the significance of preserving the forest and its inhabitants.

These experiences underscore the delicate balance between agriculture and conservation in Bhutan. Despite the challenges, protecting our forests and wildlife remains paramount. After all, our commitment to conservation is what makes Bhutan a carbon negative country. The inconvenience to farmers is a small price to pay for the preservation of our environment and the global benefits it brings.

---

[69] Martin Gilbert, 'A Himalayan Lesson – Not Every Sick Tiger is the Same!,' *Cornell K. Lisa Yang Center for Wildlife Health*, 3 December 2018, at https://wildlife.cornell. edu/blog/himalayan-lesson-not-every-sick-tiger-same.

When such incidents happen, our farmers are compensated for the damage. Two types of compensation exist for crop and livestock damages, which come from an endowment fund.[70] There are ongoing discussions in the country about the need to further invest in agriculture, including better compensation for crop loss; desperately-needed electric fencing to protect crops and ensure minimal harm to wildlife; and support for the sector itself as more Bhutanese youths enter it.

While the Bhutanese government plays a crucial role in environmental conservation, the responsibility fundamentally rests with our citizens who live amidst and cherish our country's abundant natural resources. To foster an active sense of environmental stewardship, we have implemented a series of initiatives aimed at encouraging Bhutanese people to actively participate in preserving their environment.

One such initiative is Social Forestry Day, a significant annual event held every 2 June. This date also commemorates the coronation of our Fourth King, a globally recognized environmentalist monarch who has received accolades from esteemed organizations such as the World Wildlife Fund (WWF) and the government of Japan. Since its inception in 1985, Social Forestry Day has served as a platform for students and young people to learn about trees and forests and contribute to their preservation through nationwide tree-planting activities.

In 2015, Bhutan set a Guinness World Record by planting 49,672 trees in one hour, a feat achieved by 100 male volunteers who tirelessly planted blue pine and cypress saplings in the area below Thimphu's giant Buddha statue. This effort surpassed the previous record by nearly 10,000 trees. Today, these saplings are steadily maturing into a thriving forest.

---

[70] Dechen Dolkar, 'MoF not providing funds for crop insurance premium: PAC,' *Kuensel*, 20 December 2021, at https://kuenselonline.com/mof-not-providing-funds-for-crop-insurance-premium-pac.

Not to be outdone, on Social Forestry Day in 2016, 100 female volunteers planted a staggering 49,718 trees around the Takila Guru Statue in Lhuentse, eastern Bhutan. Regrettably, this achievement wasn't officially recorded due to the absence of a representative from the Guinness World Records.

During my first tenure as prime minister, we launched additional environmental initiatives. Clean Bhutan focuses on efficient waste management, aiming to achieve zero waste by 2030 while Green Bhutan conducts annual afforestation activities. Recently, I proposed a new project to Green Bhutan that would allow individuals to offset their carbon emissions by sponsoring tree planting. As someone who now travels frequently to attend international conferences, I am keenly aware of the carbon footprint my journeys generate. This initiative, if successfully implemented, could help not only me but many others who regularly travel for work to offset our carbon emissions effectively.

Although our Constitution now decrees that at least 60 per cent of the country must have forest cover, this policy has, in fact, been already in place since 1974, after the Indian government assisted Bhutan with an inventory of our forest resources. It is a good move to take stock of our natural resources and to understand the state of our forests, but it is also potentially dangerous, as it can lead to commercial interests. So, the Fourth King implemented the minimum forest coverage policy to pre-empt any intentions of harvesting our forests in an unsustainable manner.

Thankfully, with his wise approach, our environment has been protected till date. The leadership that has guided us for so many years has also enacted other policies that have safeguarded Bhutan from unsustainable development. Instead of mining our mountains, we have been tapping into our highly lucrative hydropower capability.

Bhutan has astoundingly low carbon emissions, largely due to its extensive use of clean, renewable energy. A significant portion of global carbon emissions comes from transport vehicles that run on fossil fuel imports. Bhutan, however, has turned its back on such energy sources. Instead, we have harnessed the kinetic might of our rushing rivers, converting them into sustainable energy through hydropower.

Scattered across Bhutan are four major hydropower projects, three others in various stages of construction, and dozens of smaller electricity projects that supplement the major ones. The result of these initiatives is an abundance of electricity generated from hydropower—so much so that our surplus energy is exported to India. In fact, the volume of carbon sequestered by Bhutan's verdant forests pales in comparison to the offset achieved in India through our exported hydropower. This exportation allows India to offset millions of tonnes of carbon annually.

As we look to the future, we anticipate generating and exporting even more electricity, further reducing carbon emissions of neighbouring countries. If Bhutan were to fully exploit its hydropower capabilities and extend its energy exports to countries like Bangladesh, the impact on offsetting carbon emissions—particularly in regions still reliant on fossil fuels—would be monumental. The potential for regional carbon neutrality through renewable energy is within reach if we fully tap into our hydropower reserves. During this process, we aim to lead the transition using existing renewable energy to produce vital resources, such as green hydrogen and ammonia, in an environmentally friendly way.

Preservation and Prosperity

As part of our commitment to preserve our rich ecosystems, we have chosen not to develop all our river systems. Bhutan possesses an impressive hydropower potential, capable of generating an estimated 30,000 megawatts of energy—enough to power millions of homes. Despite this potential, only around 5 per cent has been exploited to date, and it's likely that we will never harness it in full.[71]

---

[71] 'Bhutan's Hydropower Sector: 12 Things to Know,' *Asian Development Bank*, 31 January 2014, at https://www.adb.org/features/bhutan-s-hydropower-sector-12-things-know.

This vision of clean energy was first conceived by the Third King Jigme Dorji Wangchuck in the 1960s and later brought to fruition by the Fourth King, who oversaw the development of the first hydropower project in 1974. Even with just 5 per cent of our hydropower potential being utilized, this renewable resource already generates a significant percentage of our national revenue, proving that environmental preservation and economic prosperity can indeed coexist.

In the nascent stages of a nation's growth, the allure of fossil fuels as a quick and cost-effective solution for electricity generation is undeniable. Countries worldwide often resort to coal or petroleum crude oil imports, drawn in by their immediate affordability and ease of implementation. However, while the construction of thermal plants, funded through timber sales and extensive mining, may seem feasible in the short run, it poses grave environmental threats and sustainability issues over time.

In contrast, Bhutan has chosen to tread a more challenging but prudent path, prioritizing long-term ecological balance over short-term gains. This decision has led us to hydropower, a cleaner and more sustainable energy source, despite its lengthy construction timeline.

Our journey began with modest hydropower stations, and from 1988 onwards, we embarked on larger power projects financed by the Government of India through a combination of generous grants and congressional loans. Today, Bhutan boasts four large hydropower projects and numerous small projects, all utilizing a 'run-of-river' system, which minimizes water storage or reservoir use, thereby reducing environmental impact. This system involves small dams that divert water into mountain tunnels. Exploiting altitude differences, water flows downhill to power turbines, converting potential energy into kinetic and then electrical energy. The water then returns to the river without altering its flow or levels, negating the need for large, environmentally detrimental storage dams. This approach safeguards local habitats and spares residents from displacement.

Despite our abundant hydropower potential, we have consciously opted for a measured pace of development, a testament to our kings' forward-thinking environmental stewardship. Hydropower has emerged as a crucial energy source for Bhutan, providing electricity to nearly 98 per cent of the population, from urban dwellers to rural farmers. (The remaining 2 per cent live in very remote villages in the highlands and use solar power instead.)[72] It also generates significant government revenue through the export of excess capacity, fuelled by India's demand for clean energy. Electricity access has transformed the lives of many Bhutanese who previously relied on deforestation for fuel. Unlike many developing countries, diesel generators are a rare sight in Bhutan, affirming the widespread availability of electricity.

Had we chosen the path of fossil fuels, reversing the process today would have been a Herculean task. Although transitioning to clean energy like hydropower demands substantial investment, our kings' foresight extended beyond merely adopting renewable energy. They ensured minimal environmental impact during hydropower generation and barred private companies from owning projects, preventing profiteering from this 'white gold'. Despite the temptation to fully exploit Bhutan's hydropower capacity, our kings prioritized domestic needs and exported only enough to generate fair revenue for social development.

Harnessing renewable hydropower creates a virtuous cycle. Its use reduces deforestation for fuel, enhances living standards, improves forest health, and safeguards our watersheds. This results in a more predictable and sustainable flow of rivers that feed our hydropower projects.

* * *

---

[72] Anila Qehaja, Dimitris Mentis and Eric Mackres, 'In Afghanistan, Bhutan and Nepal, Off-Grid Renewables Bring Power to Remote Villages,' *World Resources Institute*, 6 February 2019, at https://www.wri.org/insights/afghanistan-bhutan-and-nepal-grid-renewables-bring-power-remote-villages.

Policy Brief: Harnessing Hydropower

I firmly believe that all Bhutanese should have access to free hydroelectricity. Our strategy of providing rural inhabitants with free electricity was not merely a social welfare initiative. It was also an innovative step towards making them stakeholders in Bhutan's hydropower sector.

By providing 100 units of free electricity per month, we were able to meet the basic energy needs of rural households, such as lighting, television, and operating essential appliances like rice cookers or water boilers. This policy has several direct and indirect benefits.

Firstly, it has improved the quality of life for our rural population. Reliable access to electricity has transformative effects on a household. It extends the day, allowing for more productive hours. It enables children to study after sunset, improves safety, and opens up new avenues for entertainment and information through television.

Secondly, it has helped reduce the consumption of traditional fuels like firewood, thereby reducing deforestation and indoor air pollution caused by cooking and heating with firewood. This is particularly important in Bhutan, where environmental conservation is a national priority.

Most importantly, this policy created a sense of ownership among the beneficiaries towards the hydropower projects. By receiving direct benefits from the country's hydropower sector, the rural population essentially became stakeholders. They could see the tangible benefits of these projects in their daily lives, which increased their support for existing and future hydropower initiatives.

Moreover, this policy also served as an incentive for rural populations to manage their electricity usage efficiently. Since only the first 100 units were free, households had a motivation to save electricity to keep their usage within the free limit.

By providing free electricity, we aimed to involve the rural population in our journey towards sustainable development powered by hydropower. We believe that when the benefits of national resources are shared equitably, it fosters a sense of collective responsibility and pride, ultimately leading to the long-term success of such initiatives.

Immediately, this initiative reduced their reliance on firewood, protecting our forests and preserving our watersheds. This led to sustainable water flows into hydropower generation units, which in turn increased electricity production. Indirectly, it also reduced respiratory infections caused by inhaling smoke from burning firewood, improved children's study conditions with proper lighting, and boosted household productivity by extending workable hours beyond sunset.

Visionary Leadership at Work

Without visionary, enlightened leadership committed to a different path, Bhutan's environment would not be as pristine as it is today. This wisdom, courage, and compassion are much needed in the global fight against climate change. Had we chosen a less sustainable path, we might now be overdeveloped, especially considering our difficult geography and landscape. We might have towns and cities sprawling everywhere, spewing greenhouse gases and polluting the environment, and our land might be scarred by mining and mineral extraction. But our long-standing commitment to environmental preservation has saved us from that fate.

Before the Fourth King decreed that 60 per cent of Bhutan's forests must be maintained, national park reserves were protected from as early as the 1950s. Today, over half of the country comprises protected areas, including ten national parks, wildlife sanctuaries, and nature reserves, all interconnected by biological corridors established in 1999. This allows wildlife to roam freely, and flora to propagate unhindered.

Bhutan's woodlands are vibrant repositories of terrestrial biodiversity. Over 400 fern species thrive in these untouched forests, along with more than 350 mushroom species. In the alpine meadows of Bumthang, Lunana, and Laya, local villagers carefully harvest the prized wild *cordyceps sinensis*. The spores of this mushroom attack the ghost moth caterpillar that lives underground. It mummifies the caterpillar, and the cordycep grows dramatically out of its head! This rare 'Himalayan Viagra', valued for its anti-cancer properties, can fetch up to $10,000 per pound. For the highlanders of Laya and Lunana, this caterpillar fungus collection is a valuable income source.[73]

However, not everyone is permitted to harvest this precious mushroom; only highlanders can do so, under strict guidelines established in 2004 to protect the environment and ensure the sustainability of cordyceps. Harvesting is restricted to local villagers, and only for one month each year.

Our lush, biodiverse parks preserve wildlife habitats, providing vital biological corridors for animals. These 'highways' are particularly important for endangered species like the wild tiger.

Bhutan is home to approximately 131 tigers, contributing to a global population of just over 5,200. Many of these majestic creatures inhabit developing countries where rapid changes often disrupt their natural habitats. However, in Bhutan, with its expansive forests, tigers have found a thriving environment.

Camera-trap technology has been instrumental in tracking and monitoring tiger movements. The recorded data reveals that these big cats traverse a vast elevational range, from as low as 100 metres in the south to over 4,000 metres in the north. In 2013, one tiger was captured on camera in the snow of Jigme Singye Wangchuck National Park in Northern Bhutan at an altitude of about 4,500 metres. Remarkably, the same tiger (identified by its unique stripes) was spotted the following year in Royal Manas National Park in the south at an altitude of barely 150 metres.

What's particularly noteworthy is that these tigers move freely across such vast distances, seemingly undeterred by threats from poachers or illegal wildlife traders. Their journey to alpine meadows underlines the importance of high-altitude habitats for tigers and other mammals and attests to the crucial role of ecological

---

[73] 'Hunt for the World's Most Expensive Fungi,' *Taste of Bhutan*, 17 June 2022, at https://tasteofbhutan.com/harvest-of-cordyceps-sinesis.

corridors. Interestingly, Bhutan boasts the highest altitude tigers in the world, leading to speculation about possible evolutionary adaptations, such as longer tails.

After a century of decline, global tiger numbers are finally showing signs of recovery, and Bhutan hosts a significant population. In 2021, a tigress unseen for seven years was spotted with three cubs, and another tigress was also observed with her own trio of cubs. Given the extensive network of camera traps, these sightings suggest that tigers have access to large, secure habitats deep within our forests.

Bhutan's diverse environments, spanning subtropical, temperate, and alpine zones, host a rich array of wildlife. From elusive snow leopards and red pandas to Himalayan black bears and blue sheep, our forests teem with diverse species. In the subtropical plains of southern Bhutan, one-horned rhinos, elephants, golden langurs and water buffaloes roam freely.

Birdlife also flourishes in Bhutan. With over 670 species, including sixteen endangered ones like the white-bellied heron, Bhutan is a recognized avian hotspot. Of the estimated count of approximately sixty white-bellied herons worldwide, around twenty-seven live in Bhutan. Places like Phobjikha Valley in Wangdue Phodrang and Bumdeling in Trashiyangtse serve as roosting sites for vulnerable, black-necked cranes, revered as 'holy birds' in local folklore.

Bhutan's rivers provide sanctuary for the golden mahseer fish, an endangered species prized as a game fish and a decorative aquarium species. Known as the empurau in Sarawak, Malaysia, this fish can fetch hundreds of dollars per kilogram. Despite their value, these golden fish, which can grow up to 2.7 metres long and weigh up to 40 kg, thrive in Bhutan, shielded by anti-fishing regulations and religious reverence. In Vajrayana Buddhism, the golden mahseer represents fearlessness and freedom, embodying one of the Eight Auspicious Symbols.

Interestingly, a recent study revealed that the migratory mahseer fish largely remain within Bhutanese waters, stopping at the border with India. It's as if they recognize Bhutan as their sanctuary![74] Bhutan's unpolluted rivers serve as an ideal habitat for the mahseer and other fish species. However, as we develop hydropower projects along our rivers, this pristine ecosystem may be at risk. Even though Bhutan's hydropower policies require a 13 per cent 'environmental flow' to maintain the river's natural course, this could potentially disrupt fish migration. Therefore, it's crucial we only develop hydropower to the extent necessary.

Bhutan's rigorous protection of nature reserves allows endangered animals, prized fungi, and rare floral species to flourish. Each year, horticulturalists assemble for the Royal Bhutan Flower Exhibition, hosted in varying districts. Organized by Her Majesty the Queen Mother Gyalyum Tshering Yangdon Wangchuck, the exhibition is more than a showcase of vibrant flora; it's also a gathering point for the royal family and locals. The event features meticulously landscaped gardens and encourages local households and villages to beautify their areas.

One year, as I strolled through the makeshift gardens at an open space near Punakha *dzong* appreciating the beautiful landscaping, I heard a slight commotion break out from where well-known environmentalist Dasho Benji Dorji was standing. He was looking at a patch of orchids and pointing excitedly at a peculiar looking one. 'Look!' he exclaimed to me. 'This is a rare variant of the lady's slipper orchid species. There're only five of these species recorded in Bhutan. They're a vulnerable orchid in the Himalayas and very valuable too. It is said that this particular variant can fetch as much as five lakhs (US$6,870)!'

Unfortunately, someone must have overheard him, and the entire plant had vanished by the next day!

Today, even picking certain plants for scientific study requires strict permissions. Bhutan's government has enacted stringent

---

[74] Stefan Lovgren, 'How this rare, good-luck fish is thriving in Bhutan,' *National Geographic*, 22 July 2019, at https://www.nationalgeographic.com/animals/article/golden-mahseer-conservation-bhutan.

laws to protect our flora, many of which have been identified as medicinal and valuable. (For instance, our national flower, a unique species of the blue poppy, grows only between 3,700 and 4,300 metres above sea level. Its scientific name, *meconopsis gakyidiana*, is inspired by Gross National Happiness—gakyi is Dzongkha for 'happiness'. The flower is native to Bhutan and can only be found in three areas here: Merak, Sakteng, and Haa.)

Rhododendrons are another significant part of Bhutan's natural beauty, with forty-six species found within its borders, including some that are endemic. Every year, around April and May, entire mountainsides burst into a spectacular display of colour as rhododendrons bloom in various shapes, sizes, and hues. This seasonal explosion of pinks, reds, whites and purples transforms the landscape, attracting nature enthusiasts and photographers from around the world.

Our forests are the last untouched ones in this part of the Himalayas, making their protection vital. From ancient times, Bhutan was known among Tibetans as the Southern Land of Medicinal Herbs—testament to our wealth of valuable medicinal herbs and roots. Commercial exporting of such plants requires certificates, permits, and licenses, as extracting plant parts can disrupt the life cycle and lead to species fluctuation. Despite extensive legislation, illegal harvesting and trading of rare herbs occur occasionally.

With its diverse habitats stretching from monsoon-exposed lowlands to high mountains and narrow valleys, Bhutan boasts rich biodiversity. Our protected nature reserves host a variety of flora and fauna species. For example, we have over 423 species of orchids compared to Europe's 250, and over 745 bird species compared to Europe's 489. We continue to discover new species of fungi and birds, adding to Bhutan's rich environmental diversity.

The TED Stage

As a representative of Bhutan, a carbon negative country and a conservation hub, I was headed to Vancouver in 2016. My mission?

To share our unique environmental story with the world. I was also there to discuss Bhutan for Life (BFL), a trust fund initiated by our Fifth King to permanently safeguard our network of protected areas—a task requiring vast resources due to emerging threats like illegal wildlife trade and climate change. This was set to be my debut on the TED stage, a global platform viewed by millions each month. To say I was nervous would be an understatement.

For three months, my impending TED talk was all I could think about. I was honoured and excited but also anxious. How could I tell Bhutan's story in a way that would captivate the audience? Would they even know about Bhutan? And, more importantly, would they care? Despite my uncertainty, one thing was clear: This was an incredible opportunity to introduce my country to the world.

However, the journey to the stage was fraught with anxiety. Despite having given numerous speeches in Bhutan and abroad, addressing the world about my country on such a large platform was daunting. I often lack confidence, so I practised relentlessly, in front of mirrors, family, senior civil servants, and even with the TED team via video conference.

When I finally arrived in Vancouver, jet-lagged and sleep-deprived, TED curator Chris Anderson was my rock. Not only did he provide the platform for me to share Bhutan's story but he also coached me leading up to the talk. On conference day, I confided in him about my anxiety and how I had a sleepless night due to a serious case of jet lag, and he reassured me of my success. His comforting words and the knowledge that I had prepared extensively helped me step onto the stage with confidence, ready to share Bhutan's unique story with the world.

Chris's advice was a comfort, a safety net of sorts. He suggested I keep my notes by the side of the stage, along with a glass of water. If I ever found myself forgetting my lines, all I had to do was feign thirst and take a sip of water, giving me an opportunity to glance at my notes. As it turned out, I never needed that sip of water or those notes. Chris's words of encouragement and his practical tips on managing my nerves were more than enough. I am convinced that without his support, I would have faltered during my talk.

Despite having spoken in front of audiences large and small, and faced the media numerous times, I have always been plagued by self-doubt. Each time I am tasked with delivering a talk, I find myself questioning the worth of my content. Would people find it interesting? Would it be of any use to them? Alongside these concerns, I also grapple with effectively communicating my ideas in an engaging manner.

Ironically, considering these apprehensions, I find myself in the profession of politics—a field that seems to require an abundance of confidence. After all, as a politician, one is expected to represent not just oneself but also the thoughts, ideas, and convictions of the public. The general perception seems to be that politicians must exude confidence and feel adequate to represent their people. However, I have seldom felt adequate for such a task.

To me, politicians are individuals who hold strong opinions and do not hesitate at all in expressing them. They are masters at convincing others that their opinions and ideas are the best. But I have never seen myself in that light. Even today, despite being a part of the political landscape, I do not fit into that mould.

Yet, there I was, standing on the TED stage, ready to share my country's story. I was there to convince the world of Bhutan's unique approach to conservation and development, its commitment to remain carbon negative and the importance of BFL.

'I am not wearing a dress,' I began my talk, joking about my traditional Bhutanese attire, the gho. The audience roared with laughter, easing my nerves. Throughout my speech, I spoke about our unique culture, our location between two populous countries, our kings' mandatory retirement at age sixty-five, and the concept of GNH. I revealed that we were not merely carbon neutral, but carbon negative, and pledged that we would continue to be so. It was a big promise from a small country, but it was a commitment we made to the world and our people.

The eighteen-minute talk was well-received, eliciting applause and positive feedback. Most importantly, it mobilized funds for BFL and put our nation on the map. I had never imagined the talk would go viral. Bhutan, being a small country, rarely features in global discussions. I expected a few hundred thousand views, mostly from Bhutanese viewers. But I was unprepared for how widely it would be shared on social media.

The experience was humbling, and many strangers told me they decided to visit Bhutan after watching my TED talk, reminding me of the profound impact words can have. Suddenly, Bhutan was the talk of the town. Tens of millions watched the video on various platforms, and media outlets started discussing Bhutan's carbon neutrality (and negativity). Viewers admired our economic model, our unique culture, and how Bhutan could be a model for the world. Their comments were encouraging—it seemed we had inspired many with our philosophy on environment, economy, development, and democracy. Thanks in part to the TED platform, we were able to raise our targeted US$45 million. Today, the BFL fund is active, conserving forests and biodiversity while also supporting the communities living within protected areas.

The idea of BFL has also spread, inspiring similar initiatives around the world. Examples include Heritage Colombia, Peru's Natural Legacy, and Eternal Mongolia, with a combined total of $600 million in deals closed as I write. Other initiatives are currently under development, such as Bold Belize and Namibia for Life.

Despite my insecurities and doubts, I was there to make a difference, to contribute to the global conversation on environment and sustainability. And in the end, is not that what truly matters?

Part Three

Enlightened Leadership for Everyone

Chapter Eight

The Pillars of Enlightened Leadership

Irrigators channel waters; fletchers straighten arrows; carpenters bend wood; the wise master themselves.

—The Dhammapada, v. 80

Imagine, for a moment, that you find yourself in the venerable position of a king—an absolute monarch whose actions and decisions shape the destiny of a nation. The love and respect between you and your subjects are mutual and profound. With the welfare of your people at heart, you stand at the crossroads of development and tradition, tasked with guiding your country into the future.

Your kingdom faces the timeless challenges of ensuring the well-being of its citizens. How would you address the health needs of your population? Would you establish a system of free healthcare to ensure that no one is left behind, regardless of their financial standing? Consider the foundation you wish to lay for the young minds in your realm—how would you structure the education system to nurture their potential? Would education be freely accessible to all, providing equal opportunities for growth and development? How would all of this be paid for? And how would its positive effects encouraged and the negative mitigated?

The preservation of your kingdom's rich traditions and culture weighs heavily on your shoulders. How would you honour the legacy of your ancestors, building on their achievements and passing down your nation's heritage? In the face of global environmental challenges, what steps would you take to safeguard the natural beauty and biodiversity of your land for future generations to behold and cherish?

Turning to the economic landscape of your kingdom, contemplate the path you would forge. Would you allow the economy to be solely driven by the whims of the market, or would you steer it towards sustainability, ensuring equitable distribution among your people?

So much depends on your making the right decisions. But in this pivotal moment, would you entertain the notion of democracy? Would you consider transitioning from ruling as a philosopher king or a benevolent dictator to establishing a democratic system, entrusting the people with a voice in their governance?

This book has, so far, been a recounting the road Bhutan has taken from absolute monarchy to democracy, and my own small part in that process. Each successive king has seen his powers reduced and handed over to the people. It is now time to consider the values that made this possible and establish a vision for the future that will not only show it is possible to compete on a world stage while embodying them but also succeed and thrive.

Right Leading and Living

Bhutan is a land of many spiritual beings, and indeed, it is said to belong to the gods; we merely seek their permission to inhabit it. The Land of the Thunder Dragon is steeped in Vajrayana Buddhism and holds a unique place as the last independent kingdom in the world to base its governance and practices on it. Perhaps this better enables us to understand the value system that we live under and derive principles from it that allow us to exercise enlightened leadership that benefits everyone, which, indeed, everyone can and should practise.

The purpose, the objective of Buddhism is to escape this constant cycle of birth, death, rebirth, death, rebirth—a wheel of misery known as *samsara*. This life is full of suffering and it is not a good place, so the idea is to escape it by becoming enlightened. (Interestingly, this need for salvation from the evils of this life finds a parallel in the Abrahamic faiths of Judaism, Christianity, and Islam, where the solution is believed, instead, to be regeneration and obedience to God.)

In the Buddhist context, enlightenment, also known as nirvana or *bodhi*, is a state of profound spiritual insight and liberation from suffering. It represents the final goal of Buddhist practice and signifies a complete understanding of life's truths. It is seen as the end of the cycle of rebirth and suffering.

Enlightenment is intimately connected to the Four Noble Truths, which are fundamental teachings of Buddha. These truths provide a conceptual framework for understanding human suffering and how to overcome it.

1. **The Truth of Suffering (*Dukkha*):** This truth acknowledges that life inherently involves suffering. Suffering comes in many forms, including physical pain, loss, uncertainty, and dissatisfaction. Even joy and happiness are temporary and eventually give way to suffering.

2. **The Truth of the Origin of Suffering (*Samudāya*):** This truth examines the cause of suffering. In Buddhism, the primary source of suffering is identified as *tanha* or desire. This encompasses not just material desires but also the desire for permanence in an impermanent world and the desire for selfhood in a world of interconnectedness.

3. **The Truth of the Cessation of Suffering (*Nirodha*):** This truth offers hope by asserting that it is possible to end suffering. The cessation of suffering is achieved by eliminating desire or attachment. In this state, known as nirvana, one is free from all sufferings, desires, and the cycle of rebirth.

4. **The Truth of the Path to the Cessation of Suffering (*Magga*):** This truth provides a practical guideline for the cessation of suffering, known as the noble Eightfold Path.

Achieving enlightenment involves practising the Eightfold Path, which includes right view, right intention, right speech, right action, right livelihood, right effort, right mindfulness, and right concentration. The Eightfold Path does require us to work for the betterment of the lives of others. Its application to politics, management, and governance can lead to ethical, compassionate, and effective leadership.

Because the Eightfold Path is primarily a guide to a higher, better way of life rather than how to reach the next, there is nothing inherently religious about it. Here I present the Eightfold Path in a way that will benefit anyone in leadership positions:

1. **Right view:** Leaders should have a clear understanding of the realities of the world and their role in it. They should perceive the interconnectedness of all things and understand that actions have consequences.

    We are to recognize the reality of the world as it is, not as we wish it to be. It implies understanding cause and effect, acknowledging the consequences of our actions on others and the world, and accepting the necessity for change. In a secular context, this could mean recognizing social issues, climate change, or economic disparities.

2. **Right intention:** Leaders should have pure motives, free from selfish desires. Their intention should be to serve the public good rather than personal gain. They should aim to promote peace, equality, and prosperity for all, not just a select few.

    This is about setting positive, ethical goals. It means acting out of kindness, compassion, and goodwill, rather than selfishness or malice. This could mean working towards social justice, promoting equality, or striving for environmental sustainability.

3. **Right speech:** While exercising leadership, words matter. Right speech involves truthful, constructive, and compassionate

communication. Leaders should avoid divisive rhetoric, lies, or manipulative language. Instead, they should communicate in a way that fosters unity, understanding, and trust.

This principle encourages honest, kind, and constructive communication. It urges us to avoid harmful speech such as lies, gossip, or harsh words. This could apply to any form of communication, whether in personal relationships, professional settings, or public discourse.

4. **Right action:** Leaders should act ethically and responsibly. This means avoiding corruption, exploitation, and harm to others. Their actions should be guided by principles of justice, fairness, and respect for the dignity of all individuals.

    This calls for ethical behaviour and respect for the rights and well-being of others. It means avoiding harmful actions such as stealing, violence, or dishonesty. In a political context, this could mean advocating for human rights, fighting corruption, or acting with integrity in all situations.

5. **Right livelihood:** This principle encourages leaders to earn their living ethically. They should not engage in professions that harm others or are corrupt. This also means promoting policies that enable others to have a right livelihood—fair wages, safe working conditions, and opportunities for growth and development.

    In other words, we must earn a living in an ethical, non-harmful way. It means avoiding jobs or industries that harm others or the environment. This could take the form of choosing careers that contribute positively to society or promoting fair labour practices.

6. **Right effort:** Good governance requires consistent effort to create positive change. Leaders should be diligent and persistent in their endeavours, striving to overcome challenges, rectify mistakes, and improve the welfare of the people they serve.

This involves making a consistent effort to improve oneself and the world around us. It means persistently striving to overcome challenges, improve situations, and cultivate positive qualities through continuous learning and personal development.

7. **Right mindfulness:** Leaders should be fully aware and present in their roles, paying attention to the needs and concerns of the public and the impact of their policies. This mindfulness can help them make more informed and considerate decisions.

   We must be fully present and aware in each moment, paying attention to our thoughts, feelings, and actions, and their impact on others. We could consciously work to be empathetic in our interactions with others or aware of our environmental footprint.

8. **Right concentration:** Good leadership requires focus and clarity of thought. Leaders should cultivate the ability to concentrate on the issues at hand, not getting distracted by irrelevant matters or political gamesmanship. This concentration can lead to more effective problem-solving and decision-making.

   This involves developing focus and clarity of mind, enabling us to stay on task and make wise decisions. In a secular context, this could mean cultivating concentration through practices like meditation, yoga, or other forms of mind–body exercise.

In essence, the Eightfold Path can guide leaders towards a more ethical, compassionate, and effective form of governance. It promotes a leadership style that is mindful of the welfare of all constituents and committed to promoting peace, justice, and prosperity. These principles align perfectly with our national philosophy of GNH, which prioritizes holistic well-being, ethical values, and sustainable development over material wealth.

The Eightfold Path is an excellent way of thinking about how we are to live, but it is also broad and applicable to any idea. How do we specifically apply it for leadership? This is where the value system we know as Rigsum Gonpo comes in.

Rigsum Gonpo: Wisdom, Courage, and Compassion

The guiding principles that have enlightened our kings' leadership are summed up in the triad of values known as Rigsum Gonpo—wisdom, courage, and Compassion—and their ultimate fulfilment in selfless service to others. These pillars are not only the foundation of a life well-lived but also the essence of a governing philosophy that transcends the confines of time and space, and finds ready expression whatever your belief system.

Permit me a digression into our faith and why these values are held in such high esteem. In Bhutan, we revere enlightened beings known as bodhisattvas or jangchub semba in Dzongkha. These individuals are, in essence, Buddhas who have chosen to reincarnate voluntarily. They subject themselves to rebirth to assist other sentient beings, including humans, on their journey towards enlightenment. After all, what is the value of achieving enlightenment if others remain bound by ignorance and continue to suffer in the cycle of samsara? This selfless choice to aid others in their spiritual journey is a profound aspect of the concept.

As an unenlightened person, I do not have control over my rebirth. But I believe that my actions in this life will influence my state of rebirth. Bodhisattvas, on the other hand, have transcended this process. They choose to be reborn to help other sentient beings—it is the greatest sacrifice anyone can make, and the epitome of compassion. It is akin to returning to earth after attaining a place in heaven, just to help other people reach heaven as well.

There are numerous bodhisattvas, each embodying different virtues and aspects of life such as longevity, prosperity, health, and intelligence. Among these, three Bodhisattvas resonate with me particularly in the context of leadership:

1. Jampelyang, also known as Manjushri, is often associated with wisdom. He is believed to cut through ignorance and delusion with his flaming sword of wisdom.

2. Chana Dorje, or Vajrapani, represents power or spiritual strength and is often associated with courage. He is portrayed holding a vajra or thunderbolt—a symbol of the indestructible nature of enlightenment.

3. Chenrezig, or Avalokiteshvara, is the Bodhisattva of compassion. He is often depicted with multiple heads and arms, symbolising his ability to reach out and provide help to all sentient beings.

These bodhisattvas, like all Buddhist deities, are symbolic representations of different aspects of the enlightened mind. Notice that they gain nothing personally by remaining in this cycle; their motivation is purely to assist others. This ultimate act of selflessness and compassion provides an inspiring model for leadership.

Legends of the Past, Lessons for the Present

In the lore of the bodhisattvas, there are numerous tales about each of them, and I hope you'll indulge me by letting me share some relevant ones. One such story revolves around Jampelyang, the bodhisattva of wisdom. During the Lord Buddha's time, spiritual teachers were revered and when they heard about Jampelyang, they eagerly awaited his arrival. However, he was significantly late to his own meeting, which caused much restlessness and anger among his expectant audience.

When Jampelyang finally arrived, he was met with queries and rudeness due to his tardiness. He apologized and explained that during their waiting time, he was teaching the neglected segments of society—women of the night, thieves, children, farmers, and the poor. Remarkably, he had enlightened many of these people. His approach varied based on his audience—he was kind to children, angry with thieves, and compassionate to women. The moral here is that different groups require different teaching methods, and in his wisdom, he led many to enlightenment. Following this revelation, everyone sought his teachings. To this day, every Bhutanese school has a statue of Jampelyang through which we pay homage to him.

The story of Chana Dorje, the bodhisattva of courage, serves as a powerful meditation on the vital role of courage in leadership. The tale begins with Prince Siddhartha, who would later become Buddha. Despite being born into a life of privilege and comfort, he made the audacious decision of renouncing his royal status in pursuit of spiritual enlightenment. He embarked on this journey under the cover of darkness, accompanied by Chana Dorje symbolizing the courage that guided him.

This narrative holds profound lessons for leaders everywhere. Firstly, it underscores the necessity of courage in leadership. The prince's decision to abandon his luxurious lifestyle and family was undoubtedly challenging. It entailed leaving behind familiarity and security, stepping into the unknown, and embracing a life of hardship and asceticism. Yet, he had the courage to make this choice because he believed in the greater purpose it served.

Secondly, the tale highlights the additional courage required to defy societal expectations and norms. As a prince, Siddhartha was expected to lead a certain kind of life, specifically to be groomed to become king. Yet, he had the audacity to challenge these expectations, choosing a path that aligned with his personal convictions rather than societal norms.

Finally, the story illustrates the courage that comes from the right companions by your side, enabling you to go the distance. The journey to enlightenment was not easy, and fraught with obstacles and hardships. But the prince, accompanied by Chana Dorje, remained steadfast in his quest, demonstrating the perseverance that is often a hallmark of courageous leadership.

In essence, the tale of Prince Siddhartha and Chana Dorje serves as a poignant reminder of the courage necessary for leadership. It urges leaders to make tough decisions, defy societal expectations when necessary, and persist in the face of adversity. Such courage, symbolized by the presence of Chana Dorje, is what ultimately drives meaningful change and progress.

Chenrezig, the bodhisattva of compassion, is another figure with fascinating stories. In one depiction, he has eleven heads, a thousand arms and a thousand eyes. This symbolizes his commitment to alleviating others' suffering, a task so overwhelming that it figuratively shattered his head into pieces. The Buddha, moved by his plight, bestowed upon him ten more heads, and a thousand arms and eyes to assist him in his compassionate endeavours—indicating how difficult it is to practise true compassion.

The path to significant positive change is often arduous and complex. It requires a deep understanding of the interconnectedness of our actions and their impact on others. It necessitates a commitment to compromise, negotiation, and sometimes, sacrifice. Goodness is inherently selfless; it often asks us to put the needs of others above our own. (This is not always the case, hence the need for wisdom and courage.)

Chenrezig's multiplication of heads, eyes, and arms represents the truth that it is far more difficult to practise compassion than hatred or apathy, and the support we all require in doing so. A collective effort is necessary to affect meaningful, positive change; while an individual may be capable of causing harm or committing evil acts, it takes a concerted, compassionate effort by a team to do good and alleviate suffering.

In contrast, evil acts can be executed swiftly, without regard for the broader implications. They are often rooted in selfishness, lack of empathy, or a desire for power at the expense of others.

A Journey Worth Taking

Committing great evil can often be the act of a single person, driven by selfish motives or destructive intent. It requires no consensus, no collaboration, and no mutual understanding. Conversely, achieving great good is usually a collective effort that demands cooperation, shared vision, and selfless dedication.

This is at the heart of the need for enlightened leadership to embody not only wise knowledge of the way forward, but the courage to stay the course and the compassion needed to ensure no one is left behind. Evil may be easier to commit, but the capacity for good within each of us is immense. When we come together as a community, united by common goals and shared values, our potential to create positive change is limitless.

We should not be discouraged by the fact that doing good is challenging. Instead, we should see it as a testament to the value and importance of our actions. The road to goodness may be long and winding, but it is a journey worth undertaking. As Helen Keller once said, 'Alone we can do so little; together we can do so much.'

Chapter Nine

Rigsum Gonpo in Selfless Service

Only those who have learned the power of sincere and selfless contribution experience life's deepest joy: true fulfilment.

—Tony Robbins

Leadership involves recognizing that the current state is not enough and aspiring for a superior future. It is the desire to uplift your team, pushing them towards higher levels of achievement and well-being. Enlightened leadership, in my perspective, entails embodying the qualities of wisdom, courage, and compassion, much like the enlightened beings. However, the driving force behind these attributes should be a purpose rooted in selfless service. Enlightened leaders, therefore, are those who incorporate these qualities and are motivated by the desire to serve others selflessly.

If a leader is suspected of acting out of self-interest, it undermines their credibility. It creates doubts about their motivations, casting a shadow over their actions and decisions. In contrast, a leader who emulates the bodhisattva ideal—acting out of compassion for the welfare of others, without any desire for personal gain—earns the trust, respect, and loyalty of those they lead.

This is not to say that leaders must achieve the level of selflessness exhibited by bodhisattvas, as almost no one would qualify! However, everyone can draw inspiration from the bodhisattva ideal, striving to minimize self-interest and prioritize the well-being of others.

In this light, the qualities that define the bodhisattvas Jampelyang, Chana Dorje, and Chenrezig—wisdom, courage, compassion, and a selfless commitment to the welfare of all—serve as valuable guidelines for effective, credible leadership. By striving to embody these qualities, leaders can inspire trust, foster unity, and guide their communities toward a better future.

To that end, leaders striving to embody enlightened leadership equip themselves with the insight to understand their present situation, envision a desired future, and chart a course to reach that destination. This holds true whether we're discussing personal evolution, team dynamics, corporate strategy, family matters, or even national governance. After all, it is about guiding oneself or others—be it a team, a family, a society, or a nation—to a better place.

Wisdom: Knowing the Way Forward

Wisdom is the light that dispels the darkness of ignorance and sees a way forward to a better future. It does not simply involve intellectually grasping the situation and planning for the right solutions but also integrating a profound insight into the nature of reality in them.

In other words, wisdom is not just about accumulating knowledge but also about seeing the interconnectedness of all things with clear eyes. This is because knowledge refers to the accumulation of facts, information, and skills acquired through education or experience. It involves understanding specific data points, theories, and procedures—such as knowing the capital of Bhutan is Thimphu, the geography and conditions of each dzongkhag, the pillars of GNH, the science of climate change and other key concepts. Knowledge is typically gained by studying, researching, observing and learning about various subjects.

However, being intelligent does not necessarily equate with being wise. Intelligence often involves the ability to acquire and apply knowledge effectively, enabling excellence in academic or professional settings. It is by no means a bad thing, but it is not everything you need for enlightened, wise leadership.

Wisdom, on the other hand, is the ability to make sound judgments and decisions based on knowledge, experience, and intuitive understanding. It encompasses a deeper insight into life and human nature and is often acquired through reflective thinking and learning from one's successes and failures. Wisdom involves discernment, foresight, and the capacity to see the bigger picture, such as knowing when to apply a particular piece of knowledge in a given situation or understanding the long-term consequences of actions.

Despite their interrelated nature, knowledge and wisdom are in many ways independent of each other. A person can possess extensive knowledge without being able to apply it wisely. For instance, a highly educated person who has studied economics in depth might understand complex theories on how to read stock prices or the dynamics of supply and demand but still struggle with personal financial management. Conversely, a person may be wise without having extensive formal knowledge. Life experiences and emotional intelligence can cultivate wisdom, even in people who may not have an academic background, enabling them to offer invaluable practical insights and advice.

The role of wisdom in leadership is to envision a better place, to recognize that while the status quo may be comfortable for some, it may not be so for others. If maintaining the status quo is acceptable, a proficient manager can keep the wheels turning smoothly. But if the aim is to transcend the existing state, you need an enlightened leader capable of steering the team towards that better place.

For instance, in the story I shared about Jampelyang in the previous chapter, he realizes that while knowledge involves understanding facts and theories about teaching and spirituality, wisdom is reflected in the ability to apply this knowledge appropriately and effectively to diverse situations and people. He demonstrates wisdom by recognizing that different segments of society require distinct approaches to teaching. Thus, he understands the specific needs and circumstances of women of the night, thieves, children, farmers, and the poor, and tailors his methods to suit them.

Jampelyang's wisdom lies in his empathetic and strategic approach: He is kind to children to nurture their innocence, is angry with thieves to correct their ways, and compassionate to women to uplift their spirits. Through these varied methods, he successfully enlightens many people who might have been neglected otherwise. At the same time, he shows the profound understanding that the purpose of meeting his colleagues is ultimately to spread enlightenment and spiritual teachings. He does not arrive late because he is neglecting his duties. His lateness is the inevitable consequence of putting the very principles of the meeting into practice, prioritizing immediate, impactful action over formalities.

Indeed, Jampelyang recognizes that true enlightenment involves actively reaching out to those in need and applying compassionate and appropriate methods to guide them, thus demonstrating that wisdom often requires adapting knowledge to real-world circumstances. Wisdom can sometimes mean deviating from expected norms to fulfil a higher mission. Our kings understood this as they gradually (and deliberately) ceded power to the people and their elected representatives.

The key lesson here is that while knowledge of spiritual teachings is essential, true wisdom is the ability to discern how best to impart that knowledge. Jampelyang's wisdom allowed him to transform lives by meeting people where they were, using the appropriate method for each unique individual. This adaptability and deep understanding of human nature exemplify wisdom, distinguishing it from mere possession of knowledge.

To sum up, intelligence gives one the information and thinking skills needed to solve problems; it does not mean you're working on the right problems. In other words, wisdom is about discerning which problems are worth solving in the first place. It involves understanding the broader context, long-term consequences, and ethical implications of one's actions. Wisdom guides decision-making by prioritizing issues that have meaningful and positive impacts rather than just focusing on problem-solving for its own sake.

Do we not see this in the lives and work of our kings? Just as Jampelyang rightly placed the immediate and practical needs of teaching diverse societal groups over formalities, the kings of Bhutan have demonstrated their wisdom by pragmatically adapting royal traditions to better serve their people. From the days of Sir Ugyen Wangchuck to the present reign of King Jigme, they have recognized that clinging to absolute power might not be in the best interest of their nation's long-term well-being.

Instead of adhering rigidly to tradition, they chose to gradually transfer power to the people and establish a democratic system. This decision reflects their understanding that wisdom involves recognizing when and how to adapt traditions to meet contemporary needs and challenges. By setting up mechanisms for their eventual abdication and ensuring a smooth transition of power, they demonstrated foresight and a commitment to the greater good.

Their actions embody the principle that true wisdom lies in serving the broader interests of society, even if it means relinquishing personal or traditional privileges. Like Jampelyang, they understand not simply the 'what' and 'how' of leadership but also the 'why'—the deeper purpose behind their role and responsibilities, which is to ensure the well-being and prosperity of their realm. This pragmatic approach ensures that leadership remains relevant and beneficial to all members of society.

But wisdom alone is insufficient. Implementing this vision requires courage because the journey from the present to a better future demands sacrifice and involves stepping out of one's comfort zone. It requires pushing boundaries, not just for yourself but also for everyone you lead.

Courage, therefore, is indispensable. Without the courage to act on one's wisdom, the potential for change remains unrealized, preventing the implementation of one's wisdom. In essence, wisdom is about understanding where to go and how to get there, and courage is about having the bravery and resolve to implement that wisdom.

Courage: Enduring through and Completing Transformation

Wisdom, by itself, holds limited value—much like an unread book. Wisdom requires leaders who can effectively implement it. However, leadership inherently demands courage, as it places us in perilous positions. Leadership also entails making significant sacrifices, including personal ones.

The courage to bear these sacrifices is crucial to lead effectively. Leaders often become lightning rods, attracting both constructive critique and malicious attacks from those around them. To navigate these challenges, leaders must exercise courage to implement the wisdom they possess. While we may crave adulation, true leadership involves implementing change even when it is unlikely to win popular approval. This requires immense courage, as leaders must reconcile their actions with the understanding that they may not receive the accolades they desire.

As the theologian and apologist C.S. Lewis once pointed out: 'Courage is not simply one of the virtues but the form of every virtue at the testing point, which means at the point of highest reality.' His words ring true, for without courage, practising any virtue is impossible.

The figure of Chana Dorji (or Vajrapani) accompanying Prince Siddhartha on his quest for enlightenment serves as a compelling symbol, illustrating that courage cannot be mustered in isolation. He is often depicted as a protector embodying the Buddha's power and strength and shows us the necessity of a supportive community and trusted companions in any journey toward personal growth and spiritual fulfilment. This narrative powerfully conveys that even the most enlightened beings benefit from the presence of others who offer encouragement and support.

Even Siddhartha needed the encouragement of Chana Dorji to muster the courage to abandon his princely duties, his comfortable life and, critically, his wife and children. Trusted companions provide crucial emotional support, helping us maintain resilience and perseverance during challenging times. The knowledge that we are not alone can significantly bolster our courage, as companions offer words of encouragement and empathize with us, making the journey less daunting.

Furthermore, a community brings together diverse perspectives and collective wisdom, offering valuable insights and advice that can guide us in our quests for change in ourselves and our communities. Learning from others' experiences and successes provides practical strategies and inspiration while mentors offer guidance drawn from their own journeys, helping to navigate complex challenges.

Courage must originate from within, enabling leaders to overcome the myriad obstacles they face. However, relying solely on internal fortitude can be challenging. Thus, outside support is essential. While friends, mentors, and supporters can help instil and inspire courage, the ultimate responsibility to exercise it lies with leaders themselves.

Accountability is another critical aspect provided by a supportive community. Companions who hold us accountable ensure that we remain committed to our path, making consistent progress. Accountability partners help maintain discipline and motivation, offering gentle nudges when needed. They provide honest, constructive feedback that highlights areas for improvement and celebrates achievements.

Moreover, there is strength in unity, as people all over Bhutan have shown; a supportive community amplifies individual efforts, creating a synergistic effect that enhances overall resilience and courage. Working together towards common goals fosters a sense of belonging and purpose, reinforcing individual resolve and pooling resources to provide mutual aid in times of need.

Ultimately, the story of Chana Dorji alongside the Buddha on his path to enlightenment serves as a powerful reminder that courage is not down to us alone. By providing emotional support, shared wisdom, accountability, and collective strength, companions and community members all help each of us muster the courage required for personal and spiritual growth. This timeless lesson shows the importance of fostering connections and building communities where trust and mutual support are paramount.

Stepping into an unknown future by imposing democracy, building political credibility, and pushing initiatives—such as power to the people, carbon negativity, and the preservation of nature—forward requires immense political will and courage. This courage, much like the bodhisattvas', is not merely about heroic acts but also about the quiet resilience needed to confront uncertainties and lead the country with wisdom and vision.

Remember, the decision of the kings of Bhutan to transition from absolute monarchy to a democratic constitutional monarchy also took courage—this bold move entailed relinquishing traditional powers and placing trust in the Bhutanese people to shape their own destiny. It required the wisdom and foresight to recognize that a participatory political system would ensure long-term stability and prosperity for the nation.

The political credibility to bring this new democratic framework about also demanded steadfast commitment and integrity. The Fourth and Fifth Kings, alongside our chosen leaders, had to navigate the complexities of establishing a credible and effective governance system, fostering trust among the people and ensuring that democratic principles were upheld. This process involved confronting doubts and fears about the potential challenges democracy might bring and maintaining an unwavering dedication to transparency, honesty, and accountability.

Furthermore, Bhutan's pioneering initiatives in carbon negativity and environmental preservation highlight the courageous and visionary leadership of its rulers. Committing to carbon negativity and prioritizing the preservation of nature are outcomes that do not come about on their own. They require a deep-seated reverence of the environment and an acknowledgment of Bhutan's interconnectedness with the natural world. These initiatives require the political will to implement policies that sometimes went against the grain of more immediate economic gains, emphasizing sustainability and long-term ecological health over short-term benefits. They are the reason we have succeeded in raising our standard of living and building modern infrastructure while revering our nature, mountains, and forests.

The courageous leadership of Bhutan's kings also led to them championing GNH and tying it deeply to our traditions. By integrating traditional values with contemporary governance to enhance the well-being of all citizens, GNH necessitates a continuous effort to temper modernization with cultural preservation, ensuring that development remains inclusive and compassionate.

The actions of Bhutan's leaders, particularly its kings, exemplify the kind of courage Vajrapani embodies—an unwavering strength coupled with profound wisdom. They have bravely navigated uncharted waters, enabling Bhutan to forge a unique path towards sustainable development and social harmony, reflecting a profound commitment to both people and planet.

By recognizing the far-reaching implications of their decisions for current and future generations, they were compelled to act courageously for the greater good. These actions have positioned the nation as a global model of sustainable and compassionate governance, demonstrating that true courage lies in the unwavering pursuit of wisdom and collective well-being. But frequently, we find ourselves lacking compassion.

Compassion: Love and Commitment to All

Wisdom and courage form only part of the puzzle, and the heart of enlightened leadership also pulses with compassion. Change, even when it is positive, often necessitates sacrifice and a degree of discomfort or struggle. Why? Because it demands us to leave behind familiar routines, habits, or beliefs to make space for the new.

Let's explore this concept through a few examples. Many people attempt to quit smoking after many years of being habituated, finally realizing that it is detrimental to their health, socially frowned upon, and often a financial burden. It does take wisdom to acknowledge the harm caused by smoking, and quitting not only improves your health but also your quality of life.

However, knowing what to do and how to do it is only part of the equation. Courage is equally essential, as it propels us to act on this wisdom. Announcing New Year's resolutions or sharing the intention to quit with friends and family are acts of courage, signifying a commitment to change. Yet, I have always believed that while wisdom and courage are necessary for lifestyle changes, the process becomes much more manageable when compassion is involved.

Compassion plays a vital role because it allows us to be kind to ourselves. It acknowledges the pain and difficulty of sacrificing something beloved, like smoking. Understanding that quitting will be a painful process makes it easier to face, and even transforms it into a fulfilling journey. When (not if) we do slip up, compassion is the quality that enables us to forgive ourselves and persist despite the challenges.

Moreover, the concept of selfless service can provide a deeper motivation to quit smoking. While the primary reason for quitting might be personal, imagining the broader impact on loved ones— spouses, family, children, colleagues, and society—imbues the effort with a larger purpose by reminding us of the need to be there for those who depend on us. This perspective can be applied to most harmful habits, such as alcohol and drug abuse.

I faced a similar challenge with language acquisition. In Bhutan, where many people speak multiple languages—including Dzongkha, their mother tongue, other languages and their dialects in Bhutan, as well as Sharchogpa, Lhotshampa, and English—I struggled to learn languages spontaneously due to my introverted nature and lack of confidence. In 2021, I decided to learn Sharchogpa, the language of eastern Bhutan, and Lhotshampa, the form of Nepali predominantly spoken in southern Bhutan.

The wisdom here was recognizing the necessity of speaking multiple languages to be an effective public servant, especially with national elections approaching. With significant portions of the electorate speaking those languages, learning them would enable me to communicate better with voters and help bridge the gaps between us.

Courage manifested in my commitment to hire teachers for both languages, whom I thank for their hard work with me. Tshering Lham (a worker in our party offices) taught me Sharchogpa, while I learned Lhotshampa Nepali from Barsha Basnet of Kathmandu via Zoom. Committing to five classes a week for each language, learning grammar, structure, and vocabulary, and dedicating myself to this rigorous schedule required immense courage.

Compassion, however, was what truly made progress possible. I had to accept the sacrifices involved, like the time and effort required, and the humility to learn like a student again. I also had to practise consistently, understanding that making mistakes is part of the learning process and forgiving myself for these errors. With this compassionate approach, learning became easier and more enjoyable.

Finally, the aspect of selfless service was paramount. Connecting with people is a must in a political role. Speaking with me in their language brought them immense joy and allowed me to form deeper connections with them. An added bonus was our unexpected success in the elections, receiving a record number of votes in the east and sweeping southern Bhutan. This experience reminds me of the powerful synergy of wisdom, courage, and compassion necessary for selfless service to others—both in our personal or professional lives.

I'd be remiss if I didn't include an example of how I failed when I was lacking these crucial qualities. During my first tenure as prime minister of Bhutan, I made an initial push for more electric vehicles (EVs) for the country after seeing their remarkable potential.

The wisdom behind this initiative was multifaceted. Bhutan produces an abundance of renewable energy but relies heavily on imported fossil fuels for transportation, which pollutes the environment. Given our country's short travel distances, EVs would be technically more viable here than in many other places. I was convinced that EVs would not only benefit the economy but also enhance Bhutan's global image as a green, sustainable nation.

Armed with this wisdom, I mustered the courage to act. Working with the Nissan car company and the Global Environmental Facility (GEF) multilateral fund, we set up subsidies for EVs, removed all taxes on them, and provided free charging stations nationwide, creating a favourable environment for their adoption.

However, my efforts fell short because I lacked the compassion to fully understand the public's concerns. People were apprehensive about the range of EVs, the reliability and lifespan of batteries, and the overall costs involved. Some even raised the possibility of corruption! My failure to acknowledge and address these misgivings meant that, despite the comprehensive support structure, the project faced significant delays and scepticism from various quarters.

The principle of selfless service was at the heart of my push for EVs. The initiative aimed to benefit the nation at large and promote sustainability. However, without exercising compassion and empathy by genuinely listening to and addressing people's concerns, the project met with more resistance than necessary.

As we tailored our approach over time, more people thankfully came to recognize the viability of EVs. Today, they are increasingly common not just in Thimphu but across Bhutan as well.

In Bhutanese Buddhism, compassion is a fundamental principle deeply woven into the fabric of both spiritual practice and everyday life. This concept is beautifully embodied by Chenrezig, who represents the epitome of boundless compassion for all sentient beings. His devotion to alleviating the suffering of others serves as an enduring inspiration in our culture and spirituality.

Compassion manifests through an unwavering commitment to understanding and addressing the needs, wishes, and sufferings of others. This profound empathy goes beyond mere sympathy; it involves an active effort to relieve pain and foster the well-being of other people. In the context of political change, this principle of compassion has profoundly influenced the actions of Bhutan's monarchs. Despite possessing the power to outright command a transition to democracy and enforce their will, our kings chose a path that prioritized the long-term well-being and empowerment of their people. This move was not just a relinquishment of power but also a strategic and empathetic effort to secure the hearts and minds of the Bhutanese population.

After all, true governance should resonate with the aspirations and concerns of the citizens. By involving the people in the decision-making process and promoting democratic values, they demonstrated a deep respect for their subjects' autonomy and dignity. This approach required them to listen carefully to the voices of their people, understand their needs and desires, and integrate these insights into the development of national policies.

Compassion has also guided our monarchs' efforts in environmental preservation and sustainability. Recognizing the intrinsic value of nature and its vital role in the well-being of their people, they have guided the implementation of policies to ensure Bhutan remains carbon negative and maintains vast protected areas. This stewardship exemplifies an empathetic understanding of the interconnectedness of humans and the natural world, ensuring that future generations inherit a healthy and thriving environment.

Building up education, healthcare, and cultural preservation have also been priorities that emerge naturally from their compassion. By advancing these sectors, they aim to uplift marginalized communities and create opportunities for all Bhutanese to lead fulfilling lives. This compassionate approach extends beyond mere policy implementation; it involves nurturing a national ethos that values kindness, cooperation, and collective well-being. Their strategy of securing the hearts and minds of their people rather than commanding them outright aligns with the compassionate teachings of Chenrezig, highlighting the importance of empathy, understanding, and shared responsibility in governance. With their integrity and demonstrated trustworthiness, they continue to strengthen national unity and resilience.

Compassion, in this context, is rooted in the understanding that all beings are interconnected and interdependent. The pain and joy experienced by others directly impact us because we are part of a shared existence. This realization leads to a natural response of wanting to ease the suffering of others and promote their well-being. Such compassion is not limited by boundaries or conditions; it flows freely and universally to all beings, irrespective of their status, background, or relationship to us.

This must, of course, be combined with wisdom because achieving equality demands that people of different statuses be treated differently so that society as a whole may flourish, and people may be as free from suffering as possible. Letting a criminal off to re-offend and harm others is not compassion by any means; one can try restoration and rehabilitation, but this can only happen if basic safety is upheld and their ability to do harm first neutralized.

Of course, compassion by definition should be a virtue that is freely chosen and cultivated through teaching and practice rather than being imposed on others. Forcing compassion contradicts its very essence, as genuine compassion arises from a voluntary recognition of our shared humanity and a heartfelt desire to help. Teaching compassion involves creating environments and opportunities where individuals can experience and understand the interconnectedness of life, thereby naturally fostering a compassionate outlook.

In the context of governance, especially as seen in the leadership of Bhutan's monarchs, this understanding of compassion has significant implications. Effective leadership entails more than issuing commands. It requires leaders to understand the needs and aspirations of the people and work towards their holistic well-being. Our kings involved citizens in the process of governance from the beginning, encouraging active participation and feedback while not projecting an air of infallibility or accusing opponents of disloyalty. This approach aligns with the idea that compassion must be freely chosen and nurtured, not forced. By promoting education, healthcare and cultural preservation, everyone's ability to lead fulfilling lives takes primacy, thereby fostering a society where compassion is a lived value.

Indeed, while they may hold great moral and cultural authority, our Fourth and Fifth Kings have ensured that the state is protected from their capacity to make mistakes. His Majesty's person is sacrosanct and he is not answerable to courts of law, but he is not regarded as infallible or immune to human limitations. This is why major decisions, including the transition to democracy, have been taken in consultation with every part of society, from ordinary citizens to clergy and civil servants. This approach ensures that decisions are well-informed and reflect the collective interests of the populace.

Selflessness and Sacrifice

Our reverence for wisdom, courage, and compassion is profound, and we are fortunate to have real-life examples of such enlightened leaders, namely our kings. While they have built on the foundation laid by their forebears, our Fourth and Fifth Kings have epitomized selfless service throughout their reigns. This is why I refer to them as enlightened kings, not because they have escaped the cycle of rebirth but because they display qualities showing that they follow the divine examples set by the bodhisattvas.

Their tangible example is a blessing because through them we can see these divine qualities expressed in the here and now. We only need to look at Bhutan's transition from a medieval society to a modern one in a single generation with minimal sacrifice from the populace, and our monarchs' wisdom, courage, and compassion have been instrumental in this progress.

Whether it is social progress, provision of free and quality healthcare and education, or environmental conservation, our rulers have consistently demonstrated foresight. They recognized the importance of sustainability long before it became a global concern. They've had the courage to prioritize the environment over immediate economic gains, understanding that such an approach could impose hardships on our people. Yet, they've ensured that the social welfare needs of our citizens have been met, despite the sacrifices required for environmental preservation.

This is enlightened leadership—an amalgamation of wisdom, courage, and compassion, all driven by selfless service. It is a concept that can be applied by anyone across various domains from personal growth to national development. Despite the people's deep love and devotion for the Fourth King, he realized that absolute power for himself was not viable for the future and that the best way ahead is democracy. No one had asked for a democratic system, and he was at the peak of his popularity, yet His Majesty had the wisdom to initiate discussions about it, acknowledging that it was the path Bhutan needed to tread.

Then came the courage to implement this wise vision, which meant sacrificing personal power and authority. But more than that, it required faith in the people, a belief that they would successfully navigate this new system. This move also demonstrated profound compassion because democracy wasn't what the people wanted. As we have seen, they were familiar with the functioning of democracies around the world . . . and weren't particularly impressed!

Despite these obstacles, our Fourth and Fifth Kings went from house to house, explaining the importance of democracy to the entire nation—ivory tower pronouncements did not, and still do not, become them. They emphasized why peaceful times, when people are not clamouring for democracy, are ideal for initiating such a system. When people start demanding democracy, it usually indicates that it is already too late.

This is the intricate interplay between wisdom, courage, and compassion. This concept can be extrapolated to other areas, like family or even the nation, where planning bold, wise change can lead to authoritarianism and bloodshed. If such change is not ushered in with compassion, it is far more difficult right from the start. It is paramount that these three pillars of Rigsum Gonpo operate in harmony. When unified, they shape the bedrock of effective and enlightened leadership.

The peaceful and comprehensive implementation of sweeping changes, such as the transition to democracy or the achievement of carbon negativity in Bhutan, is a testament to the power of enlightened leadership. It is an affirmation that when leaders are selfless, trustworthy, and guided by wisdom and compassion, they can steer their nations through significant transformations without causing social upheaval.

Enlightened leaders have the foresight to envision a better future, the courage to make tough decisions, and the compassion to ensure the well-being of all citizens. They prioritize long-term societal good over short-term personal or political gains. This approach engenders trust among the people, fostering a conducive environment for implementing significant changes.

In the absence of such leadership, societies often resort to upheaval to bring about change. This path is fraught with conflict, suffering, and uncertainty. While it might eventually lead to transformation, the journey is much more arduous and the outcomes less predictable.

Therefore, enlightened leadership serves as a beacon, guiding societies through the complexities of change. It is a powerful force that can help nations navigate turbulent times, ensuring stability and progress while minimizing social strife. It underscores the importance of cultivating leaders who embody these qualities, for they hold the key to peaceful and effective societal transformation.

In the corporate world, a business might opt for digital transformation to streamline operations and boost profitability. While this change is positive, it comes with sacrifices. Employees may need to acquire new skills, which can be daunting and time-consuming. Some roles may become redundant, leading to job losses. The organization might have to invest heavily in new technology and training. These sacrifices might be challenging, but they are necessary steps towards the company's evolution and sustainability.

On a societal level, think about the shift to renewable energy sources as a solution to climate change. This change is undeniably beneficial, as it leads to a more sustainable and cleaner environment. However, it requires sacrifices. Industries reliant on fossil fuels may need to revamp their operations or risk becoming obsolete. Consumers might have to shell out more for energy in the short term. Jobs in certain sectors might vanish. These sacrifices are difficult but vital for our planet's long-term health.

In all these scenarios, the common thread is that positive change does not come without a price. Sacrifice, and the accompanying discomfort, is an integral part of the journey. Yet, it is these very sacrifices that clear the path for improvement and progress. Enlightened leadership understands this and employs compassion and empathy to reassure team members that the change and sacrifice are worth it. Such leaders are not afraid to make personal sacrifices, setting an example, and winning over their team's trust.

Courage is the willingness to continue in times of trial. It is the unwavering commitment to your values when they are put to the test. It is the strength required to apply your wisdom and compassion when it matters most. Yet, imagine wisdom and courage without compassion—it resembles the harsh rule of authoritarianism. Without compassion, you risk becoming a cold, inflexible dictator.

Enlightened leadership is a powerful concept, a triumvirate of wisdom, compassion, and courage driven by selfless service. Leaders who embody these principles make decisions rooted in deep understanding, empathy for others and the fortitude to weather any storm. They see beyond the surface, recognizing the intrinsic worth in every individual, and consistently place the collective good above personal benefit.

Their choices stem from a profound comprehension of the far-reaching effects of their actions, bolstered by the bravery to stand tall amid the repercussions. This potent blend of wisdom, courage, and compassion is the hallmark of enlightened leadership—shining the light of hope in the face of adversity.

Chapter Ten

Looking to the Future

Worrying does not accomplish anything. Even if you worry twenty times more, it will not change the situation of the world. In fact, your anxiety will only make things worse. Even though things are not as we would like, we can still be content, knowing we are trying our best and will continue to do so. If we do not know how to breathe, smile, and live every moment of our life deeply, we will never be able to help anyone.

—Thich Nhat Hanh, *The Heart of the Buddha's Teaching*

I have shared instances of enlightened leadership because they inspire me. I do not claim to be an enlightened leader, but nevertheless, I strive to incorporate these ideals into my work. They serve as a compass, guiding my actions and decisions. In exercising my own leadership, I remind myself to be selfless, to think and listen attentively to gain wisdom. I remind myself that I must have the courage to be vulnerable, and the compassion to understand that not everyone will share my perspectives. This is crucial for building consensus, working together to solve the problems of the future, and implementing the large-scale solutions that will be needed.

The Fourth King exemplified these principles in action, rightfully earning our admiration as an embodiment of enlightened leadership. While our bodhisattvas provide spiritual guidance and examples, the Fourth King's life and work offer a tangible role model of applying these principles in the world today. Through his efforts on behalf of his people, him handing power back to them, and his voluntary abdication and insistence on setting a retirement age even for future kings, he has shown what it truly means to lead for the benefit of his people not oneself.

Another manifestation of the enlightened leadership of Bhutan is its carbon negative status. Our commitment to preserving our forests illustrates how leadership can safeguard our planet. This links directly to the philosophy of GNH, introduced centuries ago by the Zhabdrung, the founding father of Bhutan. As we have seen, he posited that if a government fails to cultivate happiness for its people, it has no reason to exist. This belief continues to guide our leaders and shapes Bhutan's unique approach to governance.

* * *

Enlightened Leadership and the Great Fourth's Legacy

GNH is a testament to enlightened leadership in action. In the 1970s, long before global discourse caught up, the Fourth King envisioned a paradigm shift from the singular focus on economic growth to a holistic approach prioritizing the happiness and well-being of his people. This vision displayed remarkable wisdom, recognizing the limitations and potential harms of unfettered development.

Implementing such a vision required immense courage. Bhutan—which was, at the time, striving to improve its economic situation—chose a path less travelled. Sacrificing immediate economic gains for the long-term happiness and sustainability of its society was a bold move, reflecting a deep commitment to the welfare of the Bhutanese people. This decision showed the necessity of courageous leadership willing to make difficult choices for the greater good.

However, it was compassion that truly characterized the Fourth King's approach. His policies were not merely strategic decisions but were imbued with genuine care for the societal impacts of development. Compassion was the lens through which all policy decisions were made, ensuring that progress did not come at the expense of cultural preservation, environmental sustainability, or social welfare.

Central to the philosophy of GNH and the governance of the Fourth King was the principle of selfless service. By placing the happiness and well-being of the people above all else, he exemplified the essence of enlightened leadership. This approach was not merely about policy but also about cultivating a culture of empathy, foresight, and resilience—a legacy that continues to inspire leaders worldwide.

In other words, enlightened leadership goes beyond mere governance. It is about nurturing a society in which every individual feels valued, understood, and engaged in the collective pursuit of a sustainable and harmonious future. This model of leadership— rooted in the wisdom, courage, and compassion of Rigsum Gonpo— offers a blueprint for addressing the complex challenges of our times, highlighting the potential for leadership that is visionary yet compassionate and ambitious yet altruistic.

The strides made in social progress within Bhutan show all of us what enlightened leadership can achieve. The provision of free education and healthcare, spearheaded by the Fourth King's visionary policies, has transformed the lives of the Bhutanese people. It was an act of profound wisdom to prioritize these sectors, despite the nation's limited resources and numerous competing priorities. Implementing this decision must have required immense courage and deep compassion towards the well-being of the people. The results of these efforts can be seen today in our dramatically increased life expectancy and literacy rates, embodying a truly uplifted nation—the work of the Fourth King's predecessors coming to fruition.

Equally remarkable is Bhutan's stance on environmental conservation. In an age where economic development often comes at the expense of ecological balance, Bhutan has stood firm in its commitment to carbon negativity and biodiversity. This steadfast resolve has originated in the wisdom of recognizing the intrinsic value of nature, coupled with the courage to resist exploiting it for short-term gains. This environmental stewardship, safeguarded by enlightened leadership, positions Bhutan as a global exemplar in sustainability.

The transition to democracy, initiated by the Fourth King, has shown another dimension of enlightened leadership. Aware of the limitations of one-person rule and its potential unsustainability across generations, he astutely navigated Bhutan towards democratic governance. This monumental shift, rooted in wisdom, required him to courageously relinquish powers—a rarity in global political history. Even more uniquely, he abdicated in advance of his own set retirement age of sixty-five, a sign that he was serious about a new system under a new king.

His Majesty the Fifth King, following in his father's footsteps, has not only upheld these principles but has also expanded upon them. His dedication to nurturing democracy, engaging with citizens across the nation, and leading the country through the trials of the Covid-19 pandemic with minimal loss of life, exemplifies his ongoing commitment to enlightened leadership. His response to the pandemic and the proactive measures taken to mitigate its impact on the economy and societal well-being highlight a governance style that is responsive, responsible, and deeply connected to the needs of the people.

I am convinced that the Fourth King is deserving of a Nobel Peace Prize. In a world of solely capital driven economies, he has pioneered and ensured the execution of the radical idea of GNH—a development philosophy that prioritizes people's happiness, providing free education and healthcare to all citizens. Bhutan's status as the first carbon negative country can be attributed, in large part, to the Fourth King's revolutionary vision of environmentally sustainable development for the nation. Most importantly, he deserves all the recognition for being a monarch who peacefully ushered democracy in the country he was ruling—a feat practically unheard of in the modern world. For these reasons and many more, in my eyes, he sets an unparalleled example of enlightened leadership—one that the world desperately needs.

While the Fourth King has had international award committees try to nominate him, he actively shuns such recognition because the peace and prosperity of his people is his foremost priority.

* * *

Service Over Self

Leadership is not about self-gain or self-status, but self-transcendence. It is, quintessentially, about going beyond the self to serve a greater purpose. This form of leadership demands an acute awareness of the present circumstances, coupled with a visionary outlook that seeks to elevate the current state to one of higher well-being and harmony for all involved. It requires not only wisdom, courage, and compassion but a profound sense of selflessness, ensuring that the motivations behind our actions are universally beneficial, fostering a collective sense of participation and purpose among all stakeholders. This, in essence, is what I define as enlightened leadership.

My own understanding of this concept is deeply influenced by my heritage and the natural symbolism that surrounded me growing up in Haa Valley, Bhutan. This valley, marked by three large, distinctive hills, has always been seen by those who dwell there as a physical manifestation of Rigsum Gonpo—Jampelyang (wisdom), Chana Dorje (courage), and Chenrezig (compassion). These three hills, embodying the virtues of the three bodhisattvas, are not just natural features of the landscape but protectors and guides for our community. The imprint of this early association led to the connection between these virtues and the essence of leadership being indelibly marked on my consciousness.

On 17 December 2015, during the National Day celebrations, His Majesty King Jigme paid homage to his father, the Fourth King. In his speech, he referring to the Fourth King as an incarnation of Rigsum Gonpo, the bodhisattvas' virtues. This was when I realized the Fourth King is a living example of enlightened leadership. This moment was revelatory for me, connecting the dots between the principles embedded in my culture and their practical application in leadership.

It is this blend of wisdom, courage, and compassion, all driven by selfless service, that defines what I term 'enlightened leadership'. This form of leadership transcends the boundaries of personal growth to encompass the welfare of an entire organization, be it in business, governance, or societal structures. By focusing on these virtues, a leader moves beyond the confines of self-interest to champion the cause of collective well-being.

Each of these values forms a vital component of a balanced and meaningful existence. They are not exclusive to the learned or the saints but are accessible territories for every individual willing to tread their path. The cultivation of these virtues is not a luxury but a necessity for anyone aspiring towards a life of fulfilment and service.

Indeed, to practise Rigsum Gonpo in selfless service is to engage in the most profound act of rebellion against the forces of ignorance, fear, and indifference that plague our world. It is an affirmation of our shared humanity and our inherent potential to manifest goodness. Therefore, it is possible for everyone to practice these values, whatever their faith or political beliefs. Indeed, it is imperative that we all do.

Leading with these qualities requires conscious effort. It is not about claiming to have these attributes within us inherently (I certainly do not!) but about constantly reminding ourselves to prioritize selfless service over personal desires—be it fame, wealth, or recognition. The real question is whether our actions are driven by a desire to serve others.

Understanding one's position, being aware of the state of affairs, and having a clear vision of the destination are essential. It is about identifying the best path given our resources and opportunities, acknowledging the sacrifices required, and empathizing with those who make them. The courage to embark on this journey is a testament to true leadership.

Wisdom, courage, and compassion, led by selfless service, can be found threaded through the tapestry of western thought as well. From the Stoic emphasis on virtue and wisdom as the highest goods to the Christian call for compassion and courage in the face of suffering, these principles find their parallels and intersections across a multitude of worldviews. Such convergence suggests not merely a coincidence but a collective reaching towards universal truths that govern human conduct and the search for meaning.

The beauty of this shared moral landscape is that it does not demand a conversion of belief systems or an abandonment of one's faith. Rather, it encourages an expansion of understanding—a recognition that beneath the diverse expressions of human spirituality and philosophy lies a common bedrock of values that can guide us towards greater harmony, both within ourselves and with the world around us.

By acknowledging and drawing upon these universal principles, we engage in a form of spiritual and philosophical 'cross-pollination' that enriches our own traditions while fostering respect and appreciation for the wisdom of others. This approach champions the idea that wisdom, courage, and compassion exercised in selfless service are not proprietary virtues confined to any single tradition but are the collective heritage of humanity, meant to be cultivated and cherished by all.

Leadership, thus, transforms from a mere positional authority to enlightened stewardship. Such leadership does not merely seek results but prioritizes the method of achieving them, ensuring that the journey towards a better future is paved with empathy and shared sacrifices. Enlightened leaders recognize that true progress is made when everyone is brought along on the voyage, with no one left behind to suffer the consequences of unchecked ambition.

This approach fosters a culture of mutual care, respect, and collective striving towards a shared vision—a testament to the profound impact of integrating wisdom, courage, and compassion into the very fabric of selfless, honest governance.

The Continuing Role of Enlightened Leadership

Bhutan now stands at a crossroads. Our unique culture, vibrant environment and culture of GNH have set us on a path that differs significantly from the rest of the world. Despite our economic challenges, we do not experience extreme poverty thanks to a robust state-led social programme that covers education and healthcare. Our educational system, taught in English, has been one of the great successes of our focus on GNH. It has opened new doors for our youth, allowing them to access global knowledge and opportunities.

I am flattered that we in Bhutan are regarded as the last 'Shangri-La', the world's happiest people (rightly or wrongly), and pioneers of happiness as a goal in governance. This has happened because we are fortunate to have enlightened leaders guiding us. Their wisdom, courage, and compassion have shaped Bhutan's unique trajectory, making it a source of hope and inspiration for the world.

While we have had our share of successes, everything is not rosy in Bhutan—we are not a utopia filled with happy monks with no worldly cares. Throughout this book, I have discussed mysticism and wondrous miracles from Bhutan's history, but we are ultimately a real nation, facing real challenges.

Unemployment, particularly among our youth, is a pressing issue. The advent of social media has opened our society to the world, sparking desires for luxuries and access to everything the world has to offer. But with a small economy and high unemployment rates, fulfilling these desires is challenging. Moreover, we're grappling with a growing drug problem, with many abusing pharmaceutical drugs. Discreet prostitution is also on the rise, driven by an insatiable hunger for more satisfaction and fulfilment that the world cannot provide.

Our strong social fabric often masks these problems. The traditional security provided by extended family structures is a blessing, but it does not negate the fact that too many people are unemployed or experimenting with drugs. At an economic level, our challenges continue. Post-Covid recovery has been slow, with stubborn inflation, increasing national debt, and decreasing revenues. Our economy, with its foundations in agriculture and hydroelectricity, is still weak. The impact of the pandemic on tourism, a significant revenue source, has further exacerbated unemployment.

On top of this, our success has sparked an existential crisis. Our conservative economic growth, aimed at preserving our environment and culture, contrasts with the ambitions of our globally aware youth who are increasingly seeking opportunities abroad, particularly in Australia. Amid these socio-economic issues, many of our youth are opting to work abroad, primarily in the Middle East, America, Canada, and Australia. While their success abroad brings joy, it also raises concerns.

If this trend continues unchecked, we risk losing more of our young population, who are securing permanent residences and applying for citizenship in foreign lands. Who will contribute to nation-building at home? Our population is already very small, and while the prospect of losing our youth is already deeply concerning, more migration could potentially lead to a hollowing out of Bhutan and pose a significant threat to our future.

The Paradoxes of Progress

Bhutan is a living illustration of how enlightened leadership can forge a path that honours the past while boldly stepping into the future. It highlights the potential of leadership to be a force for positive transformation, guided by the principles of wisdom, courage, and compassion. Through their actions, policies, and visions, Bhutan's leaders have shown the world that governance, when rooted in these universal values, can lead to prosperity, sustainability, and harmony for all.

In my reflections on the essence of enlightened leadership, I confront a humbling truth—I am far from being the enlightened leader I want to be. Yet, for me, the true value of this guiding philosophy lies in aspiring to be one in the relentless pursuit of wisdom, courage, and compassion. It serves not just as an ideological belief but also as a practical framework through which I strive to approach leadership and governance.

There is a prevailing misconception that the issues our nation faces, particularly economic challenges and youth migration, signal the inadequacy of GNH. Contrary to this view, I posit that these challenges are, paradoxically, the outcomes of GNH's successes.

256 Enlightened Leadership

Over the span of one generation, Bhutan has transformed from a medieval society to one marked by widespread literacy, education, and proficiency in the English language. Our commitment to providing free healthcare has significantly increased life expectancy while our cultural heritage remains vibrant, safeguarded amid modernization. Environmental stewardship has rendered us a custodian of biodiversity, maintaining our status as a carbon negative country with extensive forest cover. In governance, Bhutan is unique, having transitioned peacefully to democracy at the behest of a popular king—an unparalleled feat globally.

Each of these milestones underscores the triumphs of GNH in fostering social progress, cultural preservation, environmental sustainability, and democratic governance. If there is an aspect where we perceive a shortfall, it is within the domain of economic development. Yet, even here, our modest economy is sustainable and marked by equitable distribution, harbouring vast potentials for growth. Indeed, the educational and societal frameworks nurtured under GNH have cultivated a generation of well-educated, proficient English speakers, imbued with values of hard work, humility, and trustworthiness. Such attributes render our youth highly employable, not just within Bhutan but across the global, English-speaking world, which contributes to the observed migration trends. If that is not a testament to the success of GNH, nothing is!

That said, the difficulty in retaining them at home does indicate a pressing need to channel these achievements into creating more robust economic opportunities domestically. Our focus, therefore, must shift towards leveraging the rich human capital developed through GNH to drive economic innovation and sustainability. This involves envisioning and implementing strategies that not only retain talent within our borders but attract global interest and collaboration. We have historically harmonized material well-being with spiritual and environmental stewardship. But confronted with economic challenges and the diaspora status of our youth, it becomes evident that our next phase of growth must be underpinned by bold and innovative economic strategies.

This necessitates a renewed commitment to the ideals of GNH, underscored by a courageous expansion of our economic frontiers. The potential for hydropower and clean energy in Bhutan presents a formidable avenue for economic development. Our focus should not only be on enhancing hydropower generation but also on harnessing this resource for downstream industries such as cloud computing, green hydrogen, and green ammonia production. These sectors, inherently energy-intensive, can thrive on the clean, sustainable energy that Bhutan is poised to offer, exemplifying how economic growth and environmental preservation can coexist.

Tourism, too, holds immense potential for expansion. By welcoming more visitors while preserving our cultural and natural heritage, we contribute not only to our economy but also to the global appreciation of Bhutan's unique values. Similarly, transforming subsistence farming into commercial agriculture, alongside nurturing the IT, technology and finance sectors, can create diversified, sustainable economic pathways.

In addressing these challenges, the principles of enlightened leadership remain paramount. Wisdom guides us to recognize the intricate dynamics at play between our achievements and the emerging challenges. Courage propels us to undertake bold economic initiatives that align with our values of sustainability and equity. Compassion ensures that, in our pursuit of economic vitality, we remain attentive to the welfare of all citizens, particularly those who may feel compelled to seek opportunities abroad.

'If You Could Choose . . .'

As we venture into this new phase of development, enlightened leadership beckons us to innovate, adapt, and lead with a vision that harmonizes economic aspirations with the foundational values of GNH. It is through such leadership that we can transform the paradoxes of progress into pathways for a flourishing, resilient Bhutan that continues to inspire the world.

We must leverage the successes of our GNH approach while also improving our economy. We need to provide income opportunities and salaries that are competitive with those in developed countries. Given our small but capable and agile population, and our strategic location on the border with India, I believe this is achievable. His Majesty the Fifth King is worth quoting at length on the need to attract Bhutanese living and working abroad back home:

> Our challenge is that we have barely 700,000 people in our country. Unless we find the right solution, our population may dwindle to the point when we have more shops than customers, more restaurants than diners, and more houses than tenants. [. . .] Even though you are away from home, I know your hearts are with us in Bhutan. You yearn to be home with your family and friends. If you could choose, you would be here.

In this book, I have endeavoured to show, through my experiences and observations, how Bhutan's modernization has been in line with the principles of enlightened leadership—that is, wisdom, courage, and compassion, driven by selfless service and carried out via the tenets of GNH. But the true test of whether these things are truly compatible with the future, with Bhutan's ability to throw open its doors to the world on its own terms, will take the form of a new city on our southern border with Assam, India.

Chapter Eleven

Small Land, Big Vision

The Gelephu project is to enable you to return. [. . .] My one regret has been that I could never tell you your future in Bhutan is assured. I want to change that. Young people should be excited for the future. You should look forward to it with confidence.

—His Majesty the Fifth Druk Gyalpo Jigme
Khesar Namgyal Wangchuck

What does GNH for the twenty-first century look like? Around the world, nations are dreaming up and constructing cities of the future. From Saudi Arabia to Indonesia and from Egypt to California, the global canvas is being reshaped. But imagine, if you will, a different kind of city—a city born of the GNH philosophy. Envision having 2,500 square kilometres as your canvas, a space larger than major urban territories and yet brimming with natural splendour.

Imagine this canvas not as a barren landscape but as one teeming with life, bordered by regions rich in biodiversity, including the endangered Golden Langur, Golden Mahseer, and an astonishing diversity of wildlife and birds, reflecting Bhutan's rich natural heritage. From the elusive snow leopard prowling the high mountain ranges to the Bengal tiger roaming the subtropical forests, Bhutan's fauna represents some of the world's most iconic and endangered species. Birdlife in Bhutan is equally remarkable, with over 770 recorded species, including rare and endangered birds like the black-necked crane, which migrates annually to the Phobjikha

Valley, and the critically endangered while-bellied heron, of which there are only about sixty in the world and Bhutan has twenty-six of them! Bhutan's national parks are more than just reserves; they are living, breathing embodiments of the nation's deep-rooted respect for all forms of life.

Envision protected areas, biodiversity hotspots, that are not isolated patches of wilderness but connected by biological corridors, allowing wildlife to move freely. Picture a landscape where traditional paddy fields and small hamlets are nestled amid natural water features, all under the watchful gaze of the Himalayas to the north and bordered by the expansive plains of India to the south.

Imagine a city that embodies the principles and ideals of GNH, a city designed not just for the present but as a beacon for the twenty-first century—this is GNH 2.0 in its truest form. Consider deeply, what form would this city take? Would it succumb to the dominating forces of the market or would it stand as a testament to the well-being and happiness of its inhabitants?

Picture a cityscape that diverges from the norm of towering skyscrapers. Envision, instead, structures of low-rise buildings, crafted from sustainable materials like stone, timber, and mud, harmoniously integrated with the surrounding forests. Imagine roads and transport systems that prioritize sustainability, ensuring that the its growth does not come at the expense of its environmental integrity.

Reflect on the commitment to preserving the natural wonders that frame this city—the biodiversity hotspots and national parks. These treasures would not only be protected but guaranteed to thrive for generations to come, making the entire city not just carbon neutral but audaciously aiming to become the first carbon-negative city in the world.

At the forefront of these initiatives is His Majesty's vision of the Gelephu Mindfulness City—grown from the border town of Gelephu. This visionary city transcends traditional urban development paradigms, advocating for a place designed not around market forces but the principles of harmony, community, and ecological balance. Announced on 17 December 2023, this initiative represents a bold step towards reimagining urban spaces in alignment with GNH values.

Gelephu will be a centre for mindful living, where the urban environment facilitates a deep connection among its inhabitants and with nature. It embodies the essence of enlightened leadership, demonstrating wisdom in its foundational vision, courage in its realization amid challenges, and compassion in its intent to serve the broader well-being of Bhutan and its future generations.

The Special Administrative Region Model

Our enlightened leaders have never been afraid to build on what's worked and innovate for the future. Unique to the Gelephu Mindfulness City is its designation as a special administrative region (SAR). This model, typically seen in contexts like Hong Kong and Macao during transitional periods from colonial rule to local sovereignty, is employed here as a strategic move to create an independent executive, legal, and judicial structure tailored to the city's unique objectives.

An SAR within Bhutan, equipped with its own independent government, legislature, and judiciary, is groundbreaking. It allows for the autonomy necessary to experiment with and implement policies that reflect the city's ethos of mindfulness and harmony, setting a precedent for how regions can operate independently within a national framework.

This pioneering approach marks the first instance where an SAR is established strategically for purposes beyond colonial transition, aiming instead to foster a community focused on GNH principles. By granting Gelephu the flexibility to innovate within its administrative and legal frameworks, Bhutan is not only creating a new 'country' within its borders but also offering the world a novel model of development—where mindfulness, sustainability, and community are the cornerstones of progress.

This city symbolizes a pivotal shift for Bhutan, seamlessly blending our time-honoured values with the exigencies of the twenty-first century. As we chart our path forward, we must ensure that our progress does not inadvertently erode our cultural heritage or displace our people. By proactively addressing these challenges, we can secure a prosperous and sustainable future for our land.

Innovation and Tradition, Hand in Hand

Before running in the 2023 election, I spent much time serving His Majesty by traversing the world, helping investors grasp the profound ripple effects of their contributions to our project. This endeavour is not merely a lucrative opportunity for them, but a lifeline for the people of Bhutan. It offers a platform for Bhutanese talent to thrive within their homeland, and when it succeeds, we know it will be a gift to the entire world.

A harmonious fusion of ancient Bhutanese tradition and cutting-edge innovation, it will be a place where the past meets the future in a vibrant dance of cultural preservation and technological advancement. Accordingly, it will have executive, legislative, and judicial independence, and once complete, the future Gelephu Mindfulness City will be spread across 2,500 square kilometres (5 per cent of Bhutan's total area).

This strategic location on the India–Bhutan border will offer it connectivity to South and Southeast Asia, through an international airport, railway connections, and a hydroelectric dam. This will create a platform for sustainable growth and economic opportunities in green technology, education, infrastructure, finance, and health and well-being while preserving our status as a carbon negative country. Given its strategic location along the Bhutan–India border in addition to the already exceptionally friendly ties between our two nations, the Gelephu Mindfulness City could become another gateway to India's huge and growing market.

Imagine approaching Gelephu as a visitor to Bhutan, your senses instantly captivated by the majestic panorama of lush green mountains that serve as a backdrop to the city. The air is crisp and clean, with a hint of earthy aroma from the surrounding forests, a testament to Bhutan's commitment to environmental conservation.

The cityscape is a blend of traditional Bhutanese architecture and futuristic buildings, all designed with sustainability in mind. Solar-powered lhakhangs with intricate carvings coexist harmoniously with smart buildings covered in vertical gardens, reducing the urban heat island effect and improving air quality. Despite the technological advancements, the city retains its pedestrian-friendly layout, with people preferring to travel on foot or bicycles along the beautifully landscaped paths.

Gelephu's economy thrives on ecotourism, organic farming, digital technology, finance, education, and health and well-being. Local markets are thriving with fresh produce from nearby farms while tech startups operate out of green coworking spaces. The city is also a global centre for Vajrayana Buddhism and a hub for meditation and wellness tourism, attracting visitors from around the world seeking solace and tranquillity. Yet, the heart of these institutions remains deeply rooted in Bhutan's unique philosophy of GNH, emphasizing holistic well-being over materialistic gain.

In the evenings, the city comes alive with traditional music and dance performances at public squares while restaurants serve a delicious fusion of Bhutanese and international cuisine. The people of Gelephu are warm and welcoming, their smiles as radiant as the city itself. Gelephu is an example of sustainable living, a place where technology enhances rather than overtakes human life, where modernity enriches rather than erodes tradition.

It is a cradle for growth and innovation, while remaining deeply connected to its cultural roots and the country's unique philosophy of GNH. Its architecture, which combines traditional aesthetics with modern design elements, reflects this harmonious blend of past and future. Embracing local materials such as wood, stone, and bamboo, the city's architecture incorporates traditional motifs like *rabsel*, cornices, ornaments, and roofscapes, marrying tradition with innovation.

Moreover, the city is planned with a strong emphasis on sustainability, aligning with Bhutan's status as a carbon negative country. It incorporates green spaces and aims to be powered entirely by renewable energy sources, including solar energy, but more importantly, a 5,000 MW hydroelectric project. All transport will also be sustainable, contributing to a healthier environment and improved quality of life for its residents. To safeguard against monsoon flooding, terraced paddy fields are made. Biodiversity corridors help preserve local flora and fauna and maintain undisturbed migratory routes for elephants and other wildlife.

The city's numerous bridges connect people and places. And each bridge hosts key destinations: a new airport; a Vajrayana spiritual centre offering insights into mindfulness practices; a healthcare centre blending eastern and western medicine; a university showcasing academic activities; a greenhouse demonstrating ancient farming practices and modern agricultural science; a cultural centre promoting Bhutanese culture and customs; and a market featuring Bhutanese textiles.

The final bridge on the city's western edge houses a dam that includes a temple and step-well retaining wall for viewpoints and meditative walks—a complex known as the Sankosh Temple-Dam, symbolizing Gelephu's harmonious fusion of culture and nature.

In essence, the future Gelephu Mindfulness City represents a hub for growth and innovation, deeply rooted in Bhutanese nature and culture. It aims to preserve and evolve tradition, creating a unique city that stands as a testament to the sustainable coexistence of humans and nature on Earth. As Bjarke Ingels, Founder and Creative Director of BIG, describes it: '[The] Sankosh Temple-Dam [. . .] will be a manmade monument to the divine possibility of a sustainable human presence on earth. Turning engineering into art and turning the forces of nature into power.'

Given the potential benefits, it is imperative that we bring this vision to life promptly. As His Majesty has rightly challenged us, what will we be able to tell future generations of what we have built? It cannot be that we merely preserved what was given to us but that we found new heights of achievement and prosperity, leaving behind a legacy we can be proud of—as our ancestors did, we will enable our descendants to do.

In this book, I have recounted my experiences and given my perspective on Bhutan's journey towards democracy, the selfless dedication of its leaders and their bravery in launching significant initiatives that have managed our development, preserved our values, and prevented many of the social issues that other nations now struggle to mitigate. It illuminates the relationship between progress and tradition, and the indispensable role wisdom, courage, and compassion play in steering our lives and efforts effectively. I firmly believe our story serves as a testament to the power of enlightened leadership, the significance of selfless service, and the enduring value of our cultural heritage.

What the Gelephu Mindfulness City does best, however, is encapsulate our vision for the future—a thriving nation anchored by its roots while welcoming the changes to come with the same qualities of selfless wisdom, courage, and compassion that have guided us thus far.

While navigating these promising times, the Government of Bhutan remains steadfast in its commitment to serving our people and our King, ensuring the spirit of Bhutan endures for centuries to come. As His Majesty so aptly put it:

> Some will think that the main goals of the Gelephu project are to attract investments, boost trade and businesses, and create employment. While these remain important, the larger vision of all our endeavours is to serve and protect our three precious jewels: our inheritance—Bhutan, our spiritual legacy of Ugyen Guru Rinpoche and Zhabdrung Nawang Namgyal, and thirdly, the future of our children.

This path, illuminated by enlightened leadership, beckons us forward—not just as a nation, but as a global community in search of sustainable, harmonious ways of living that benefit the world around us.

Afterword

Welcome to Bhutan

Nothing could be more striking than the pristine, haunting beauty of the landscape of Bhutan, or the atmosphere of peace and sacredness, which pervades the land from end to end. Bhutan is a place blessed with an almost magical power to transform the mind, whenever I am there I feel as if transported into a pure realm.

—His Eminence Sogyal Rinpoche

In the course of compiling this book, my commitment to the principles of enlightened leadership and GNH has been not only a guiding light but also a steadfast vision for the future of Bhutan. As I reflect upon the recent culmination of the 2024 electoral process, it is with profound humility and a deep sense of responsibility that I find myself entrusted by the people of Bhutan to serve another term as prime minister.

Throughout the final stages of compiling this manuscript, I was actively campaigning, mindful of the fact that the outcome of the elections could sway in any direction. Thus, I articulated within these pages a sentiment of contingency and hope—should the trust and confidence of the people be placed in me again, the insights and reflections shared here would directly inform my tenure. The ideas I share here, however, extend beyond my own political fortunes because the world still resonates with the paradigms of leadership and happiness that Bhutan champions.

My comrades in the People's Democratic Party and I now stand at the threshold of another term. The principles of wisdom, courage, compassion, and selfless service at the core of this book will be integral as I endeavour to meet the expectations of my fellow citizens and further the vision of a prosperous, harmonious Bhutan.

The Essence of Leadership

Our Constitution stipulates: 'No person shall hold the office of Prime Minister for more than two terms.' I have often been asked if the terms served by the prime minister must be consecutive or if they could be staggered. The interpretation of the law, which allows only two terms, ultimately lies with the judiciary. However, my personal view is that it amounts to two terms, consecutive or otherwise. Each term lasts five years, and after I serve this upcoming second term, that's it for me.

The point here is not about the titles or the tenure; it is about the service rendered during those five years. At the end of the term, I return to being a private citizen. But what truly matters is the commitment and dedication during those years of service, as that's where the essence of leadership lies.

Recognition, fame, and prestige often accompany high office, but as a politician, I find myself drawn to the essence of public service rather than these superficial trappings. When people recognize me, it is not just my past role they see but also the values and principles I stand for. How I perceive myself today, and how I will perceive myself in five years, would be largely shaped by my second tenure as the prime minister. Do I wish to bask in the warmth of my past achievements, enjoying the respect and kindness of people who wish to meet me, listen to me, and learn from my experiences? Or do I want to utilize this time for selfless service, continuing to contribute to the well-being of Bhutan and its people?

The driving force behind my actions is not a sense of superiority or a desire for recognition. Instead, it is the unwavering belief that I still have much to offer in terms of public service. There's a reservoir of dedication, passion, and commitment within me that I believe can still make a difference.

My journey as Bhutan's prime minister may or may not have concluded (we will know by the time you read this), but my journey of service continues. The opportunity to serve my king, my country, and its people is a privilege I cherish deeply. As we look to the future, I am excited to channel my energy, expertise, and love for Bhutan into meaningful initiatives that uphold our values and propel us towards a brighter tomorrow.

In facing the paradoxes wrought by our developmental successes, Bhutan stands on the cusp of a new era. Through the courageous expansion of our economy, grounded in the values of GNH, and the visionary project of the Gelephu Mindfulness City, we chart a course to a future where economic growth and human well-being are inextricably linked. This path, illuminated by enlightened leadership, beckons us forward—not just as a nation but also as a global community in search of sustainable, harmonious ways of living.

This book, therefore, serves not merely as a personal reflection or an academic undertaking but as a manifesto of sorts—a pledge to uphold the ideals that have shaped our unique approach to governance, society, and development. It is a promise to carry forward the legacy of enlightened leadership, to innovate while preserving, and to lead with a heart as steadfast in compassion as it is ambitious in vision.

In preparing for my term, I revisit the pages of this book with a renewed sense of purpose. But it is not about me—it is about Bhutan, and a testament to the vision and values that have guided it through the years. If you resonated with the questions posed about leadership, governance, and development then you, too, share the belief in GNH and its wish for a harmonious balance between economic advancement and the pillars of social progress, cultural vitality, environmental stewardship, and exemplary governance.

Of course, we have been buoyed by the unwavering support and camaraderie extended by the government and people of India. Their generosity and solidarity have been instrumental in our successes, for which our gratitude knows no bounds.

Rigsum Gonpo and the Future of GNH

The Gelephu Mindfulness City symbolizes a new era—not merely an innovative approach to urban living or an experiment in urban design but a bold step forward in the evolution of GNH. It is a leap towards GNH 2.0 for the twenty-first century, offering a legacy for Bhutan and a model for the world. This city represents a gift not only to our nation and to our future generations but also extends its promise as a gift to India and to the broader international community.

It is a demonstration of how urban environments can thrive in harmony with both humanity and nature, guiding us all toward a more sustainable, joyful, and interconnected world. Sustainability, community, and harmony with nature are not just ideals but the very foundations upon which every street, building, and policy is built. This dream is not just about constructing a city; it is about crafting a living, breathing embodiment of GNH, an urban environment that nurtures the well-being of its inhabitants and the natural world alike.

As the values of Rigsum Gonpo—wisdom, courage, and compassion—enlighten us along this path of selfless service and understanding, let us use them as the potent tools for personal and communal evolution that they are. All of them are accessible to every one of us, regardless of our worldly positions or beliefs.

Wisdom teaches us to see the world with clarity and insight, to understand the impermanent and interdependent nature of all things. It empowers us to make decisions that align with the deeper truths of existence, guiding us away from the shadows of ignorance and towards enlightenment. In practising wisdom, we learn that true mastery over our lives comes not from exerting control over the external world but from understanding and shaping our inner landscapes.

Courage, then, is the strength to act in accordance with our wisdom, even in the face of adversity. It is the audacity to uphold our convictions, to venture beyond the comfort of the known, and to act with integrity even when the path is arduous. Courage propels us forward on our personal journeys and inspires those around us to pursue their highest selves.

Compassion binds us to one another, reminding us that we are not isolated entities competing for survival but fellow travellers sharing a common destiny. It teaches us to act with kindness and empathy, to alleviate suffering where we find it, and to extend our love beyond the boundaries of self. In compassion, we find the motivation to work for the betterment of our communities, understanding that our own well-being is intimately connected to the happiness of others.

The king, venerable and an enlightened leader though he may be, operates within the same constraints and opportunities as the humblest of his subjects. His power lies not in the ability to command or control but in the capacity to inspire, guide, and uplift through the embodiment of these timeless virtues. Similarly, each of us possesses the potential to shape our destinies and contribute to the tapestry of our communities by putting the values of Rigsum Gonpo into practice.

Closing Words

United in wisdom, courage, and compassion, and the selfless service that they bring to pass, we can transcend the limitations imposed upon us by circumstance or fate. Our dreams for ourselves and our societies are not mere fantasies but potential realities waiting to be brought forth through collective effort and enlightened action. Thus, in every moment, with every thought, word, and deed, we are invited to participate in the co-creation of a world of understanding, bravery, and profound care for one another.

My final invitation in this book is to you, the reader—wherever you are in the world, I know I speak for us all when I say Bhutan looks forward to welcoming you. Whether in the vibrant bloom of spring, the cool respite of summer, the colourful tapestry of fall, or the clear, sunlit days of winter, Bhutan offers a unique experience across all seasons. Your visit is more than just travel; it is a gesture of support, an act of friendship, and a step towards bolstering the ties that bind us together. See you there!

Acknowledgements

In the journey of penning this memoir, there are countless hands that have shaped its narrative, and I am deeply grateful for each one:

To my beloved wife Tashi, whose unwavering support and boundless patience have been the cornerstone of my endeavours. Your presence in my life is a blessing beyond measure, and I am forever indebted to your grace and resilience.

To my children, Gyamtsho and Galek, whose support, youthful curiosity, and invaluable assistance in research have breathed life into these pages.

To my revered parents and their generation, whose noble service to our kings laid the foundation for our nation's transformation from isolation to enlightenment.

To Dominic Scriven, Matt Harris, Karen Lim, and many other international friends who encouraged me to write about Bhutan's unique journey. Their guidance and support have been instrumental in seeing this project through to completion.

To Pearlin and her dedicated team at Boss of Me[75], for their exceptional talent in translating my thoughts into eloquent prose and for their relentless encouragement throughout this journey.

---

[75] Boss of Me is a boutique book-writing agency run by Pearlin Siow that specializes in helping people write as well as publish books. Together, with Pearlin's team of content specialists, Boss of Me has produced several bestselling biographies for top entrepreneurs and companies in Singapore. Their clients range from billionaires to politicians. Connect with Pearlin at www.bossofme.sg.

To the Penguin Random House SEA team—Nora Nazerene Abu Bakar, Amberdawn Manaois, Sneha Bhagwat, and Adviata Vats—for believing in the power of this story and for their unwavering commitment to its publication.

And most importantly, to the illustrious line of kings who have guided and inspired me with their wisdom and enlightened leadership, I offer my deepest gratitude. Your lessons continue to shape my path, and I am humbled by the privilege of serving our king, country, and people.